D0886707

THE TRANSMISSION
OF *BEOWULF*

A VOLUME IN THE SERIES

MYTH AND POETICS II

GREGORY NAGY, EDITOR

LEONARD MUELLNER, ASSOCIATE EDITOR

For a full list of titles in this series,
visit our website at www.cornellpress.cornell.edu.

A complete list of titles published in the original
Myth and Poetics series is available at the back of this book.

THE
TRANSMISSION
OF
BEOWULF

Language, Culture, and
Scribal Behavior

LEONARD NEIDORF

Cornell University Press
Ithaca and London

First published 2017 by Cornell University Press

Printed in the United States of America

Library of Congress Cataloging-in-Publication Data

Names: Neidorf, Leonard, author.
Title: The transmission of Beowulf : language, culture, and scribal behavior / Leonard Neidorf.
Description: Ithaca : Cornell University Press, 2017. | Series: Myth and poetics II | Includes bibliographical references and index.
Identifiers: LCCN 2016035593 (print) | LCCN 2016037074 (ebook) | ISBN 9781501705113 (cloth : alk. paper) | ISBN 9781501708275 (epub/mobi) | ISBN 9781501708282 (pdf)
Subjects: LCSH: Beowulf--Criticism, Textual. | Epic poetry, English (Old)--Criticism, Textual. | Transmission of texts--England--History--To 1500. | Language and culture--England--History--To 1500.
Classification: LCC PR1586 .N45 2017 (print) | LCC PR1586 (ebook) | DDC 829/.3--dc23
LC record available at https://lccn.loc.gov/2016035593

Cornell University Press strives to use environmentally responsible suppliers and materials to the fullest extent possible in the publishing of its books. Such materials include vegetable-based, low-VOC inks and acid- free papers that are recycled, totally chlorine-free, or partly composed of nonwood fibers. For further information, visit our website at www.cornellpress.cornell.edu.

TO

R. D. FULK

JOSEPH HARRIS

RAFAEL J. PASCUAL

Beowulf is a work, as we have it, of a single hand and mind—comparable to a play (say *King Lear*) by Shakespeare: thus it may have varied sources; minor discrepancies due to imperfections in the handling and blending of these; and may have suffered some "corruption" (e.g. occasional deliberate tinkering or editing, and many minor casual errors) in the course of tradition between author and our copy. But it makes a unified artistic impression: the impress of a single imagination, and the ring of a single poetic style. The minor "discrepancies" detract little from this, as a rule.

J. R. R. Tolkien, *Beowulf: A Translation and Commentary*

There is one kind of corruption which our text has escaped, viz. that which is imported by a too clever scribe who thinks he knows what his author ought to have written and "mends his book" accordingly. Our two scribes were immune from this weakness; they were conscientious, if unintelligent, copyists who set down what they saw or thought they saw in their book (perhaps itself a copy) without worrying about sense or metre. There is one great advantage in this faithful form of transcription; for, by studying the different kinds of involuntary error to which it is subject, we can usually correct with confidence either nonsense or wrong sense...

S. O. Andrew, *Postscript on Beowulf*

Die Überlieferung ist also gerade für die Dichtungen der klassischen Zeit, des 7. und 8. Jahrhunderts, durchschnittlich um 200 bis 250 Jahre jünger als die Texte selbst und gibt alle anglischen Gedichte in fremder Dialektform wieder. Es ist selbstverständlich, daß bei einer solchen Art der Überlieferung auch das Metrum vielfach gestört worden ist, durch Einsetzung jüngerer und dialektisch abweichender Sprachformen, von eigentlichen Textverderbnissen ganz abgesehen. Doch lassen sich die meisten Fehler dieser Art mit ziemlicher Sicherheit erkennen und beseitigen.

Eduard Sievers, *Altgermanische Metrik*

CONTENTS

ILLUSTRATIONS

All illustrations from London, British Library, Cotton MS Vitellius A.xv.

SERIES FOREWORD

Gregory Nagy

As editor of the renewed and expanded series Myth and Poetics II, my goal is to promote the publication of books that build on connections to be found between different ways of thinking and different forms of verbal art in preliterate as well as literate societies. As in the original Myth and Poetics series, which started in 1989 with the publication of Richard Martin's *The Language of Heroes: Speech and Performance in the "Iliad,"* the word "myth" in the title of the new series corresponds to what I have just described as a way of thinking, while "poetics" covers any and all forms of preliterature and literature.

Although "myth" as understood, say, in the Homeric *Iliad* could convey the idea of a traditional way of thinking that led to a traditional way of expressing a thought, such an idea was not to last—not even in ancient Greek society, as we see, for example, when we consider the fact that the meaning of the word was already destabilized by the time of Plato. And such destabilization is exactly why I prefer to use the word "myth" in referring to various ways of shaping different modes of thought: it is to be expected that any tradition that conveys any thought will vary in different times and different places. And such variability of tradition is a point of prime interest for me in my quest as editor to seek out the widest variety of books about the widest possible variety of traditions.

Similarly in the case of "poetics," I think of this word in its widest sense, so as to include not only poetry but also songmaking on one side and prose on the other. As a series, Myth and Poetics II avoids presuppositions about traditional forms such as genres, and there is no insistence on any universalized understanding of verbal art in all its countless forms.

PREFACE

The present book addresses philological questions that are fundamental to the study of *Beowulf*. When was it first composed and committed to parchment? How substantially did scribes alter the text during its transmission? Should the poem be regarded as the product of unitary or composite authorship? These are difficult questions, but readers of *Beowulf* wishing to obtain a historically accurate understanding of this work must answer them, at least tentatively. A special difficulty attending these questions is that they must be addressed in unison, since answers offered to one of them will raise questions about the others. Most philologists are now prepared to credit the argument that *Beowulf* was composed around the year 700, three centuries prior to the production of its sole extant manuscript (from ca. 1000), but their consensus leaves many observers wondering what, if anything, happened to the poem during the long period separating its date of composition from the date of its sole extant manuscript. Does the text generally preserve the lexical and metrical characteristics it possessed when it left the pen or the mouth of the *Beowulf* poet? Or did scribes so thoroughly recompose the text during its transmission that *Beowulf* ought to be regarded as a work more or less contemporary with its extant manuscript? For linguists, historians, and literary critics, these questions are vital, since they delimit what *Beowulf* can reasonably do for them. It matters a great deal whether the poem reflects the language and culture of the year 700 or the year 1000, or whether it is a composite work, containing passages of varying antiquity and authority.

A central argument of this book is that the text of *Beowulf* preserved in its late manuscript witness essentially remains the unified work of one archaic poet. This conclusion is grounded, above all, in the presentation of evidence for the structural homogeneity of the transmitted text. Lexical and metrical archaisms are not limited to one portion of the poem, but can be found in it from beginning to end. Furthermore, the detection of a number of subtle linguistic regularities, which pervade *Beowulf* and distinguish it from other works of Old English literature, furnishes strong evidence for compositional unity, while casting serious doubt upon hypotheses of composite authorship or scribal recomposition. Credence in the integrity of *Beowulf* does not imply, however, that nothing happened to its text after the lifetime of its author. To the contrary, more than three hundred scribal errors crept into the text during the course of its transmission. In most cases, the graphemic resemblance between the scribal error and the authorial form has enabled textual critics to recover the antecedent reading with considerable certainty. The accumulated errors thus present no grave impediment to our understanding, but form a thin veneer that can be removed. Indeed, editors of *Beowulf* do remove this layer of superficial corruption, relegating it to the apparatus criticus and printing emended forms in their texts. The present book differs from editions and traditional works of textual criticism in that it foregrounds the accumulated errors and makes them the subject of concerted analysis. In its central chapters, these errors are demonstrated to contain valuable evidence for language history, cultural change, and scribal behavior.

The scribal errors in the transmitted text lend independent and overwhelming support to the hypothesis that *Beowulf* existed in writing centuries before the production of its extant manuscript. When brought together and studied comprehensively, these errors reveal several chronologically significant patterns. Many corruptions can be seen under this light to be the textual consequences of linguistic and cultural changes that took place in England during the three centuries of the poem's transmission. Such corruptions result not from the random carelessness of the scribes, but from their unfamiliarity with the language and culture of the earlier Anglo-Saxon period. Diachronic change is reflected in the myriad errors induced by archaic words, antiquated orthography, and obsolete letterforms. Similarly, the serial corruption of the names of ancient heroes and peoples reflects the cessation of legendary traditions essential to the composition and comprehension of *Beowulf*. The systematic character of these patterns of corruption indicates that we are not dealing with idiosyncratic flaws of individual scribes, but with their vulnerability to impersonal and inexorable processes of linguistic and cultural change. The scribal errors thus confirm the relative antiquity of *Beowulf* and shed considerable light on the difficulties this archaic poem presented to late Anglo-Saxon audiences. The particular forms these errors take also reveal a great deal about the aims and methods of the scribes responsible for the poem's transmission.

The lexemic theory of scribal behavior emerges upon recognition of the fact that the vast majority of the aforementioned corruptions possess the form of genuine lexemes. Personal names become common nouns of similar appearance, archaic words become current ones, heroic vocabulary becomes theological vocabulary, and so forth. Throughout the extant manuscript, scribal error tends not to have resulted in the transmission of gibberish, but in the conversion of authorial readings into genuine Old English words that are contextually implausible. In case after case, these words disrupt the meter and make nonsense of the narrative, such that their spuriousness would be immediately apparent to any reader paying careful attention to the poem. The scribes, however, were not concerned with the formal or literary properties of the work they transmitted. For them, *Beowulf* was not a masterwork of Old English literature, but a sequence of discrete lexemes that required continual modification in order to assume the forms they should possess in the Late West Saxon written standard in which the scribes were trained. The aim of the scribes was to modernize and Saxonize the spellings of an antecedent manuscript copy, not to understand, interpret, or recompose Old English poetry. The theory that scribes concentrated on individual lexemes, not continuous sense, gains empirical support outside of *Beowulf* by accounting well for the variation in parallel texts of Old English poems and by accommodating the kinds of corruption found in the Exeter Book, the Junius Manuscript, and the Vercelli Book.

The composition of the present book was greatly facilitated by the compendious resources of the fourth edition of Klaeber's *Beowulf* (ed. Fulk et al. 2008), which represents the culmination of two centuries of textual criticism on the poem. Because it would be impossible for the bibliographical references provided here to be as comprehensive as those provided in *KB*, no attempt has been made to cite every contributor to the unwieldy critical literature on any given textual problem. References to *KB* are thus often intended to direct readers to the complete critical background on a particular issue. Similarly, because it would needlessly swell the book without contributing to its arguments, no attempt has been made to name the first individual responsible for proposing a particular emendation. Readers interested in such matters can readily satisfy their curiosity by consulting the apparatus criticus in *KB* or the tables printed in Birte Kelly's studies (1982, 1983) of the formative stages of *Beowulf* textual scholarship. Throughout this book, citations of *Beowulf* refer to the edited text of *KB*, though reference is also frequently made to unedited manuscript readings. Translations of *Beowulf* are everywhere taken from Fulk's Dumbarton Oaks volume (2010a), since it follows the edited text of *KB*, though argument occasionally necessitates slight modifications. Citations of other Old English poems refer to the editions of Krapp and Dobbie (1931–1953) except when different editions are cited. Translations of other works are my own throughout unless otherwise noted.

ACKNOWLEDGMENTS

It is a pleasure to record my gratitude to the many scholars who contributed in various ways to the production of this book. The three scholars to whom this book is dedicated exerted the greatest influence on its final form and refined its argumentation considerably. Rafael J. Pascual, my collaborator and closest friend, read every word of this book twice and systematically improved every discussion pertaining to meter. Joseph Harris, my former doctoral advisor, read this book as it was composed and generously discussed its arguments with me for many hours in his office. Robert D. Fulk, whom I regard as the greatest Germanic philologist of the twentieth century, read the final version of this book's manuscript and eradicated many of its infelicities. I thank these three scholars not only for their service to this book, but also for setting in life and work a scholarly standard to which I have constantly aspired. They have ennobled the field of Old English philology and made me feel proud to devote myself to its advancement.

Four other scholars, who played decisive roles in my intellectual life in recent years, read portions of this book or offered valuable comments on the research informing it. For memorable conversations and insightful suggestions, I thank George Clark, Daniel Donoghue, Geoffrey Russom, and Tom Shippey. Large debts of gratitude are owed to each of these scholars for reasons too numerous to list here. Suffice it to say that I feel exceedingly fortunate to have enjoyed the friendship and support of these tremendous scholars over the past few years.

There are many other colleagues in the field of Old English studies to whom I incurred intellectual and professional debts in the years during which this book was composed. For myriad reasons, I thank Carl Anderson, Rolf Bremmer, Michelle Brown, Tom Cable, Graham Caie, Christopher Cain, Juan Camilo Conde Silvestre, Paul Cavill, Howell Chickering, Dennis Cronan, Susan Deskis, Mark Griffith, Megan Hartman, John Hines, Carole Hough, Stefan Jurasinski, Michael Lapidge, Francis Leneghan, Anatoly Liberman,

Donka Minkova, Haruko Momma, Andrea Nagy, Rory Naismith, Andy Orchard, Caroline Palmer, Susan Pintzuk, Brittany Schorn, Jun Terasawa, Greg Waite, Charlie Wright, and Hee-Cheol Yoon. I am also grateful to several colleagues at Harvard University—especially Tom Keeline, Michael McCormick, Stephen Mitchell, Greg Nagy, James Simpson, Matthew Sussman, Maria Tatar, and Thomas Wisniewski—for insightful conversations and for creating an atmosphere of intellectual excitement during my time there. Lastly, I must thank my new colleagues at Nanjing University— especially Wang Shouren, Yang Jincai, He Ning, Wang Jinghua, Chen Bing, Zhang Yi, and Liu Yang—for providing me with conditions so conducive to research while I prepared the final version of this book.

Much of this book was composed in Cambridge, Massachusetts, in the office granted to me by the Harvard Society of Fellows, but important portions of this book were also composed in Granada, Spain, during two long and salubrious stays at the Universidad de Granada. For their hospitality, I am most grateful to José Luis Martínez-Dueñas and Rafael J. Pascual. For its generous financial support of my research, I thank the William F. Milton Fund of Harvard University. For permitting me to print images from the *Beowulf* manuscript in this book, I thank the British Library. Finally, I thank everyone involved in the production of this book at Cornell University Press for their diligent and supportive labor.

ABBREVIATIONS

CCCC = Cambridge, Corpus Christi College

DrR = *Dream of the Rood* (Swanton 1987)

EWS = Early West Saxon

Gen A = *Genesis A*

HOEM = *A History of Old English Meter* (Fulk 1992)

KB = *Klaeber's Beowulf* (Fulk et al. 2008)

KB:Par. = *Klaeber's Beowulf: Parallels*

KB:Lang. = *Klaeber's Beowulf: Language*

KB:T.C. = *Klaeber's Beowulf: Textual Criticism*

LWS = Late West Saxon

OES = *Old English Syntax* (Mitchell 1985)

SBI = *Soul and Body I*

SBII = *Soul and Body II*

SnS = *Solomon and Saturn*

WS = West Saxon

1

INTRODUCTION

1. The Duration of Transmission

§1. The text of *Beowulf* was transmitted to the modern world by means of a single medieval manuscript: London, British Library, Cotton MS Vitellius A.xv. Two scribes copied the poem into this codex, alongside three fantastical prose texts—*The Life of St. Christopher*, *The Wonders of the East*, and *Alexander's Letter to Aristotle*—and the poetic *Judith*.[1] The characteristics of the scribes' handwriting enable the act of copying to be dated to a relatively narrow period. Scribe A's vernacular minuscule script was not regularly used before 1001, whereas Scribe B's square minuscule was not regularly used after 1010.[2] The probability that the extant manuscript of *Beowulf* was written out during the first decade of the eleventh century is thus considerable. The hundreds of transcription errors that pervade the transmitted text indicate, however, that this manuscript is a copy of a copy, written out at a vast remove from the authorial archetype.[3] Philological investigation into the dating of *Beowulf* has generated compelling reasons to believe that the poem was first composed and committed to parchment around the year 700 (§§3–12). Because language and culture did not remain static for three centuries, the scribes who produced the surviving copy of *Beowulf* faced considerable difficulties in their effort to reproduce and modernize this centuries-old poem. Scribal unfamiliarity with

---

[1] On the textual history of the codex's contents, see Sisam 1953b:65–96 and Lucas 1990. For possible literary connections between its works, see Orchard 2003b.

[2] The reasoning behind this conclusion is presented in Dumville 1988. See also Ker 1957:282 and the explication of Ker's dating in Leneghan 2005. On the methodology to be employed in the dating of the manuscript, see Dumville 1998.

[3] Cf. Kemble: "The numerous blunders both in sense and versification, the occurrence of archaic forms found in no other Anglo-Saxon work, and the cursory illusions [*sic*] to events which to the Anglo-Saxons must soon have become unintelligible, are convincing proofs that our present text is only a copy, and a careless copy too" (1835:xxi).

the ancient content of *Beowulf* is registered throughout the transmitted text in the serial corruption of unfamiliar words and forgotten names.

§2. The present book offers the first comprehensive study of scribal errors induced by the linguistic and cultural changes that took place between the period when *Beowulf* was composed (ca. 700) and the period when its extant manuscript was copied out (ca. 1001–1010). Because the authorial reading can be identified in these cases with a high degree of probability, these errors shed significant light on the modus operandi and reading practices of the scribes. Understanding the behavior of the two scribes is essential for the textual criticism of *Beowulf*, but it also has significant implications for the editing of the rest of the corpus of Old English poetry. A substantial body of theoretical literature has been written about Anglo-Saxon scribes and their participatory role in the transmission of poetic texts, yet the concrete evidence upon which such theories have been erected is often rather slim. The transmitted text of *Beowulf* is shown in subsequent chapters to yield valuable evidence for testing and refining prominent theories of Anglo-Saxon scribal behavior. Before the transmission of *Beowulf* can be analyzed, two complicated subjects must first be addressed: the evidence bearing on the dating of *Beowulf* must be surveyed, so that the duration of the transmission can be apprehended; and the delicate methods for distinguishing scribal errors from authorial readings must be explicated. Consequently, this introduction addresses these two topics and the epistemological considerations they necessitate.

§3. The dating of *Beowulf* has long been a controversial subject in Anglo-Saxon studies, with opinions ranging from the seventh to the eleventh century,[4] but recent philological research has reduced the range of plausible dates to a fairly narrow period of time, extending from ca. 685 to 725. The most compelling arguments for this range of dates emerged in R. D. Fulk's *A History of Old English Meter* (1992) (hereafter *HOEM*), which comprehensively assessed the metrical and phonological evidence for the relative and absolute dating of Old English poetry. The chronological conclusions based in meter and phonology make particularly strong demands on credence at present because they have been repeatedly corroborated in subsequent studies concerned with the dating implications of many independent forms of evidence. The hypothesis that *Beowulf* was composed around 700 has been shown to find strong support in lexical (§7), semantic (§8), onomastic (§9), and paleographical research (§§10–11). The ability of a unitary

---

[4] See the conspectus of views presented in Bjork and Obermeier 1997. Another sound overview is offered in Evans 1997:41–63. For a history of the dating controversy focused on methodology and reasoning, see Neidorf 2014c.

hypothesis to explain so many disparate pieces of data, whose chronological significance derives from independent linguistic and cultural developments, is the clearest sign that this hypothesis is probably correct. A review of all of the evidence pertaining to the dating of *Beowulf* is beyond the scope of this introduction, which focuses instead on the forms of evidence related to diachronic changes that affected the transmission of *Beowulf*.

§4. The meter of classical Old English poems, such as *Beowulf*, is remarkably regular.[5] Every verse alliterates with another verse and consists of four metrical positions, which are realized either as a long stressed syllable, a resolved sequence of a stressed short syllable and its successor, or a variable sequence of unstressed syllables.[6] Some verses appear at face value to possess three or five metrical positions, until it is realized that the verse contains a word that either lost or gained a syllable due to early Old English sound changes. In verses such as *deaþwic sēon* (*Beowulf* 1275b), the poet must have treated *sēon* as disyllabic **seohan*, the form of this verb before it underwent contraction during the seventh century, since the verse would otherwise contain only three metrical positions. Conversely, in a verse such as *wundorsmiþa geweorc* (1681a), the poet must have treated *wundor-* as monosyllabic **wundr*, the form of this noun before it underwent parasiting during the seventh century, since the verse would otherwise contain five metrical positions. Fulk demonstrated that verses requiring archaic phonology for scansion occur with the highest incidence and greatest lexical variety in *Beowulf*, *Genesis A*, *Exodus*, and *Daniel*. The incidence of metrical archaisms declines in Cynewulfian poetry, regresses further in Alfredian poetry, and reaches its nadir in poems externally datable to the tenth and eleventh centuries.[7] The broad consistency of this distribution indicates that metrical criteria such as parasiting and contraction can reliably adumbrate a relative chronology of Old English poetry, in which *Beowulf* is one of the earliest extant works.[8]

---

[5]   Eduard Sievers (1885, 1893) is responsible for identifying the formal principles of verse construction behind the ostensibly random fluctuation of syllables exhibited in the poetry. On the enduring validity of Sievers's conclusions, see Pascual 2016. For an accessible and reliable introduction to Old English metrics, see Terasawa 2011.

[6]   On the four-position principle, see Cable 1974:84–93 and Pascual 2013–14. There are some licensed exceptions to this rule, most prominently represented in types A3 and expanded D*.

[7]   A summary of Fulk's findings is presented in *HOEM*:§376; on verses requiring noncontraction for scansion, see *HOEM*:§§99–130; on verses requiring nonparasiting for scansion, see *HOEM*:§§76–98.

[8]   Fulk's conclusions have been corroborated in several subsequent studies of the relative chronology of Old English poetry, including Russom 2002, Cronan 2004, Lapidge 2006, Neidorf 2013–2014, and Bredehoft 2014.

§5. Metrical studies have also yielded an absolute terminus ad quem for the composition of *Beowulf*. The poem is unique in its treatment of resolution, a structural feature of Old English poetry designed to preserve the principle that every verse must contain exactly four metrical positions.[9] When a short, open syllable receives metrical stress (i.e., ictus), the following syllable is resolved, and the two syllables are made to occupy a single metrical position. Resolution was operative throughout the Anglo-Saxon period, but in *Beowulf* its application under secondary stress is governed by distinctions of etymological length that became phonologically indistinct before 725 in Mercia and before 825 in Northumbria (*HOEM*:§§170–183). In sixty-two verses like *frēowine folca*, a historically short desinence is subject to resolution, whereas in forty-four verses like *eald æscwiga*, a historically long desinence suspends resolution. In the case of *frēowine folca*, the lexeme *-wine* reflects prehistoric **winiz* and its short desinence must be resolved, since the verse would otherwise contain five metrical positions (SsxSx). In the case of *eald æscwiga*, the lexeme *-wiga* reflects prehistoric **wigô* and its long desinence must block resolution, since the verse would otherwise contain three metrical positions (SSs). This linguistic regularity—the restriction of resolution under secondary stress in *Beowulf* to desinences that were short in Proto-Germanic or shortened in prehistoric Old English—is known as Kaluza's law, though Fulk was the first scholar to identify the law's conditioning and explain its chronological implications.[10] Because *Beowulf* contains Mercian features and its structural phonology is less conservative than that of the Épinal-Erfurt glossary (ca. 685), Fulk concluded that the poem was most likely composed between 685 and 725 (*HOEM*:§§406–420).

§6. Scholars who object to the use of metrical criteria to date Old English poems tend to discount parasiting, contraction, and Kaluza's law by relating them to nonchronological variables such as poetic style or the conscious desire to sound archaic.[11] The credibility of such theoretical objections vanishes, however, when it is recognized that they cannot adequately explain how an Old English poet could possess such accurate knowledge of prehistoric phonology. With regard to contraction, for example, it is remarkable that the *Beowulf* poet knows that *ēam* is eligible for disyllabic treatment

---

[9]   On the linguistic origin of resolution and its probable connection to the Northwest Germanic lengthening, see Kuryłowicz 1949 and Fulk 1995.

[10]   The law originates in the observations of Kaluza 1896 and 1909:57–59. The evidence was reviewed and augmented (but not adequately explained) in Bliss 1967:§§34–40.

[11]   See, for example, Frank 2007 and Kiernan 1981:23-63.

(as *ēa-am* < Proto-Germanic *awa-haim*), but *tēam* and *bēam* must always be monosyllabic, since they developed from original diphthongs.[12] The linguistic knowledge exhibited in the poem's regular and extensive adherence to Kaluza's law is even more impressive. In *nȳdwracu nīþgrim* (193a), the poet is aware that the feminine *ō*-stem nominative singular is historically short and hence resolvable (*wracu* < *wracō*), whereas in *gearo gyrnwræce* (2118a), the poet knows that the feminine *ō*-stem genitive singular is historically long and hence unresolvable (*wræce* < *wræcôz*). In *frēowine folca*, moreover, the poet recognized that the masculine *i*-stem nominative singular is resolvable (*wine* < *winiz*), whereas in *frome fyrdhwate* (1641a, 2476a), the masculine adjective nominative plural is unresolvable (*hwate* < *hwatai*). Although many desinences would come to be realized as –*e,* they were etymologically distinct, and the *Beowulf* poet recognized the distinction. The only credible explanation for the poet's ability to make such distinctions consistently is that they remained audible in the language he spoke. Consequently, it is probable that *Beowulf* was composed in Mercia before 725, since distinctions of etymological length crucial to the law's operation had collapsed by that time.[13]

§7. Lexical investigations into the relative chronology of Old English poetry have independently corroborated the conclusions of metrical dating studies.[14] Dennis Cronan (2004) observed that fourteen poetic simplexes are restricted to six Old English poems: *Beowulf, Genesis A, Exodus, Daniel, Maxims I,* and *Widsið*. For many of these words, their restriction to a corpus of archaic poetry—and their absence from texts known to have been composed during the ninth and tenth centuries—is a probable sign that they became obsolete at an early date. The earliest English poems therefore appear to preserve an archaic lexical stratum consisting of words that fell out of use before the ninth century. The reasoning behind this conclusion can be clearly illustrated with the case of *suhtriga* 'nephew'. As a simplex, *suhtriga* is attested only in *Genesis A* and in glossaries that derive from seventh-century *glossae collectae*. Elsewhere in the corpus of Old English, *suhtriga* is found only in *Beowulf* and *Widsið*, in the copulative compound *suhtor(ge)fædren* 'uncle-and-nephew', a type of word-formation that ceased to be productive

---

[12] For this particular example, see Amos 1982:338. On the gradual loss of the linguistic knowledge required for metrical archaisms, see Fulk 2007b.

[13] The argumentation of this paragraph draws on Neidorf and Pascual 2014. Other objections to the chronological interpretation of Kaluza's law are answered in Clark 2014 and Fulk 2014:28–32.

[14] For an overview, see Neidorf 2013–2014, which builds on Menner 1952 and Cronan 2004.

in prehistoric Old English.[15] The natural explanation for the restriction of *suhtriga* to *Genesis A*, seventh-century glosses, and a fossilized compound is that this word fell out of the English language very early, having been supplanted by comparable words such as *nefa* and *brōðorsunu*.[16] Similar conclusions are required to explain, for example, the restriction of *missere* 'half-year' to *Beowulf*, *Genesis A*, and *Exodus*, and the restriction of *þengel* 'prince' to *Beowulf* and *Exodus*.

§8. The language of *Beowulf* differs markedly from that of works known to have been composed during the ninth and tenth centuries not only with respect to its phonology and lexicon, but also its morphology, syntax, and semantics. The most striking morphological archaism in *Beowulf* is the conservation of the original *i*-stem genitive plural desinence in the forms *Deniga* and *winia*.[17] Syntactically, the poem is exceptional for its close observance of Kuhn's laws and its regular use of the weak adjective without a determiner.[18] The poem's archaic semantics are evident in many fascinating cases. Fred C. Robinson (1985:55–57) observed that *Beowulf* is unique in its use of *synn*, *bealu*, and *fyren*, because these words retain their original, preconversion meanings, which are absent from later works where they regularly bear theological connotations. Tom Shippey (1993:173–175) identified a similar case of archaic semantics in the poet's use of the noun *hrēow*, which carries only its older meaning 'sorrow' and never exhibits its later, specialized meaning 'penitence'. Rafael J. Pascual (2014) recently noted that *scucca* 'instigator' and *þyrs* 'ogre' must also possess only their preconversion meanings in *Beowulf*—a feature that aligns the poem's semantics with early glossarial evidence, but renders it distinct from texts composed after 800, by which time these words had become synonymous with "devil." Semantic change is also the probable reason for the restriction of *gædeling* 'kinsman, companion' to *Beowulf*, *Daniel*, and the Corpus Glossary, three notably archaic works (Neidorf 2016b).

---

[15] The significance of *suhtergefæderen* in *Beowulf* is discussed below in §§42–43 (chapter 2).

[16] For the attestations of *suhtriga*, see Cronan 2004:35–39; the word receives further discussion in Neidorf 2013–2014:11–13, 26–27.

[17] See Fulk 2007a:271 and Fulk 2014:26, as well as the discussion below in §§48–49, 105.

[18] Both features are discussed in Fulk 2014:27–28 and below in §§173–174. On Kuhn's laws, see Donoghue 1997. Pascual (2015) demonstrated that many perceived exceptions to Kuhn's laws actually conform to a distinct, but complementary regularity (Pascual's law) and therefore do not constitute genuine violations. On the use of weak adjectives without determiners, see Yoon 2014 and Amos 1980:110–124.

§9. The unambiguous conclusion to be drawn from the linguistic evidence pertaining to the dating of *Beowulf*—that the poem was composed around 700—is lent further support by the evidence for the circulation of Germanic legend in England. H. M. Chadwick first observed that many of the names in *Beowulf* and related poems were borne by historical Anglo-Saxons during the seventh and eighth centuries, but were no longer in use during the ninth and tenth centuries.[19] The onomastic data suggest that Germanic legend circulated vigorously during the early Anglo-Saxon period, but gradually fell out of circulation during the ninth century. This suggestion is borne out by the chronological distribution of the works that exhibit genuine awareness of heroic-legendary traditions. The seventh and eighth centuries yield the *Liber Monstrorum*, the *Vita Sancti Guthlaci*, Alcuin's *Letter to Speratus*, the Franks Casket, the Anglian genealogies, and *Widsið*. The ninth and tenth centuries, on the other hand, yield no contemporary compositions that bear unambiguous witness to the oral currency of Germanic legend.[20] The serial corruption of proper names in the manuscript of *Beowulf*, moreover, is a clear sign that heroic-legendary traditions were no longer as widely known as they had once been.[21] Two scribes were evidently able to reach maturity in England without hearing of many of the heroes and peoples who inhabited the migration-era world of *Beowulf* and its antecedent tradition.

§10. While the scribal errors of proper names lend broad support to the hypothesis of archaic composition, clearer dating implications attend the many transliteration errors that pervade the transmitted text of *Beowulf*.[22] Because these errors must have entered into the text as it was copied from earlier scripts into later ones, they indicate that the poem had been committed to parchment long before the eleventh century. Most significantly, the transmitted text of *Beowulf* contains fourteen readings in which the letters *a* and *u* have been confused: for example, *unhar* for *anhar* (357a),

---

[19] See Chadwick 1912:42–44, 64–66. Recent discussions of the onomastic evidence that corroborate Chadwick's conclusions include Wormald 2006, Neidorf 2013a, and Shippey 2014.

[20] The evidence for the circulation and cessation of knowledge of Germanic legend in England is surveyed in Neidorf 2014b and discussed below in §§120–124 (chapter 3).

[21] See Neidorf 2013b, which is substantially expanded in chapter 3 of the present book. The corruption of proper names in the transmitted text of *Beowulf* is also noted in Sisam 1953b:37; Tolkien 2006:32; and Shippey 2007:474–476. Tolkien's prescient apprehension of this regularity, recorded in his recently published textual commentary (2014), is discussed at greater length in the appendix to the present book.

[22] See Wrenn 1943:18; Gerritsen 1989b:24; Clemoes 1995:32–34; Lapidge 2000; Clark 2009.

wudu for *wadu* (581a), *banū* for *banan* (158b), and *gumū* for *guman* (2821b).[23]
These errors were probably induced by the use of the open-headed *a* letterform in an earlier manuscript of *Beowulf*. This letterform is common in
eighth-century manuscripts, such as the Épinal Glossary and the Moore MS
of Bede's *Historia Ecclesiastica*, but it is rarely used after the ninth century;
its latest documentary occurrence is in a charter of King Æthelwulf from
847 (Clemoes 1995:32n77). Late scribes who copied out *Beowulf* naturally
misread this obsolete letterform as *u*. The transmitted text also exhibits
frequent confusion of *r* and *n*, *c* and *t*, *p* and *þ*, and *d* and *ð*. Michael Lapidge
(2000) devised an economical explanation for the totality of these transliteration errors by hypothesizing that the archetype of *Beowulf* was written in
Anglo-Saxon set minuscule script prior to 750. Such an archetype would
have contained all of the peculiarities of script and orthography needed to
induce the five sets of transliteration errors found in the extant manuscript
of *Beowulf*.[24]

§11. The transmitted text of *Beowulf* contains many additional signs
that the poem had been committed to parchment long before the eleventh
century. The orthography of the manuscript is predominantly Late West
Saxon (LWS), but there are more than a few archaic spellings in the text that
evidently escaped modernization. The lexeme typically spelled *ecg* in LWS
is thrice spelled *ec*, much as it was in eighth-century manuscripts of Bede's
Historia Ecclesiastica; the same phenomenon is evident in the spelling *sec* for
later *secg*. The lexeme typically spelled *þeow* in LWS is frequently spelled
þeo in the poem's personal names, which reflects composition before the *w*
in inflected forms of *þēo* had been attached to the nominative case through
analogy; the *þeo* spelling is also found in the Vespasian Psalter and the Laws
of Æthelberht.[25] Ritchie Girvan noted that the spelling *hrærg* (for LWS *hearg*)
appears to represent the corruption of a notably archaic form, since smoothed
æ before *r* is preserved only in the early glossarial evidence.[26] In this case
and others, archaic spellings were retained because scribal misapprehension
prevented modernization. For example, Daniel Donoghue (1987:36–40)
observed that the manuscript's *seah on* probably represents the infinitive

[23] See the fuller discussion of these errors in §53 (Chap. 2); the related confusions of *d* and *ð* are
discussed at length in §54.

[24] Lapidge's argument is corroborated in Doane 2013:37–41, where it is shown that the same transliteration errors occur in the transmitted text of *Genesis A*. The objections to Lapidge's argument
raised in Stanley 2002 are refuted in Clark 2009.

[25] On the *ec* and *þeo* spellings, see Fulk 2014:25–26 and the discussion below in §56.

[26] See Girvan 1935:14; *HOEM*:§289; and §52 below.

sēon, spelled in the poem's archetype as uncontracted **seohon* (§51). The ability of the scribes to modernize was not infallible: various relics of archaic orthography are to be expected in a late copy of a text composed centuries earlier. The twelfth-century copy of the Laws of Æthelberht, which were issued around the year 600, offers an apt parallel in its preservation of a smattering of archaic forms in a predominantly Late West Saxon matrix (see Oliver 2002:25–34).

§12. Examined in isolation, a relic of archaic orthography or an error induced by diachronic change might be dismissed on the grounds that its chronological significance is uncertain or that a nonchronological explanation for its genesis is conceivable. Discussing the *merewioing* form,[27] E. G. Stanley (1981:201) contended that its dating implications are negligible because "some single, odd, ancient-looking spelling provides no firm basis for early dating." Such reasoning would be sound if the transmitted text of *Beowulf* contained only one or two peculiar forms that might be archaic. The manuscript contains, however, many textual aberrations that are readily explained under the hypothesis of archaic composition. The ability of a single hypothesis to explain what caused a wide array of disparate phenomena is the clearest sign of its validity. Rational observers readily credit such a hypothesis, since doubting it demands credence in an improbable coincidence: in this case, one would need to believe that each of the archaic forms in the *Beowulf* manuscript has an independent cause unrelated to chronology and that the poem's apparent antiquity is an accidental illusion. Accordingly, when choosing between competing hypotheses that have been marshaled in attempts to explain a peculiar spelling or a scribal error, it is essential to reason holistically and halt the proliferation of unnecessary conjectures. A contested form should not be examined in a vacuum, where it might be dismissed as a meaningless accident, but should whenever possible be related to significant patterns that have been observed in the transmitted text.

§13. The chronological significance of scribal errors and archaic spellings is often evaluated in isolation, though, due to the piecemeal nature of the scholarship in which the pertinent forms have been identified and analyzed. Relevant observations are scattered throughout works of text-critical and linguistic scholarship, in notes, articles, monographs, and grammars. Editions of *Beowulf* offer extensive compilations of data, but considerations of space necessarily render their discussion rather terse and often impenetrable to nonspecialists. Consequently, one purpose of this book is to explicate and

---

[27] The significance of which is explicated below in §§34, 107.

consolidate what is already known of the transmission of *Beowulf*. By synthe-
sizing and augmenting that body of knowledge, this book presents a wealth
of material for scholars to consult when they must evaluate textual evidence
bearing on the dating and editing of *Beowulf*. The macroscopic assessment of
the condition of the transmitted text conducted herein leaves one with little
doubt about the duration of the poem's transmission. The hypothesis that
the extant manuscript of *Beowulf* contains a late copy of a work composed
centuries earlier is so frequently required to explain the evidence that its
probability approximates virtual certainty. Kevin S. Kiernan (1981:270)
complained that previous studies of the *Beowulf* manuscript were "founded
on the premise that the MS is a late, corrupt copy of an early poem ... though
there has never been an attempt to justify this premise." His complaint is not
quite correct, since the aforementioned premise had been implicitly justified in much philological scholarship. Yet a comprehensive and pedagogical
account of the reasons for regarding the extant manuscript of *Beowulf* as
a late copy of an early poem remains a desideratum, which this book is
intended to fulfill.

2. The Detection of Scribal Error

§14. The most significant insights into the transmission of *Beowulf* derive
from those manuscript readings where the scribes responsible for copying
the poem have evidently misconstrued and corrupted the text before them.
These errors reveal a great deal not only about the history of the *Beowulf* text,
but about language history, cultural change, scribal behavior, and the relative intelligibility of archaic Anglian poetry in the later Anglo-Saxon period.
Since the text of *Beowulf* is preserved in a single manuscript, readers might
wonder how it is possible for scholars to conduct textual criticism—that is, to
identify scribal errors and restore authorial readings. Indeed, it has been said
that textual criticism is an entirely futile branch of research into Old English
poetry because "the task of identifying the poet's work versus the scribe's
work is impossible" (Pasternack 1995:193). This statement is grounded in
a dubious theory of scribal behavior scrutinized in chapter 4, but its senti-
ment is commonly found in the work of scholars who are not adequately
informed about the methods and reasoning employed in *Beowulf* textual criticism. Scholars opposed to the use of emendation in editions of Old English
poetic texts—known as editorial conservatives for their desire to conserve
as much of the transmitted text as possible—apparently hold the conviction

that the methods for detecting scribal errors and restoring authorial readings are unreliable and hence not worth employing in critical editions.[28] Since editorial conservatism has saturated Old English scholarship for more than a century, it appears necessary to explain in detail how scribal errors in the *Beowulf* manuscript can be detected and emended.

§15. The detection of scribal error is an inductive process dependent upon the recognition of regularities and the identification of passages that constitute deviations from those regularities.[29] In this context, the term "regularities" refers both to the regular features of the particular text under scrutiny—its meter, syntax, style, morphology, semantics, etc.—and to the regular features of the linguistic and cultural material that informed the composition of the work. The textual criticism of *Beowulf* necessarily looks beyond the poem's sole extant manuscript to embrace what is known of the history of the English language, the corpus of Old English poetry, and Germanic heroic-legendary tradition (*inter alia*). When a passage appears to deviate from the regularities observed in *Beowulf*, or in the pertinent sets of external data, it should not immediately be regarded as a corruption, but the possibility of scribal error must be investigated. As A. E. Housman remarked, the reasoning employed in the investigation of a suspected corruption is circular, but circularity should not be equated with futility:

> Rules of grammar and metre ... are formed by our own induction from what we find in the MSS.... The MSS. are the material upon which we base our rule, and then, when we have got our rule, we turn round upon the MSS. and say that the rule, based upon them, convicts them of error. We are thus working in a circle, that is a fact which there is no denying; but, as Lachmann says, the task of the critic is just this, to tread that circle deftly and warily; and that is precisely what elevates the critic's business above mere mechanical labour.
>
> 1961:145

In other words, circular reasoning is an inherent feature of hypotheticism; such reasoning is fallacious only if the circle of evidence the critic embraces is too narrow to justify credence in the hypothesis of scribal error. As the circle widens to embrace considerations pertaining to independent forms of evidence, the probability of scribal error can become so

---

[28] For discussion of the theoretical underpinnings of editorial liberalism and conservatism, see Lapidge 1994 and 2003. The longstanding prevalence of conservatism in *Beowulf* textual criticism is recounted and critiqued in Lapidge 1993 and Fulk 1997.

[29] See Patterson 1987:55–91 and Fulk 1996b.

considerable that it demands credence from reasonable observers.[30] This is why the charge of corruption is most convincing when grounded in data internal and external to *Beowulf*: to doubt that these passages contain errors forces one to regard the agreement between disparate bodies of evidence as an accidental coincidence.

§16. The corruption of a word in the manuscript of *Beowulf* is often revealed through a confluence of signs that an error has crept into the text. A clear illustration is available in the passage printed in *KB* as follows:

> siþðan Cāin wearð
> tō ecgbanan   āngan brēþer,
> fæderenmǣge

> 1261b–1263a

after Cain turned out to be the murderer of his only brother, his father's son

In the transmitted text of *Beowulf*, the name *Cain* is not present here. A scribe at some point in the transmission has corrupted this name into the word *camp*, which means "strife" or "combat" (cf. German *kampf*). The substitution of *camp* for *Cain* not only deprives the passage of its obvious sense—Grendel's mother dwelt in wastelands as an exile because Cain, her ancestor, murdered Abel—it also results in a verse that is metrically defective. The distribution of stressed and unstressed syllables in the manuscript's *siþðan camp wearð* (xxSS) finds no secure parallel in *Beowulf* or in any classical Old English poem because it represents a violation of the four-position principle.[31] Emending *camp* to disyllabic *Cāin* restores sense to the passage and results in a standard type B verse that contains the four requisite metrical positions (xxSxS). This combination of semantic and metrical considerations possesses such probabilistic force that one cannot reasonably doubt that *camp* is a scribal corruption of authorial *Cain*.

§17. The hypothesis of scribal error can always be subject to unreasonable doubt, however. Kiernan (1981:183) contended that "the modern critic need not assume that *camp*, at line 1261, is a corruption of the proper name, Cain," on the grounds that some sense can still be wrested from the passage as it stands. In his view, the manuscript reading should be retained because the passage in which it occurs can be translated as "when strife arose [*siþðan*

---

[30] The distinction between narrow and holistic circularity in reasoning is elucidated well in *HOEM*:§14.

[31] Comparable verses are attested only in nonclassical poems composed late in the Anglo-Saxon period; see Russom 1987:54 and *HOEM*:§291.

camp wearð] as a sword slayer to an only brother" (1981:183). Many untenable arguments in the text-critical literature on *Beowulf* employ this sort of ad hoc reasoning and cling to the belief that if a passage can be shown to contain intelligible Old English lexemes, the possibility of scribal corruption is nullified. Such reasoning is misguided because the rational textual critic prefers the reading that makes the best overall sense, not a mere modicum of grammatical sense. It is therefore not surprising that editors of *Beowulf* since Grundtvig, with the exception of Kiernan, have routinely emended *camp* to *Cāin*. Yet there is a more fundamental problem with Kiernan's reasoning: it implies that in order for a word to be regarded as a scribal error, the resultant form must be unintelligible gibberish. To credit argumentation like Kiernan's, one would need to believe that scribes were capable of erring only by corrupting a word in their exemplar into a string of letters devoid of any discernible meaning. The errors discussed in this book demonstrate, to the contrary, that the scribes who transmitted *Beowulf* often corrupted authorial words by converting them into other recognizable words, which, although intelligible, are contextually nonsensical and transparently spurious.

§18. Several of the passages that contain transliteration errors illustrate the tendency for corrupt readings to take the form of genuine lexemes. When emended, these passages read as follows:

(a)   mægenrǣs forgeaf
            hildebille,   hond swengne oftēah;

                                                            1519b–1520

he gave a powerful thrust to his war-sword—his hand did not spare the blow

(b)   ond his mōdor þā gȳt
            gifre ond galgmōd   gegan wolde
            sorhfulne sīð,   sunu *dēoð* wrecan.

                                                            1276b–1278

and his mother still, ravenous and gallows-minded, intended to mount a grievous undertaking, to avenge her son's death

(c)   of þām lēoma stōd,
            þæt hē þone grundwong   ongitan meahte,
            wrǣtte giondwlītan.

                                                            2769b–2771a

light glinted from it, so that he could make out the ground, look over the treasures

(d)   Þā wæs gesȳne   þæt se sīð ne ðāh
                 þām ðe unrihte   inne gehȳdde
                 wrǣtte under wealle.

                                                     3058–3060a

It was then apparent that the attempt by the one who had wrongly hidden
the valuables within walls had not succeeded

In each passage, the visual confusion of letterforms (*r* for *n*, *d* for *ð*, *c* for *t*)
led a scribe to misconstrue a word in his exemplar and commit a different
Old English word to parchment. The resultant word has an established place
in the lexicon of Old English, but it produces nonsense in its immediate
context. In (a), the manuscript reads *hord* 'hoard' in place of *hond* 'hand';
in (b), the manuscript reads *þēod* 'nation' in place of *dēoð* 'death'; and in
both (c) and (d), the manuscript reads *wræce* 'misery' in place of *wrǣtte*
'treasure'. Readers can substitute the meanings of the manuscript forms into
the translations provided above to apprehend the not infrequent absurdity
of the transmitted text.[32] These transliteration errors are the products of
a purely mechanical method of copying, in which each individual lexeme
in the exemplar is scrutinized independent of its larger semantic context.[33]
The scribe aimed either to reproduce the form as he saw it or to modernize
the form according to Late West Saxon orthographic conventions. In the
cases of *þeod* and *wræce*, the scribal preoccupation with form rather than
sense is most apparent. Some care was evidently taken in each case to
produce an orthographically correct form: the archaic spelling *deod must
have been misconstrued as *ðeod* and then spelled *þeod*; and the exemplar's
wrætte must have been misconstrued as *wræcce* and then spelled *wræce*.[34]
The scribes were not mindless, but their minds were focused on committing
plausible forms to parchment, not on the sense that these forms collectively
yielded. Accordingly, to argue that a manuscript reading cannot be an error
on the grounds that it is an intelligible form is to misunderstand fundamentally the behavior of the scribes, as the following chapters of this book will
demonstrate.

---

[32] For a recent demonstration of the literary incoherence that results from the corruption of *hond*
into *hord*, in view of the poet's characterization of Beowulf as a *hondbona*, see Sebo 2011.

[33] The lexemic theory of scribal behavior reflected in this remark is expounded below in §§126–133.

[34] It should be noted that *þ* and *ð* were interchangeable graphemes; the tendency for *þ* to be used at
the beginning of words accounts for the scribe's replacement of the perceived *ð* with *þ*. For more on
the corruption of *dēoð* into *ðeod*, see §54. Scribal unfamiliarity with *wrætte*—a poeticism or archaism
confined to *Beowulf* and the *Riddles*—might have facilitated the corruption of this word into *wræce*.

§19. Each of the methodological considerations articulated above (§§15–18) bears on the detection and emendation of two scribal errors located in the same verse (2523a). The verse appears in a speech Beowulf delivers prior to fighting the dragon:

> Nolde ic sweord beran,
> wǣpen to wyrme,   gif ic wiste hū
> wið ðām āglǣcean   elles meahte
> gylpe wiðgrīpan,   swā ic giō wið Grendle dyde;
> ac ic ðǣr heaðufȳres   hātes wēne,
> [o]reðes ond _ǣ_ttres;   forðon ic mē on hafu
> bord ond byrnan.

2518b–2524a

> I would not bear a sword, a weapon against the reptile, if I knew how I could otherwise honorably grapple with the troublemaker, as I once did with Grendel; but I expect hot war-flame there, exhalations and poison; therefore I have on me shield and mail-shirt.

In the manuscript, the text comprising line 2523a reads *reðes ond hattres*. Sense can be wrung from each of these forms: *reðes* can be construed as the genitive singular of an adjective that means "cruel"; and *hattres* can be construed as the genitive singular of an otherwise unattested nomen agentis formed from the verb *hātian*, meaning "hater." In an article that exhorted editors to retain the manuscript reading, Allan H. Orrick (1956:554) offered the following translation of the clause containing the problematic verse: "But there I should expect hot battle-fire, I should expect a fierce one, a hater." Orrick's defense of the manuscript is based upon his belief that emendation is justified only "when a passage makes absolutely no sense" or "when the one essential of the form, i.e., at least one occurrence of the alliterative stave in each half-line, is absent" (1956:556). In his view, then, the manuscript reading has been successfully defended because a modern mind has managed to make sense of it and because the *h* of *hattres* could be thought to alliterate with *hafu* in the off-verse.

§20. Defense of the manuscript's *reðes ond hattres* is untenable, however, because there are several unmistakable signs that the verse is corrupt, which are discernible in the defects of sense, style, and meter that scribal error has here generated. John C. Pope (1957) composed a comprehensive refutation of Orrick's argument, and some of his most salient observations are worth recapitulating in the present context. First, although the manuscript reading is intelligible Old English, it deprives the passage of its required sense.

Beowulf is explaining why he arms himself with sword and shield to fight the dragon, though he went unarmed when he fought Grendel: this time, he anticipates hot battle-fire (*heaðufȳres hātes*), noxious breath (*oreðes*), and poisonous venom (*āttres*). These are the threats that distinguish the dragon from Grendel, necessitate the wearing of a shield and mail-shirt (*bord ond byrnan*), and eventually result in Beowulf's death. The entire train of thought is derailed if "breath" and "poison" are eliminated. Second, Orrick's claim that the manuscript reading results in a line with acceptable alliteration is incorrect. For *hattres* to alliterate with *hafu* in the off-verse (*forðon ic mē on hafu*), the final lift of the line would need to participate in alliteration—a circumstance ubiquitously prohibited in classical Old English poetry (Sievers 1893:§21). The scansion of the off-verse indicates that postpositive *on* constitutes its first ictic position; vocalic alliteration is therefore to be expected in the on-verse, and it is supplied in the emendation *oreðes ond āttres*. There are several other technical problems with the manuscript's *reðes ond hattres*: the verse is stylistically anomalous;[35] and if alliteration were to fall on *hattres*, the second ictic lexeme, the verse would violate the rule of precedence.

§21. As the preceding example illustrates, the mere addition or omission of a letter can disrupt the text so severely, and in so many different respects, that it is often rather easy for the discerning textual critic to detect corruption in the transmitted text of *Beowulf*. The emendation of scribal errors can be a more difficult matter, and it is admittedly futile in cases where lengthy sequences of text have been accidentally omitted. Yet the scribes' method of mechanically reproducing the words they saw in their exemplar ensured that, in most corrupt passages, the authorial form was preserved beneath a thin layer of textual corruption. Recognition of the pertinent regularities internal and external to *Beowulf* enables the textual critic to penetrate through the corrupt form and identify the reading that would remedy the aberrations generated by scribal error.

§22. Erasures and superscript letters in the extant manuscript of *Beowulf* indicate that the scribes altered approximately 150 words after they were committed to parchment.[36] In some cases, these alterations function

---

[35] Stevick (1959:341) lent support to Pope's (1957) defense of the emendation by noting: "Whenever the on-verse consisting of an *x ond y* construction appears, alliteration of the two key words is the unvarying pattern unless the half-line is a common formula.... [W]e have 121 half-lines constructed in precisely the same manner as 2523a. In all these 121 occurrences, both key terms alliterate. The original MS reading *reðes ond hattres* is, therefore, not only unprecedented in the poem, but stands in a 121 to 1 ratio of improbability."

[36] A list of the instances of scribal self-alteration is conveniently printed in the appendix of Orchard 2003–2004.

to correct mechanical errors, while in others they function to standardize the orthography of the text. Kiernan (1981:191) regarded this evidence for scribal self-correction as a conclusive sign that the scribes proofread their work and subjected it to "intelligent scrutiny." He then argued that if the text had been proofread, the scribes could not have "overlooked up to 350 additional mistakes, about one every ten lines, as the modern editions maintain" (1995:209). Closer examination of the alterations that the scribes made to their work does not inspire confidence in the hypothesis that the scribes thoroughly proofread the poem they copied. The alterations confirm, rather, that the scribes were concerned solely with form, not with sense, since they affect isolated words and exhibit no regard for their larger semantic context (see §§44, 56, 66, 102, 110, 112–116, 186). The scribes corrected errors when they resulted in gibberish, but errors that resulted in genuine lexemes escaped their scrutiny. When the scribes sporadically proofread their work, they scanned the text for words spelled incorrectly; they do not appear to have made any effort to comprehend the text and determine whether it made sense. It is not an accident that so many of the uncorrected errors in the transmitted text, such as the seven discussed above, take the form of plausible words: *camp* (for *Cāin*), *hord* (for *hond*), *þēod* (for *dēoð*), *wræce* (for *wrætte*, twice), *rēðes* (for *oreðes*), and *hattres* (for *āttres*). To a scribe concerned only with the superficial dimensions of the text, rather than its sense, these forms did not look suspicious. The nonsense engendered by these errors would be apparent only to someone who took the time to comprehend the poem.

§23. An understanding of scribal behavior is thus an essential tool for textual criticism. The demonstrable tendency of the scribes to corrupt words into visually similar words should remain ever at the forefront of the textual critic's mind. When it is recognized that this tendency was combined with an indifference to the sense of the text and a desire to modernize its spellings, the cause of many errors becomes apparent. For example, at the close of the Offa digression, the poet alludes to the great king's successor:

> wīsdōme hēold
> ēðel sīnne;   þonon *Ēomēr* wōc
> hæleðum tō helpe

1959b–1961a

(Offa) ruled in wisdom his native land; from him arose Eomer as a help to heroes

In the manuscript, the name Eomer has been corrupted into the adjective *geōmor* 'mournful', which yields manifest nonsense in the present context. Because the scribe was unfamiliar with the legendary traditions known to the *Beowulf* poet, he evidently saw no proper name in the graphemes comprising the name *eomer* and believed this sequence of graphemes to be a nonstandard form of the lexeme that should be spelt *geōmor* (§91). This error exemplifies well the scribal tendency to copy the text on a word-by-word basis, without regard for the sense or the formal properties of the poem. For in addition to depriving the text of its sense, the corrupt *geōmor* results in a line without alliteration. Because of the virtually certain identification of the authorial form here—the Anglian genealogies (Dumville 1976: 33) confirm that Eomer was the name of Offa's heir—this case independently corroborates the reliability of alliteration as a criterion for the detection of scribal error.

3. Meter and Alliteration

§24. Defective alliteration is the most easily apprehended sign that a line is corrupt, but it should not on account of its salience be considered the only criterion of poetic form relevant to textual criticism. Orrick's argument for the retention of the manuscript's erroneous *hattres* was erected upon the premise that alliteration is "the one essential of the form," though a century of metrical scholarship has shown this premise to be rather mistaken. Statistically, the transmitted text of *Beowulf* is as regular in its adherence to various metrical rules of classical Old English poetry as it is to the requirement that alliteration must be present in every line. The reliability of meter as a tool for the detection and emendation of scribal error receives independent corroboration in a case similar to the corruption of Eomer, involving the name of the son of Scyld Scefing. The transmitted text gives *Bēowulf* as the name of this character, though in every iteration of the West Saxon genealogies, the son of Scyld is named Beow (*KB*:291–292). The genealogies lead the textual critic to suspect corruption—has the scribe once again regarded the name of an unfamiliar hero as an orthographical error requiring correction?—but meter confirms it beyond reasonable doubt. The off-verse *Bēowulf Scyldinga* (53b) would need to be scanned as an expanded type D* (SxSsx), yet verses of this sort are restricted to the on-verse and require double alliteration.[37] Emendation of the verse to *Bēow Scyldinga* not only

---

[37] See Bliss 1967:§64 and Fulk 1989:314n4.

brings the poem into accord with the genealogies, but also results in a metrically acceptable arrangement (§§89–90).

§25. Scholars opposed to the emendation of Old English poetic texts often contend that verses exhibiting deficient meter or alliteration should not be regarded as corrupt, since poets might deliberately compose defective verses for artistic purposes.[38] On a theoretical level, this argument might seem reasonable, but confrontation with the actual evidence of the transmitted text of *Beowulf* suggests that it is incorrect. The notion that the *Beowulf* poet genuinely composed unmetrical or nonalliterative verses is falsified by the frequent co-occurrence of defects of form and sense in passages where corruption is suspected.[39] Verses deficient in alliteration (such as *reðes ond hattres* or *þonon geōmor wōc*) tend also to be deficient in sense or syntax; the same holds true for verses deficient in meter (such as *siþðan camp wearð* or *Bēowulf Scyldinga*). The transmitted text contains few unmetrical or nonalliterative verses that are not objectionable on independent grounds. Because defects of meter and alliteration emerge so often in patently corrupt verses, these defects must be understood as the consequences of scribal error, not as the products of authorial deliberation.

§26. The charge of ethnocentrism has often been leveled against scholars who favor the emendation of verses on the basis of meter. John D. Niles, for example, wrote:

> Emendations that are made *metri causa* eliminate poetic license by fiat. They can take no account of departures from the norm for special reasons or effect. If poets are not metrical automatons but poets, it seems presumptuous to remake them in our own metrical image and likeness.

> 1994:452

There is considerable irony in such allegations, since the proposition that the *Beowulf* poet would deliberately compose unmetrical verses for poetic effect is itself a salient example of ethnocentrism. Argumentation to this effect is predicated upon a modern notion of the poet as an individual reacting against tradition, who violates conventions to distinguish himself from his predecessors and express his unique literary sensibilities. By imagining that Old English poets must have fashioned themselves in this manner, scholars resistant to metrical emendation anachronistically project a product of the

[38] Remarks to this effect appear in Busse 1981, Taylor and Davis 1982, Niles 1994, and Kiernan 1995.

[39] For an illuminating discussion of this phenomenon of co-occurrence, with several additional examples provided, see Fulk 1997:38–46.

Romantic period a thousand years into the past.[40] The extant Old English poetic texts offer no compelling reasons for scholars to believe that Anglo-Saxon poets or audiences regarded defective meter or alliteration as a mark of literary sophistication.[41] On the relatively rare occasions when transmitted verses are deficient in meter or alliteration, there tend to be independent signs of scribal corruption, not poetic subtlety. By all appearances, poets strove to be as metrically regular and linguistically conservative as they could be. Anglo-Saxon aesthetics plainly differed from the aesthetics of modern literary culture, and the surest way to apprehend the difference is to acquire a technical understanding of the formal features of their poetry, not to disregard such features on the basis of theoretical reasoning appropriate to works composed a millennium later.

§27. Although some degree of ethnocentrism is unavoidable in modern scholarship on medieval works, textual critics can reduce their susceptibility to ethnocentric assumptions by regarding meter as one of the most decisive criteria for the detection and emendation of scribal errors. The reliability of meter as a tool for textual criticism stems from the fact that it enables the probability of corruption to be determined on a statistical basis, with the pertinent statistics drawn from the extant corpus of Old English poetry. Arguments for the retention or emendation of a suspected corruption focused solely on its apparent sense (or lack thereof) are far more likely to involve ethnocentric assumptions than arguments grounded in metrical considerations. For example, the transmitted text's naming of Scyld's son as Beowulf, rather than Beow, struck the postmodern sensibility of James W. Earl (1994:22–25) as a poet's clever manipulation of tradition rather than a scribe's blunder. His argument for the retention of the manuscript reading is based in the application of contemporary aesthetics to a medieval poem, whereas the argument for emendation has the support of metrical probabilities that are inductively derived from the poem itself. Since a human subject is required to discern metrical rules, both criteria can be said to be subjective, but the degree of subjectivity involved is obviously different. When metrical regularities and aesthetic impressions collide in the evaluation of a textual crux, meter must be regarded as the more reliable criterion. The problem with argumentation such as Earl's is not that it is subjective, but

---

[40] This claim is insightfully elaborated in *HOEM*:§§35–40, which builds upon the contention of Calder (1979:1) that "Romantic notions of 'The Poet' offer no help in explicating these largely anonymous and formulaic poems, because their impersonality and remoteness call attention to style without reference to biography."

[41] For empirical substantiation of this claim, see Neidorf 2016a.

that it is unreliable and hence more likely to lead to improbable conclusions about the textual history of *Beowulf*.

§28. Metrical analysis, far from being an excessively subjective tool, actually constrains the subjectivity of the textual critic and impedes the proliferation of implausible conjectures. More than a few *Beowulf* emendations that have been proposed can be discarded because they would result in unmetrical verses. A recent example pertains to the critical effort to identify the word that has been omitted from a defective verse:

> Breca nǣfre gīt
> æt heaðo-lāce,   nē gehwæþer incer,
> swā dēorlīce   dǣd gefremede
> fāgum sweordum   —nō ic þæs [fela] gylpe—
> þēah ðū þīnum brōðrum   tō banan wurde,
> hēafod-mǣgum;

> 583b–588a

> Breca has never yet at sword-play, nor either of you, accomplished so daring a deed with chased swords—I boast little about it—though you turned out to be your brothers' killer, your closest kinsmen's

Editors have traditionally supplied *fela* in line 586b because it remedies both the alliterative and metrical defects of the manuscript reading, *no ic þæs gylpe*: it alliterates with *fāgum* and produces a standard type C verse. Alfred Bammesberger (1996:380) challenged this emendation on the grounds that it results in a statement that is "incongruous with the tone and style of the epic." He proposed that *sōþes* was the omitted word and rendered the defective verse as *nō ic þæs sōþes gylpe* ("I do not brag about this truth"). Bammesberger's emendation might strike the subjectivity of a modern reader as a plausible solution—indeed, it was persuasive enough to be credited by Andy Orchard (2003a:252)—but metrical considerations expose its improbability. Because *sōþes* places the first alliteration of the line on *sweordum*, the second stressed lexeme in the on-verse, this emendation results in a violation of the alliterative rule of precedence. More decisively, *nō ic þæs sōþes gylpe* must be scanned as a type A verse with trisyllabic anacrusis in the off-verse (xxxSxSx)—a metrical contour that is not attested in *Beowulf* and is prohibited in classical Old English poetry. In the wars fought over textual criticism, meter is an impartial weapon: it undermines conservative efforts to defend corrupt readings as effectively as it constrains liberal efforts to bring about specious improvements of sense or style.

4. Probabilistic Reasoning

§29. In textual criticism, competing hypotheses are validated or falsified on the basis of relative probability, not absolute certainty. Editors and critics deem one hypothesis superior to another not because it is definitely correct, but because it is more coherent and plausible than all of the alternative hypotheses. With regard to the preceding example, it is conceivable that *fela* was not the reading that appeared in the archetype of *Beowulf*. Yet *fela* remedies the defects of meter and alliteration in the transmitted text more effectively than any other reading that has been proposed. Another consideration in its favor is that *nō ic þæs [fela] gylpe* exemplifies the type of litotes of which the *Beowulf* poet was demonstrably fond. *Sōþes* is rejected not because it is certainly incorrect, but because it makes inferior claims to probability: this word fails to remedy the line's faulty alliteration, while introducing new metrical defects. The same considerations of probability that led textual critics to suspect corruption in the manuscript lead to the rejection of Bammesberger's emendation. Editors doubt the authenticity of the manuscript's *nō ic þæs gylpe* because regarding it as a genuine verse demands credence in an improbable coincidence: one would need to believe that a poet who imposed strict regularities of meter and alliteration on his poem decided to compose, in this particular instance, a verse that is deficient in both meter and alliteration. Credence in Bammesberger's hypothesis is equally costly, since it forces adherents to maintain the collateral belief that a metrical pattern not attested in *Beowulf* (xxxSxSx) would actually have been found in the poem in this one verse, had it not been corrupted during the text's transmission. Credence in the hypothesis that *fela* is the missing word, on the other hand, necessitates belief in no stunning coincidences—one must merely believe that a scribe, while copying a standard type C verse, accidentally omitted a word.

§30. Probabilistic reasoning is not a medium for arriving at definitive truth, but for determining what it is rational for observers to believe about an unknown reality on the basis of the available evidence.[42] Whether the unknown reality is the archetype of *Beowulf* or the evolution of the human species, absolute proof of the veracity of the hypothesis cannot materialize, but that is a precondition for scientific research, not a sign of its futility. To

---

[42] I am indebted for this formulation to Hirsch 1967:174–175, who draws in turn on Keynes 1921:7. On the role of probabilistic reasoning in philological argumentation, see *HOEM*:§§8–23 and Fulk 2003.

reject a valid text-critical hypothesis on the grounds that it is not absolutely certain is thus to misunderstand the epistemological character of claims generated through probabilistic reasoning. Determining whether a passage in the transmitted text of *Beowulf* is corrupt or genuine is a matter of rational belief, centered on the following question: Is it more reasonable to believe that the passage was genuinely composed by an Old English poet or is it more reasonable to believe that it is the outcome of scribal error? The issues can be illustrated with any proposal of corruption, such as the hypothesis that the manuscript's *geōmor* is a corruption of authorial *Ēomēr*. To regard this word as a scribal error, one must simply believe that a scribe has mistaken the identity of a word in his exemplar. To regard the manuscript reading as genuine, however, one must believe that the poet deliberately composed a verse deficient in alliteration and sense. Advocates for the authenticity of *geōmor* must also believe in a stunning coincidence: that the name of Offa's son is not mentioned in the poem, but that a word formed from many of the same graphemes happens to appear in the one verse where we should expect to find this name. The hypothesis that *geōmor* is a corruption can be doubted—indeed, Kiernan (1981:184) has doubted it—but such doubt is patently unreasonable, since it forces the doubter to maintain collateral beliefs that are overwhelmingly improbable.

§31. Two centuries of collaborative scholarship on the detection and emendation of scribal error in the transmitted text of *Beowulf* have generated an impressive body of what Sir Karl Popper (1985: 112) labeled "conjectural knowledge." Such knowledge is said to be conjectural because hypotheses retain an aspect of their hypothetical character even after validation, insofar as they are continually subject to scrutiny and refinement in the light of new insights. Most contributions to human knowledge are conjectural in origin and character, since they stem from the formulation and testing of hypotheses that cannot be strictly proven, but can be validated when rendered probable beyond reasonable doubt. The reliance upon probabilistic reasoning in text-critical research should therefore not be construed as a unique feature of this field of inquiry. Nor should it be imagined that the absence of definitive proof erects an insurmountable barrier to the advancement of our knowledge of the transmission of *Beowulf*. Even without definitive proof, the probability of many text-critical hypotheses can approximate virtual certainty. Considerations of probability are entirely sufficient to justify the firm investment of credence in the hypothesis that *Ēomēr* was the authorial reading in line 1960b. If a second manuscript of *Beowulf* were discovered that contained the correct reading, its bearing on the validity of the hypothesis that *geōmor* is a corruption of *Ēomēr* would be negligible, since that hypothesis has already been rendered probable beyond reasonable doubt. Apprehension of a variety of probabilistic considerations provides, in fact, a much firmer foundation for credence in a hypothesis than the emergence of a single piece of apparently definitive proof.

§32. To apprehend fully the probabilistic force of an argument for corruption or emendation, intricate knowledge of several complicated subjects is often required. For *Beowulf*, these subjects include meter, orthography, phonology, morphology, syntax, and dialectology. It is frequently the case that corruption in the transmitted text can be identified only in the light of these specialized disciplines. Scholars unequipped with the knowledge required for *Beowulf* textual criticism may therefore express unreasonable doubt about valid hypotheses without perceiving why such doubt is unreasonable. If the reasoning behind these hypotheses is not understood, corruption may not be apparent and emendation may appear superfluous. Accordingly, the existence of intense disagreement over text-critical questions should not be regarded as a sign that these questions are genuinely undecidable. Rather, such disagreement is usually a sign that certain contributors to the text-critical literature have not possessed an adequate understanding of the philological probabilities involved. Simply put, the less knowledge a critic possesses, the less corrupt the text will seem.[43] It is for this reason that some editors will emend verses with alliterative defects, but not metrical defects: any scholar can recognize the absence of alliteration, whereas only scholars with considerable philological knowledge can perceive metrical problems. Since the statistical underpinnings of metrical and alliterative rules are roughly equivalent, no principled rationale could support the practice of emending on the basis of one criterion, but not the other.[44] Such contradictory practice is a product of insufficient understanding of the conclusions that have been reached in philological scholarship. In an

---

[43] The role that knowledge differential plays in the formation and dissipation of text-critical consensus has also been observed by Housman (1926:xxvii): "It would not be true to say that all [editorially] conservative scholars are stupid, but it is very near the truth that all stupid scholars are conservative. Defenders of corruptions are therefore assured beforehand of wide approval; and this is demoralizing. They need not seriously consider what they say, because they are addressing an audience whose intelligence is despicable and whose hearts are won already; and they use pretexts which nobody would venture to put forward in any other cause. Emendators should thank their stars that they have the multitude against them and must address the judicious few, and that moral integrity and intellectual vigilance are for them not merely duties but necessities."

[44] This argument has been articulated and illustrated with many examples in Fulk 1997 and Fulk 2007e.

effort to improve understanding of these conclusions, clear explication of the reasoning behind them is provided throughout this book.

5. General Prefatory Remarks

§33. The most common objection leveled against text-critical scholarship on *Beowulf* is that the enterprise is futile because it is impossible for modern scholars to reconstruct the "original version" of the poem in its entirety: stretches of unrecoverable text have been omitted, some scribal alterations may be undetectable, and the extant manuscript is charred around the edges.[45] This objection reflects a misunderstanding of the practical aims of textual criticism. Modern editors of *Beowulf* emend roughly three hundred scribal errors in the transmitted text, yet they never imagine that these emendations combine to generate the pristine original of *Beowulf* as it left the poet's pen or mouth. In recent editions, no effort is made to supply verses to fill in lacunae of indeterminable length, nor is there any attempt to rewrite the transmitted text with archaic and dialectal spellings. Editors refrain from engaging in such futile undertakings because their aim has not been to recover the unrecoverable, but to restore authorial readings whenever compelling probabilities permit (Fulk 1996b:8). In this respect, editors of *Beowulf* have adhered to the conception of textual criticism articulated by Eugène Vinaver (1939: 366), who regarded an edition as "a *partial* reconstruction of the lost original." As Vinaver states, textual critics aim "not at restoring the original work in every particular, but merely at lessening the damage done by copyists" (1939:366). This aim has yielded considerable fruit in *Beowulf* textual criticism, which has not recovered the poem's original version, but has probabilistically detected and emended over three hundred instances of scribal error in the transmitted text. Like most sciences, this scholarly enterprise does not offer unmediated access to definitive truth, but it improves our understanding of observable phenomena.

§34. Since this book studies the received text of *Beowulf* for information about the poem's transmission, the question of whether a passage requires emendation in a modern critical edition is not always relevant to its argumentation. Of course, the detection of scribal alteration requires the textual critic to formulate a tentative hypothesis about the authorial or antecedent

---

[45] The various forms that this objection has taken in Anglo-Saxon studies are reviewed in Fulk 1996b:7–8.

reading that has been altered. Yet there are many cases of scribal alteration in the transmitted text that shed light on the poem's textual history or the scribes' difficulties that do not require emendation in modern editions. For example, the aberrant spacing in the manuscript's *mere wio ingasmilts* for *Merewioingas milts* 'the Merovingian's mercy' furnishes a significant indication that a scribe could not correctly discern the lexemes that were to be extracted from the series of graphemes encountered in the exemplar.[46] Scribal confusion induced by unfamiliarity with the Merovingian name is evident, yet emendation (as conventionally understood) is not required: the authorial reading is recovered merely by altering the spacing of the manuscript.[47] Similarly, many peculiar spellings in the transmitted text contain probable indications of scribal misapprehension, yet it is conventional to print the transmitted spellings rather than to regularize them and bring them in line with the orthographical norms of the manuscript. The merits and demerits of this policy are not relevant to the present study, which aims only to extract information from the aforementioned peculiarities about the transmission of the text and the behavior of the scribes.

§35. There is a tendency in text-critical scholarship to attribute the genesis of every corruption in the transmitted text of *Beowulf* to the two scribes who copied out the extant manuscript. Since there are compelling reasons to believe that at least one copy of the poem stands between the archetype and the extant manuscript (see Gerritsen 1989b:20), this tendency is not altogether justified. While the two latest scribes are doubtless responsible for introducing many errors into the transmitted text, it is possible that they uncritically reproduced errors that were already present in the exemplar from which they were copying. In most cases, no decisive method can enable the textual critic to determine whether an error was generated by the final scribes or by antecedent copyists.[48] While it is an acceptable convention to attribute an error to the final scribe, it would be more accurate to regard a given corruption as the product of scribal behavior in general

[46] On the *merewioing* form, see Shippey 2005 and Neidorf 2013b:255. J. Gerritsen (1989b:23) wrote in passing of the manuscript reading: "One can only marvel who or what [scribe B] thought *mere wio ingasmilts* was." See also the discussion below in §107.

[47] Emendation is generally understood to involve the editorial modification of at least one letter. Editorial rejection of the word divisions in the transmitted text is not considered a form of emendation; if it were, the number of emendations in a given edition would increase exponentially, since sense constantly requires editors to combine or divide the units of words transmitted by the scribes.

[48] Only in the cases of scribal self-corrections, which appear to have been conducted without consultation of the exemplar, can we be certain that we are bearing witness to innovations (often trivial or erroneous) introduced into the transmitted text by the two final scribes (see §§186, 188).

rather than as the product of the unique methods of a particular scribe. The patterns of errors that are discernible throughout the extant manuscript suggest, in any event, that the scribes who played a role in the transmission of *Beowulf* were not markedly different in their aims or their methods. The errors that pervade the text indicate that the entire poem was reproduced in a mechanical, word-by-word manner by scribes who were preoccupied with orthographical regularization and indifferent to meter and sense. If the scribes differ in any respect, it is in the degree to which they systematically modernized the spellings encountered in the exemplar.[49] Beyond that, there is no salient difference between the labors of the two scribes who produced the poem's extant manuscript.

§36. Contemporary scholarship on medieval literature places increasing emphasis on the material contexts in which works were preserved and transmitted. Practitioners of Old English literary criticism regularly generate new readings of poems in their manuscript contexts, in which they relate the reception of these works to the religious and political issues of the tenth and eleventh centuries. The spread of uncritical agnosticism concerning the relative chronology of Old English poetry has lent this approach considerable appeal. Many scholars now reject the prospect of interpreting a poem in the century in which it was probably composed, and prefer instead to read the poetic corpus "in the late Anglo-Saxon period, the period in which we know the poems to have been read" (Magennis 1996:5). For example, Stacy Klein (2006: 57) situates her interpretation of Cynewulf's *Elene* "during the period of the manuscript's reception" because an audience of that era is the "one, and indeed the only, group of Anglo-Saxon readers whom we can be reasonably certain had access to the poem." A curious feature of literary criticism purportedly performed on Old English poems in their manuscript contexts is the indifference shown to scribal errors and questions of relative intelligibility. Critics routinely presume that the language of the poetry was transparent to late audiences, yet the condition of the transmitted text of many poems indicates that archaic Anglian poetry was not entirely comprehensible to late scribes. Linguistic and cultural changes that intervened between the period of composition and the period of reception created difficulties for eleventh-century readers of eighth-century poetry comparable to those facing modern readers of *Paradise Lost* or *Hamlet*. These difficulties should

---

[49] There is reason to believe that the second scribe modernized the spellings of the exemplar less assiduously than the first scribe; see Sisam 1953b:92–93.

not be effaced, but should be placed in the foreground of genuine efforts to read Old English poems in their manuscript contexts.

§37. Formalist efforts to produce plausible interpretations of Old English poems are also aided by an understanding of textual transmission and scribal error. Interpreters of *Beowulf*, discovering that long-standing dispute surrounds a particular manuscript reading, are often forced to take a side in the dispute in order to generate a coherent interpretation of the passage containing the crux. Sound judgment in matters of textual criticism can therefore be a prerequisite for the construction of a persuasive interpretation. More than a few interpretive essays on *Beowulf* have been vitiated by their authors' inability to gauge the probability of corruption and weigh the merits of emendation. For example, two scribal errors in the Finnsburh episode converted the Jutes (*Ēotan*) into giants (*eotenas*). Scholars aware of the scribes' propensity to corrupt unfamiliar proper names into common nouns of similar appearance will readily apprehend the probability that the manuscript's *eotenum* is a mechanical corruption of *Ēotum* (see §§103–105). A surprising number of critics, however, have regarded *eotenum* as an authorial form and maintained the belief that giants played a mysterious role in the conflict between the Danes and the Frisians at Finnsburh.[50] A great deal can hinge on a scholar's text-critical acumen: mistaking a scribal error for an authorial reading in this case alters the character of the poem and generates an untenable interpretation of the episode. If literary critics intend to respect the intelligence and artistry of the *Beowulf* poet, it is imperative for them to interpret the text of his work "in a form more nearly resembling what the author is judged to have written than what the scribe has happened to transmit" (Lapidge 1993:132).

§38. The transmission of *Beowulf* is a subject that should command the attention of all scholars who work closely with the poem. Whether one is a historical linguist mining the text for data or a literary critic developing a fresh interpretation of a passage, one must handle the transmitted text in a critical manner in order to produce accurate scholarship. The extant manuscript is not a divine relic; it is the product of fallible human laborers. To treat the transmitted text as a set of immutable and inevitable facts is to deny the material realities of medieval textual production. This book presents those who wish to make critical use of *Beowulf* with the knowledge required to understand how the poem was transmitted. Patterns of error in the transmitted text are identified and explained, so that scholars can

---

[50] For references, see Neidorf 2015a:616n60.

more easily gauge the relative probability of hypotheses directed at textual cruces. Beyond this instrumental value, the transmission of *Beowulf* is a subject with considerable interest in its own right. Traditional textual criticism aims to detect scribal errors in order to emend them and establish a more accurate text of an author's work. The present study embraces those aims, while marshaling scribal errors for other purposes as well: contending that they furnish valuable evidence for language history, cultural change, and scribal behavior. In addition to forming the basis for modern critical study of *Beowulf*, the text of the poem transmitted in Cotton Vitellius A.xv bears eloquent witness to the immense historical changes that took place in England between the eighth and the eleventh centuries.

2

LANGUAGE HISTORY

1. Diachronic Variation

§39. Medieval manuscripts that transmit classical Latin works invariably contain corruptions that reflect their scribes' limited command of a dead language. The scribe, whose native language was a European vernacular, can be expected to have experienced difficulties with rare words or unfamiliar constructions. The gap in knowledge of classical Latin between the author of the work and the scribe who transmitted its earliest extant witness is likely to be considerable. It is therefore entirely reasonable for modern editors of classical Latin works to explain peculiarities in the transmitted text by hypothesizing that the scribe has failed to comprehend the text in his exemplar. For Old English textual criticism, however, it has been argued that the hypothesis of scribal incomprehension is inherently implausible, since each work was composed in the native language of the scribe. This view was memorably articulated by E. G. Stanley (1984:257) in his defense of textual conservatism:

> We in our subject have to remember with constant humility that though perhaps, not certainly, most scribes may not have been the equals in Old English of the best Old English poets, every one of them, sleepy and careless as he may have been at times, knew his living Old English better than the best modern editor of Old English verse.

The claim that scribal fluency in Old English should ensure the accurate transmission of literary works illustrates the perils of purely theoretical reasoning, since this claim sounds reasonable in theory, but it crumbles upon confrontation with the evidence. Close analysis of the transmitted text of *Beowulf* reveals, contrary to Stanley's dictum, that fluency in Old English could be an impediment to accurate transmission, especially when the fluent scribes were preoccupied with form and indifferent to sense. If the scribes who transmitted *Beowulf* knew no Old English, many of the lexical, syntactic, and onomastic corruptions discussed below could never have materialized.

§40. A more fundamental problem with Stanley's argument is that it effaces diachronic and dialectal variation in its presumption that the "living Old English" of the scribe should be identical to the Old English of a poem composed in a different part of the country over two centuries before the scribe's birth. Scribal errors induced by diachronic and dialectal variation are salutary reminders that Old English was not a homogeneous language that existed in stasis for five centuries. The language of the eighth century was not the language of the eleventh century. Salient differences in lexicon, phonology, and morphology distinguished the Mercian dialect of the *Beowulf* poet from the Late West Saxon dialect of the scribes. The artificial and elevated diction of the Old English poetic tradition was another source of difficulty for prosaic scribes: poetic vocabulary long removed from colloquial speech and syntactic archaisms conditioned by the demands of meter made the language of *Beowulf* even more remote from the language of the scribes. Accordingly, textual critics dealing with late manuscripts of Old English poetry have sound reason to emulate editors of classical Latin texts and explain textual peculiarities by hypothesizing that linguistic barriers impeded scribal comprehension. A modern editor trained in historical linguistics, metrics, and dialectology could be in a much better position to understand the language of *Beowulf* than a late scribe whose knowledge of Old English was synchronic, provincial, and unaided by scholarly resources.

§41. The failure of the scribes to comprehend the language of *Beowulf* would not be relevant to the transmission of the text if the task of the scribe were to reproduce the letters encountered in the exemplar without modification. Problems arose because the scribes programmatically altered spellings that deviated from the orthographical norms of the Late West Saxon written standard in which they were trained. Several varieties of corruption in the *Beowulf* manuscript indicate, moreover, that the scribes felt obligated to "correct" the forms in their exemplar when they believed them to be in error. For the Anglo-Saxon scribe, the task of the mechanical reproduction of the text was complicated by the imperative to modify its superficial, nonstructural features.[1] Language change frequently induced the scribes to make minor alterations to the text that inadvertently deprived it of sense,

---

[1]   The term "nonstructural" refers to the features of an Old English poetic text that are not bound to its metrical or alliterative regularities. Structural features of the text, in Sisam's terms, are those that are "confirmed by the metre" (1953b:123).

grammar, alliteration, or meter. These alterations offer valuable insights into the history of the English language—particularly, into some specific ways that the language had changed between the period when *Beowulf* was composed and the period when its extant manuscript was produced. Moreover, the errors induced by language change lend compelling support to the hypothesis that the composition of *Beowulf* antedated the production of its extant manuscript by several centuries. If the poem were contemporary with the manuscript, as Kiernan (1981) maintained, the transmitted text would not exhibit errors that must be attributed to language change.

§42. Two cases of scribal misunderstanding conditioned by the archaic language of *Beowulf* materialize in the rendering of copulative compounds in the transmitted text. In the corpora of early Germanic languages, only four such compounds are attested: *sunufatarango* 'son and father' in the *Hildebrandslied*, *gisunfader* 'son and father' in the *Heliand*, *āþumswēoras* 'son-in-law and father-in-law' in *Beowulf*, and *suhtorfædran* 'nephew and uncle' in *Beowulf* and *Widsið*. The rarity of this type of word-formation, combined with its restriction to poetic texts, led C. T. Carr (1939: 40) to conclude that "the type was obviously not productive at the time when the earliest texts of Germanic were written down." For the *Beowulf* poet and his original audience, the copulative compound remained an intelligible archaism, but for the scribes of the extant manuscript, it was an inexplicable anomaly. Some context is required to apprehend the consequences of these corruptions. The first copulative compound refers to Ingeld (the *āþum* 'son-in-law') and Hroðgar (the *swēor* 'father-in-law') in a passage that alludes to their future conflict and reads as follows in the edited text of the poem:

> Sele hlīfade,
>
> hēah ond horngēap,   heaðowylma bād,
>
> lāðan līges—   ne wæs hit lenge þā gēn
>
> þæt se *e*cghete   āþumswēoran
>
> æfter wælnīðe   wæcnan scolde.

81b–85

The hall towered, tall and wide-gabled; it awaited battle-surges, dreaded flame; it was sooner yet that the blade-hostility should be roused for father- and son-in-law after deadly violence.

In place of *āþumswēoran*, the transmitted text reads *āþum swerian* 'to swear oaths'. The scribe evidently misconstrued *āþum* as the dative plural of *āþ* (oath), which then led him to regard *swēoran* as an erroneous spelling of *swerian* that required correction (*KB*:120). This chain of confusion, preceded by the miswriting of *se ecghete* as *secghete*, illustrates how the scribal preoccupation with form and indifference to sense could result in drastic disruption of the text. The resultant forms are all sense-bearing Old English words (*secg, āþum, swerian*), but they conspire to produce a line deficient in sense and alliteration. By obliterating the reference to the two principal agents of the feud, moreover, the error deprives the entire passage of its import. That a late scribe should find the copulative compound an unrecognizable formation is suggested by a verse in Cynewulf's poetry: *swēor ond āðum* (*Juliana* 65b). Composing perhaps a century after the *Beowulf* poet (*HOEM:*§376), Cynewulf divided the obsolete *āþumswēoras* into a phrase that would have been easier for his audience to comprehend (Carr 1939:41).

§43. The other copulative compound attested in Old English is recorded in *Widsið* as *suhtorfædran* (46b) and in *Beowulf* as *suhtergefæderan* (1164a). In both poems, this word is used in reference to Hroðulf (the *suhtor* 'nephew') and Hroðgar (the *fædera* 'uncle'). Editors avoid emending the form transmitted in *Beowulf* by construing it as *suhterge-fæderan*, though Carr (1939:41) rejected that construction on the grounds that in compounds "weak nouns do not normally appear with a composition vowel in OE." There is thus reason to believe that the form transmitted in *Widsið* reflects the form that had been present in the archetype of *Beowulf* and that the *-ge-* in *suhtergefæderan* is the product of scribal tampering. Two motivations for its insertion are conceivable. The letters could serve to convert *fædera* into the contextually incorrect, but formally viable *gefædera* 'godfather' (= Lat. *compater*). Alternatively, the inserted *ge-* might serve to connect the two lexemes, on analogy with compounds such as *aldorgedal*.[2] The scribe, unfamiliar with the copulative compound formation, appears to have regarded the form in the exemplar (*suhtorfædran*) as a syntactic aberration that required correction through the insertion of a connective element. In this case, the sense of the text is not disrupted, but scribal difficulty with the archaic language of *Beowulf* may nonetheless be apparent.

§44. Minor tampering motivated by misapprehension of a linguistic archaism is evident in the scribal treatment of the instrumental inflection of *dōgor* 'day'. This noun occurs in the instrumental case three times in *Beowulf*:

Ðȳs dōgor þū	geþyld hafa (1395)
þegnes þearfe,	swylce þȳ dōgor (1797)
ðǣr hē þȳ fyrste	forman dōgore (2573)

---

[2] On the use of the *ge-* prefix in compounding, see Fulk 2007b:312–317.

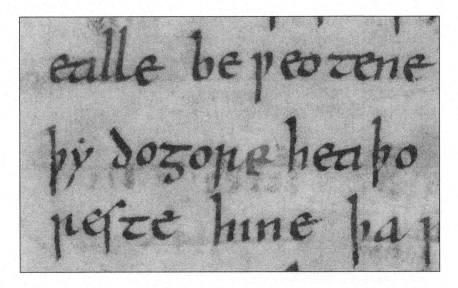

Figure 1. Scribal addition of *e* to *dōgor*, line 1797b (fol. 172r).

In 1395a, the archaic inflectionless form of the instrumental is preserved in the transmitted text, whereas in 2573b, the later analogical form is recorded.[3] The meter provides no decisive indication of which form is authorial, since the medial vowel would be syncopated when an inflectional ending is added (§66), but the third instance of instrumental *dōgor* suggests that the *-e* in 2573b is a scribal insertion. In the portion of the manuscript corresponding to 1797b, it is clear that Scribe A originally committed *dōgor* to parchment and that Scribe B later added an *-e* to this form (see figure 1). Since Scribe B's alterations of Scribe A's work appear to have been effected without consultation of the exemplar, the editors of *Klaeber's Beowulf* prudently restore the form that Scribe A had committed to parchment in 1797b (*KB*:xxxii–xxxiii). The thirteen alterations that Scribe B made to Scribe A's work reveal that he skimmed his collaborator's portion in search of superficial errors or nonstandard spellings. Because the scribe was unaware of the archaic instrumental ending of *s*-stem nouns, he probably regarded *þȳ dōgor* as an ungrammatical construction that required correction. The addition of the *-e* in 1797b and 2573b was therefore motivated by language change—in particular, by the reduction in intelligibility of an archaism over the period that separated the composition of *Beowulf* from the production of its extant manuscript.

---

[3] On this archaism, see *KB:Lang.* §21.4; Weyhe 1906:85–87; Brunner 1965:§289n1; Fulk 2007a:270; Hogg and Fulk 2011:§2.96n2.

§45. Another morphological archaism in *Beowulf* that the scribes mechanically obscured is the use of the uninflected infinitive after *tō*.[4] In two instances, the uninflected form escaped scribal scrutiny and was preserved in the transmitted text: *Mæl is mē tō fēran* (316a) and *frēode tō friclan* (2556a). Elsewhere in the manuscript, the inflected form of the infinitive uniformly appears after *tō*. In four verses, such as *tō healdanne* (1731a; cf. also 174b, 1003a, 1805a), the meter requires the syllable generated by the inflection and thereby indicates that the *Beowulf* poet varied his deployment of this feature. In five verses that contain inflected infinitives, however, defective meter reveals that the inflection is scribal, not authorial:

> Sorh is mē tō secganne (473a)
> Wundor is tō secganne (1724b)
> idese tō efnanne (1941a)
> Tō lang ys tō reccenne (2093a)
> sæcce tō sēceanne (2562a)

Because the inflection in these verses generates various problems—converting verses of type A into implausibly heavy type D verses, if not violating the stricture against protracted second drops (Sievers 1893:§82.6)—it is clear that the final syllable of each verse is not genuine. The scribes, concerned with the superficial correctness of the text rather than its meter, inflected these infinitives in the evident belief that the inflection is not optional in a grammatically regular work. Tampering with this feature might have extended beyond the five cases listed above: inflected infinitives appear in eight other verses (257a, 1419a, 1851a, 1922a, 2416a, 2445a, 2452a, 2644a) where scansion can accommodate either the inflected or the uninflected form. As Fulk observed, the scribal inflection of the uninflected infinitive demonstrates, contra Stanley (1984), that "the scribes' own language interfered with their copying, prompting them to write metrically incorrect forms because the forms in their exemplar were foreign to their own speech" (Fulk 1997:40).

§46. Scribal alteration motivated by language change produces a similar metrical aberration in verse 25a, *in mægþa gehwǣre*. As it stands, the verse would need to be scanned as type A with anacrusis (xSxxSx), but double alliteration is standard in verses requiring this scansion.[5] It is probable that a scribe has substituted analogical *gehwǣre* for an original *gehwǣm*, since

---

[4]   This feature has engendered considerable discussion: see *KB:Lang.* §25.8, *T.C.* §21; Sievers 1885:255, 312, 482; Brunner 1965:§363n3; *OES:*§921; *HOEM:*§3; Pope 1966:237; Bliss 1967:§44; Hutcheson 1995:146–149.

[5]   See *KB:T.C.* §35; Bliss 1967:§§46–7; Sievers 1885:485; Fulk 1996b:3.

the restoration of *gehwǣm* converts 25a into a standard type B verse. In the original paradigm of the indefinite pronoun *gehwā* 'everyone', masculine and feminine genders were not distinguished, and the dative singular *gehwǣm* accorded with nouns of all three genders. In Late West Saxon, analogy with the paradigm of the demonstrative pronoun led to the creation of *gehwǣre*, the feminine counterpart to *gehwǣm* and *gehwǣs* (Hogg and Fulk 2011:§5.20). That this neologism was foreign to the language of the *Beowulf* poet is evident in verses 1365a (*Þǣr mǣg nihta gehwǣm*) and 2838a (*þēah ðe hē dǣda gehwǣs*), in which the original pronominal forms are used in reference to feminine nouns (*KB:T.C.* §20). In each case, the meter confirms that the *Beowulf* poet never used *gehwǣre* and that the presence of this neologism in 25a is due to the scribal belief that the use of *gehwǣm* in connection with *mǣgþa* (f.) is ungrammatical. Once again, the language of the scribes is at odds with the language of the poet, and the discrepancy results here in a palpable vitiation of the poet's artistry.

§47. Before other alterations induced by language change are discussed, two observations pertaining to the preceding three examples (in §§44–46) are worth registering. First, there is reason to believe that the scribal effort to regularize the superficial features of the text is not a reflection of the individual preferences of the scribe, but of a programmatic imperative, connected to training in a late written standard, that informed the labors of many contemporary scribes. Corruptions similar to those noted above are discernible in all of the major codices of Old English poetry: the scribal inflection of the infinitive spoils the meter, for example, in *nīðas tō nergenne* (*Daniel* 284a), *Micel is tō hycganne* (*Riddles* 28.12b), and *weorc tō geþolianne* (*Juliana* 569b); and the scribal substitution of *gehwǣre* for *gehwǣm* generates metrical defects in *ond þē wyrda gehwǣre* (*Andreas* 630b), *þā þe her on mǣgðe gehwǣre* (*Precepts* 74a), and *in ceastra gehwǣre* (*Elene* 972). Second, although late scribes plainly strove to correct nonstandard features that were perceived to be erroneous, inattentiveness often led to inconsistent and imperfect results. Many archaisms escaped obliteration and persisted into the transmitted text of *Beowulf* due to the precarious nature of scribal performance. Consequently, in the three preceding paragraphs, the transmitted text was seen to contain both the authorial and the scribal treatment of the particular feature: alongside *dōgor* (1395a), there is *dōgore* (2573b); alongside *frēode tō friclan* (2556a), there is *sǣcce tō sēceanne* (2562a); and alongside *gehwǣm* (1365a), there is *gehwǣre* (25a). Recognition of the fallible nature of scribal modernization is essential to the interpretation of much subsequent data. Since it is implausible that late scribes should introduce archaic features into the text, the transmitted archaisms must represent features that were present—and more prominent—in the poem's archetype.

§48. One of the most remarkable archaisms preserved in the transmitted text of *Beowulf* is the retention of the original genitive plural desinence of the light *i*-stem nouns *Dene* 'Dane' and *wine* 'friend': the form *Denig(e)a* is transmitted fourteen times, and *winia* is transmitted twice.[6] *Beowulf* is the only work that contains these forms, with the exception of *Guthlac B*, where *winiga* (1365a) escaped modernization due to scribal error—it is preserved in the manuscript as *wiinga* or *wunga* (*HOEM*:§281). Analogy with the paradigm of *a*-stem nouns led to the replacement of the -*i(g)a* desinence with the widespread genitive plural -*a* desinence. The original *i*-stem paradigm must have eroded at an early date, since poetry and prose of all periods exhibit the analogical forms. Meter confirms that the *Beowulf* poet used the original desinence: all of the verses with *Denig(e)a* and *winia* would become unmetrical if the analogical form were substituted (e.g., *Deniga leodum* and *winia bealdor* would turn into three-position verses). Conversely, in the seventeen verses where the manuscript records the analogical forms (*Dena* and *wina*), the older forms can be substituted without disturbing the meter, with the sole exception of *Dena land ofgeaf* (1905b), where *Dena land* may in any event represent an alteration of an antecedent *Deneland* (*HOEM*:§§279–280). A scribe has evidently modernized the text whenever the substitution of the analogical form would not generate a metrically defective verse. An original **Deniga ond Wedera* was therefore altered to the equally viable *Dena ond Wedera* (498b), but *folces Denigea* (1582a) was left unaltered because the reduction of a syllable would have rendered the verse unmetrical.

§49. It is surprising that metrical considerations should have constrained the modernization of *Denig(e)a* and *winia*, since other modernizations, such as the scribal inflection of the uninflected infinitive, were imposed upon the text without regard for their metrical consequences. The discrepancy is perhaps best explained by attributing the selective modernization of *Denig(e) a* and *winia* to an intermediate copyist, closer to the *Beowulf* poet, who apprehended metrical nuances to which later scribes were indifferent. The frequent and obvious corruption of the meter in the transmitted text suggests that the final scribes paid little attention to the meter of what they were copying. The distribution of *Denig(e)a*, *winia*, *Dena*, and *wina* in the extant manuscript is therefore a likely reflection of the distribution found in an antecedent copy of the poem. The final scribes might have refrained from modernizing the

---

[6] On this archaism, see *KB:Lang.* §21.5; Fulk and Hogg 2011:§2.61; Fulk 2014:26.

rest of the -*i(g)a* forms because the significance of the desinence was obscure to them. Scribal unfamiliarity with this archaism is registered in the curious manuscript reading *de ninga* (for *Deniga*, 465b), in which the -*i(g)a* desinence has been misconstrued as the -*ing* suffix.

§50. Unfamiliarity with another morphological archaism led a scribe to distort the sense of the passage in which Beowulf thanked Unferð for lending him his sword:

> Heht þā se hearda   Hrunting beran
> sunu Ecglāfes,   heht his sweord niman,
> lēoflic īren;   sægde him þæs lēanes þanc,
> cwæð, hē þone gūðwine   gōdne tealde,
> wīgcræftigne,   nales wordum lōg
> mēces ecge;   þæt wæs mōdig secg.

1807–1812

> The hardy man directed that Hrunting be brought to the son of Ecglaf, told him to take his sword, the valued iron; he offered thanks to him for the loan, said, he regarded that war-friend as good, strong in battle, by no means explicitly found fault with the sword's edge; that was a magnanimous man.

The transmitted text is defective in reading *lēan* 'reward' for the word that the narrative requires to be *lǣn* 'loan': Beowulf is here thanking Unferð for the loan of Hrunting and returning the heirloom to its rightful owner.[7] The probable motivation for the scribal substitution of *lēan* for *lǣn* is that the gender of *lǣn* had changed after the poem's composition. Elsewhere in Old English, *lǣn* is always a feminine noun, but it was originally a neuter noun like all of its Germanic cognates (Brunner 1965:§288). Composed before the analogical reassignment of the word's gender had set in, *Beowulf* appears uniquely to retain the etymological gender of *lǣn*. Since *lǣn* was a feminine noun in the language of the scribe, however, the sequence *þæs lǣnes* must have struck him as an ungrammatical construction that required correction. Disregarding the sense of the passage, the scribe resolved the difficulty by presuming that *lǣnes* was an error for *lēanes* and altering the word accordingly. Diachronic change created a rift between the language of *Beowulf* and the language of its copyists, which once again induced a scribe to introduce a corruption into the text when he probably believed he was removing a corruption from it.

§51. Contraction upon loss of intervocalic *h*, a sound change relevant to the establishment of a relative chronology of Old English poetry, might also

---

[7]   See *KB*:217–218; Hoops 1932b:196; Kock 1922:90.

play a role in the textual history of *Beowulf*. This sound change had taken effect by the middle of the seventh century, well before the composition of *Beowulf*, yet meter frequently indicates that the poet used the precontracted forms of certain words (*HOEM*:§§99–130). Verses such as *man geþeon* (25b), *on flet teon* (1036b), *metodsceaft seon* (1180a), and *deaþwic seon* (1275b) require the substitution of the earlier, disyllabic form in order to possess four metrical positions. It is therefore not improbable that an earlier manuscript of *Beowulf* should have contained spellings that reflected the archaic pronunciations of these words. One anomalous passage in the transmitted text is readily explained under the hypothesis that such spellings had been employed in an antecedent copy of *Beowulf*. Wounded by the dragon, the dying hero sits down in order to gaze upon the work of giants:

> Ðā se æðeling gīong
> þæt hē bī wealle   wīshycgende
> gesæt on sesse;   seah on enta geweorc,
> hū ðā stānbogan   stapulum fæste
> ēce eorðreced   innan healde.

> 2715b–2719

The sagacious prince went then to sit on a seat by the wall, to gaze at the work of giants, how stone arches affixed to pillars supported the ageless earth-hall inside.

The transmitted verse *seah on enta geweorc* is metrically defective: it would need to be scanned as an expanded type D*, but verses requiring that scansion are confined to the on-verse and require double alliteration.[8] This long-standing textual crux is satisfactorily resolved by Donoghue's argument (1987: 36–40) that *seah on* is a corruption of *seohon, an archaic spelling of the precontracted form of the infinitive *sēon*. Because this emendation removes the passage's metrical difficulties and improves its syntax, with the infinitive dependent on *gīong*, the probability that it is correct is considerable. The suggestion that a late scribe would misconstrue the unfamiliar *seohon* as two distinct morphemes, *seah on*, is consistent with and corroborated by the patterns of scribal error that are discernible in the transmitted text and adumbrated throughout this book. Considering the rarity of spellings that preserve the intervocalic *h* even in the Épinal-Erfurt glossary (*HOEM*:§405), the evident use of the spelling *seohon* in an earlier manuscript of *Beowulf*

---

[8]   See *KB:T.C.* §31; Sievers 1885:255; Sievers 1893:§84.7; Bliss 1967:§§64–65; *HOEM*:§66.

lends additional support to the hypothesis that the poem was first committed to parchment prior to 725.

§52. The existence of an archaic written text of *Beowulf* is also indicated in the transmitted text's *hrærgtrafum* 'heathen temples' (175a). Comparable spellings, which reflect a stage of the language when smoothed *æ* before *r* had not yet been raised to *e*, are found exclusively in the early Mercian glossaries, in forms such as *haerg(a)*, *faerh*, *mærh*, *spærca*, and *uaergrōd*.[9] Later Anglian texts, such as the Vespasian Psalter, consistently exhibit *e* in the place of *æ* in this environment. That the shift had taken place by the middle of the eighth century is evident, for example, in a charter of King Offa from 767 (Sweet 1978:203), where the lexeme spelled *hærg* (or *haerg*) in *Beowulf* and the glossaries is already spelled *herg(ae)*, the form it would continue to possess in Anglian texts composed throughout the Anglo-Saxon period. The remarkable preservation of the *æ* in *Beowulf* is the probable consequence of the dittography of an antecedent copyist, who corrupted *hærg* into *hrærg*. As Girvan argued:

> Once miswritten, it was copied mechanically and preserved because no longer understood. If the scribe had understood the word he would have made it *herg* or *hearg* as it appears elsewhere, but by an accident we can restore an older and more original spelling (1935:14).

The reasoning behind this conclusion is holistic, since the transmitted *hrærg* is not the only corruption that has alerted textual critics to archaic orthographic features of the archetype of *Beowulf*.

§53. A variety of transliteration errors entered the transmitted text of *Beowulf* because the orthographic conventions that obtained in the earliest period of English literacy were foreign to scribes educated in later centuries. As noted above (§10), the corruptions that involve the confusion of *a* and *u* are particularly significant, since the open-headed *a* letterform that evidently induced these corruptions fell out of regular use before the middle of the ninth century.[10] There are eight unambiguous instances of *a/u* confusion in the extant manuscript, which are distributed evenly between the stints of the two scribes: MS *banū* for *banan* (158b), *unhar* for *anhār* (357a), *wudu* for *wadu* (581a), *walan* for *walu* (1031b), *gumū* for *guman* (2821b), *geongū* for *geongan* (2860a), *sweordū* for *sweorda* (2961b), and *strade* for *strude* (3073b).

---

[9] See Campbell 1959:§222–225; Hogg 1992:§5.98; *HOEM*:§289.

[10] For discussion of this phenomenon and its chronological significance, see *KB:T.C.* §8; Lapidge 2000:10–20; Clemoes 1995:32–34; Gerritsen 1989b:24. Objections to this criterion are answered in Clark 2009 and Clark 2014.

Three other probable cases of *a/u* confusion are MS *sporu* for *spora* (986a), *eaferū* for *eaferan* (1068a), and *eaforū* for *eafora* (1710a). Of possible, but uncertain, significance in this connection are the four instances where *sunu* is transmitted in place of what would have been *suna* in the original paradigm of this noun (344b, 1278b, 1808a, 2013a).[11] In any event, the secure instances of *a/u* confusion are sufficient to justify credence in the hypothesis that the open-headed *a* letterform had been employed in an earlier manuscript of the poem. The distribution of these errors throughout the transmitted text confirms that they are not random or idiosyncratic accidents, but are rather the consequences of a systematic problem that created difficulties for both of the scribes (and perhaps for their predecessors). It is worth noting that *a/u* confusion is discernible in the transmission of other archaic poems as well, including *Cædmon's Hymn* (MS *aeldu* for *aelda*, *fudur* for *fadur*), *The Dream of the Rood* (MS *unforht* for *anforht*), and *Genesis A* (MS *garū* for *garan*, *ærenda* for *ærendu*, *iabal* for *Iubal*).[12]

§54. Corrupt readings that involve the confusion of *d* and *ð* form another category of transliteration error with potential chronological significance. There are twelve clear instances of this confusion in the transmitted text: MS *hādor* for *haðor* (414a),[13] *að* for *ād* (1107a), *þeod* for *dēoð* (1278b), *hwæþer* for *hwæder* (1331b), *standeð* for *standeð* (1362b), *drysmaþ* for *ðrysmaþ* (1375a), *freoðe* for *frēode* (1707a),[14] *geþinged* for *geþingeð* (1837a), *wiðcuðne* for *wīdcūðne* (1991a), *aðsweorð* for *āðsweord* (2064a), *ford* for *forð* (2959b), and *wonreðing* for *Wonrēding* (2965a). The significance of these errors derives from the fact that in the earliest Old English manuscripts, the letter *d* was used to represent both the dental fricative and the alveolar stop. In the word spelt *mōdgidanc* [= LWS *mōdgeþanc*] in the Northumbrian version of *Cædmon's Hymn*, for example, *d* can be seen to represent both consonants. Scribes continued to use *d* in this dual manner until the middle of the eighth century, when it became standard to use *ð* to represent the dental fricative and *d* to represent the alveolar stop.[15] Following Wrenn (1943:18) and Clemoes (1995:32–

---

[11] See Lapidge 2000:12n36; Campbell 1959:§613; *KB:Lang.* §19.2.

[12] See Orton 2000:22; Lapidge 2000:10–11n32; Doane 2013:37–41.

[13] The need for MS *hādor* to be emended to *haðor* is discussed in this book's appendix and in Fulk 2005b, which also explains why MS *drysmaþ* must represent a corruption of *ðrysmaþ* (1375a). I single these readings out because editorial treatment of them has not been uniform, but the probability of corruption is nevertheless considerable.

[14] There has been some dispute about the reading of the MS in this instance, but the question now appears settled; see Fulk 2005a:196–197.

[15] See Lapidge 2000:31–34; Seiler 2008; Shaw 2013.

34), Lapidge (2000:29–34) contended that the confusion of *d* and *ð* in the transmitted text of *Beowulf* is a probable indication that the poem had been committed to parchment prior to 750. Stanley objected to this argument on the grounds that the confusion could be attributed to mere sloppiness, that is, to "the not uncommon failure in the practice of some scribes to cross <d> to produce <ð>" (2002:65). The objection is theoretically valid, but the particular cases in the *Beowulf* manuscript point to a cause other than scribal inattentiveness. It is remarkable that in eight of the twelve instances identified above, *ð* (or *þ*) is erroneously transmitted where *d* is required. Because this inversion suggests that the scribes had grown accustomed to altering *d* to *ð*, it supports the notion that *d* frequently stood for *ð* in the exemplar from which the scribes were copying. The transmitted *þeod*, for example, must represent a scribe's rationalization upon encountering the form **deod* in the exemplar: instead of converting this form correctly into *dēoð* 'death', the scribe presumed it stood for *ðēod* 'nation', and thus rendered it as *þēod*. The readiness of the scribes to convert *d* to *ð* is best explained as a psychological consequence of dealing with an archaic text where *d* could represent either the dental fricative or the alveolar stop.

§55. Other orthographic features that figured into the poem's textual history are indicated in the occasional errors they appear to have induced. On three occasions where *c* is erroneously written in place of *t*, the confusion is preceded by *e*: MS *secan* for *sētan* (1602b), MS *wræce* for *wrǣtte* (2771a, 3060a). The miswriting of *et* as *ec* reflects the probable use of *et* ligatures in an antecedent copy of the poem, since the *t* in this ligature is especially difficult to distinguish from *c* (Lapidge 2000:27–28). Like the open-headed *a* letterform, the *et* ligature is a common feature of set and cursive minuscule scripts. There is also reason to believe that the poem's archetype made use of the *œ* ligature (or *oe* digraph) to represent the *i*-mutation of *ō*. The variation between *ē* and *ǣ* in the transmitted spellings of the name of Beowulf's grandfather—*Hrēþel, Hrēþles, Hrǣdles, Hrǣdlan* (PGmc. **Hrōþilaz*)—is the probable consequence of a scribe's erroneous decision to render the *œ* ligature as *æ*.[16] The unetymological *Hrǣd-* forms may also preserve the archaic use of *d* to represent the dental fricative (§54), if this is not an instance of phonetic change of *ð* to *d* before *l* (Campbell 1959:§424). Finally, the transmitted form *fæðmię* (2652b) merits consideration in the present context. In the manuscript's *reced* (1981a) and *beļ* (2126b), the hook under the *e* plainly

---

[16] See *HOEM*:§353.17. The transmitted form *reote* (2457a) has been explained as an inversion of an earlier *rœte*; see *KB:Lang.* §7.3.

serves to convert *e* to *æ*, thereby converting an Anglian form into its West Saxon equivalent. Fulk (2005:197) concluded from the Saxonizing function of these hooks that the instances of *ę* are scribal in origin and constitute probable deviations from the exemplar. The rationale behind the scribal insertion of a hook on *fæðmię* is therefore puzzling. If the hook were intended to restore the reading found in the exemplar, it would hint at the existence of a notable orthographic archaism, *fæðmiæ*. While it would be unexpected for a scribe to restore an archaic spelling after transmitting the modernized form, it is possible that the restoration was effected mechanically. The only other way to explain the transmitted *fæðmię* is to contend that the hook is meaningless or accidental.

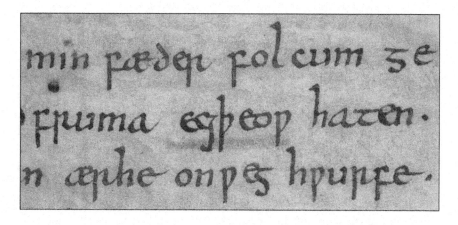

Figure 2. Scribal insertion of *g* into *ecþeow*, line 263b (fol. 137v).

§56. The scribal modernization of the archaic spellings that had been used in the poem's archetype was extensive, but not exhaustive. Indifference or inattentiveness resulted in the occasional transmission of both the archaic and the modernized spellings of certain words. Thus, alongside *ecg-*, the archaic *ec-* spelling of this word is transmitted on three occasions: *Ecþeow* (263b), *Ecþeowes* (957b), and *Eclāfes* (980b). In one instance (263b), the scribe committed *ec* to parchment, then altered it to *ecg* through the insertion of a smaller *g* (see figure 2). The occurrence of *sec* (2863a), in place of *secg*, elevates the probability that the archetype regularly used the *ec-* spelling, which is common in eighth-century Bede manuscripts.[17] Archaic orthography is also preserved in the transmission of *þeo* spellings alongside

---

[17] On the significance of these spellings, see Fulk 2014:26; *KB*:174, 258, Lang. §20.1; Hogg 1992:§2.67n1; Ström 1939:134, 167.

the later, analogical *þeow* spellings. Each form occurs roughly fifteen times, yet the meter confirms that the *þeo* forms reflect authorial usage (*KB:T.C.* §17). In two instances, scribal self-alteration exposes the process of modernization: in 612b, Scribe B has appended a *p* to *wealhþeo*, the form that Scribe A had committed to parchment (see figure 3); and in 2961a, Scribe B added a *p* to his own *ongenðio* (figure 4). Modernization may also be evident in the scribal alteration of -*ungum* to *ingum* in *Sigescyldingum* (2004a): other spellings with -*ung* for -*ing* are transmitted in 2052b, 2101b, and 2159a.[18] Another probable vestige of archaic orthography is *gūðrēouw* (58a), where the early use of *uu* (for *p*) has been incorrectly modernized into *up*, thereby creating an illusory *ēou* triphthong.[19]

Figure 3. Scribal addition of *p* to *wealhþeo*, line 612b (fol. 146r).

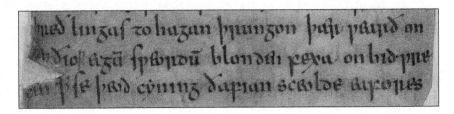

Figure 4. Scribal addition of *p* to *ongenðio*, line 2961a (fol. 197v).

---

[18] On the rationale behind construing -*ung* (for -*ing*) as an archaism, see Kluge 1922:§22.

[19] See *KB:T.C.* §10; on the graphic representation of /w/ and the introduction of the *p* character, see Seiler 2008.

§57. In sum, the transmitted text of *Beowulf* contains a wide variety of peculiarities that are adequately explained only under the hypothesis that the poem had been committed to writing before the middle of the eighth century. To withhold credence from that hypothesis is to demand credence in the perverse belief that, although a chronological explanation can accommodate so many disparate errors and inconsistencies in the transmitted text, an ad hoc multitude of nonchronological explanations for these phenomena is to be preferred. The evidence for a process of scribal modernization of the nonstructural features of an archaic poem is overwhelming. The scribes made numerous superficial alterations to the language of *Beowulf* in an effort to counter the effects of diachronic change and improve the legibility of the text for an eleventh-century readership. Their effort was not always successful: incomprehension and inattentiveness led to the transmission of many nonstructural archaisms; unfamiliarity with the older language and orthography led, in certain places, to errors that preserve or indicate their archaic sources. These errors confirm that diachronic variation created a range of difficulties for scribes charged with the task of reproducing and modernizing a centuries-old poem. A similar picture emerges upon consideration of the scribal effort to convert the Anglian features that characterized the poem's archetype into the West Saxon features that predominate in the transmitted text.

2. Dialectal Variation

§58. Southern scribes active during the tenth and eleventh centuries systematically altered the phonology of the Anglian works they transmitted in order to produce texts in linguistic conformity to the Late West Saxon (LWS) written standard in which they were trained. The ability of southern scribes to understand and alter the vocalism of the Anglian dialects is demonstrated in the LWS versions of *Cædmon's Hymn*, *Bede's Death Song*, and the *Leiden Riddle*, three poems also preserved in their original Northumbrian dialect. Comparison between the archaic, Northumbrian versions and the LWS versions reveals that the process of dialect translation could obliterate the majority of the nonstructural dialectal features and leave only a few traces of the poem's original dialect. Two versions of *Cædmon's Hymn* illustrate how complete the process could be:

Nū scylun hergan hefaenrīcaes uard,	Nū sculon herigean heofonrīces weard,
metudæs maecti end his mōdgidanc,	meotodes meahte and his mōdgeþanc,
uerc uuldurfadur, suē hē uundra gihuaes,	weorc wuldorfæder, swā hē wundra gehwæs,
ēci dryctin, ōr astelidæ.	ēce drihten, ōr onstealde.
Hē āērist scōp aelda barnum	Hē ǣrest sceōp eorðan bearnum
heben til hrōfe, hāleg scepen;	heofon tō hrōfe, hālig scyppend;
thā middungeard moncynnæs uard,	þā middangeard moncynnes weard,
ēci dryctin, æfter tiadæ	ēce drihten, æfter tēode
fīrum foldu, frēa allmectig.	fīrum foldan, frēa ælmihtig.

Now we must praise the guardian of the heavenly kingdom, the might of the maker, and his conception, the work of the glorious father, as he, the eternal lord, established the origin of every wonder. He first created for the children of men [LWS: of earth] heaven as a roof, the holy creator; then the guardian of mankind, the eternal lord, wrought the earth, plains for men, the almighty lord.

Because of the length of *Beowulf*, the occasional traces of the poem's original dialect are cumulatively so considerable as to establish beyond reasonable doubt that its poet was an Anglian, and most probably a Mercian.[20] Since the language section of *Klaeber's Beowulf* provides readers with a complete discussion of the text's transmitted Anglian features and its correctly Saxonized words, the present section of this book will focus on cases where dialectal variation impeded scribal comprehension and resulted in readings that disturb the sense or meter of the text. These cases of failed or detrimental Saxonization shed considerable light on scribal behavior and on the ability of late, southern audiences to comprehend archaic, Anglian poetry.

§59. Saxonization was usually a straightforward process. The scribes responsible for the LWS version of *Cædmon's Hymn* easily recognized, for example, that Northumbrian forms such as *uard* and *barnum* should be Saxonized into *weard* and *bearnum*. The process was complicated when the scribes encountered a lexeme restricted to the Anglian dialects, which had no

---

[20] See *KB:Lang.* §29; *HOEM*:§§353–375.

equivalent in southern dialects and was therefore unfamiliar to them. Faced with dialectal vocabulary of this sort, the scribes had three options: they could transmit the word more or less as they found it; they could mechanically alter the vowels in an attempt to generate a rough LWS equivalent; or they could trivialize the text, replacing the unfamiliar word with a word that was more familiar to them.[21] Other difficulties arose when the Anglian spellings of certain words resembled the LWS forms of different words. Misled by their superficial similarity, the scribes transmitted genuine forms that are contextually implausible. The cases of faulty Saxonization are not signs of the scribes' agency and participation, but of their alienation from a text that they could not entirely comprehend.

§60. Three cases of trivialization in the transmitted text of *Beowulf* stem from the notorious inability of southern scribes to comprehend Anglian *wærc* 'pain'. That this word circulated exclusively in the midlands and the north is confirmed by its restriction to Anglian works and by the frequency with which southern scribes corrupted it into *weorc* 'labor' or *wræc* 'misery'.[22] The word's putative LWS equivalent **wierc* has no secure attestations. Confronting the unfamiliar *wærc*, the scribes who transmitted *Beowulf* presumed it stood for *weorc* each time it occurred:

(a)   Denum eallum wæs,
winum Scyldinga,   weorce on mōde
tō geþolianne,   ðegne monegum,
oncȳð eorla gehwǣm,   syðþan Æscheres
on þām holmclife   hafelan mētton.

                                        1417b–1421

For all the Danes, friends of Scyldings, it was painful to endure in their hearts, for many a thane, a distress to each of the men, when on the water-cliff they encountered Æschere's head.

(b)   fēower scoldon
on þǣm wælstenge   weorcum geferian
to þǣm goldsele   Grendles hēafod

                                        1637b–1639

---

[21] Trivialization is the probable reason for the replacement of *aelda* with *eorðan*; see the discussion in §§135, 148, below.

[22] See Fulk 2004; Jordan 1906:51–53; *HOEM*:§366; *KB:Lang.* §27.

It took four to carry Grendel's head with painful effort to the gold-hall on a battle-shaft.

(c)   drēamlēas gebād
þæt hē þæs gewinnes   weorc þrōwade,
lēodbealo longsum.

1720b–1722a

Estranged from contentment, he lived to see it that he suffered the pain of that struggle, a long-lived bane to the people.

In these three passages, it is clear that the transmitted *weorc* must stand for *wærc*. Readers can substitute "labor" for "pain" in each of the translations cited above to apprehend the nonsense generated by scribal trivialization here. Because it deprives the text of sense in each instance, the substitution of *weorc* for *wærc* cannot be regarded as a sensible attempt to improve the legibility of the text for contemporary audiences. The substitutions appear to have been generated, rather, by the scribes' assumption that *wærc* was a nonexistent word, an error committed by antecedent copyists, which must be corrected into the lexeme it superficially resembles, *weorc*. This substitution is yet another product of the scribal preoccupation with form and indifference to sense, which played a role in the genesis of so many of the transmitted text's peculiarities.

§61. A similar case of trivialization emerged due to the unfamiliarity of the scribes with the conjunction *nefne/nemne* 'unless, except'. While *wærc* is distributed widely in Anglian texts, *nefne/nemne* is attested only in works with Mercian connections, and is consequently one of the clearest indications that *Beowulf* was originally a Mercian composition.[23] The absence of this word from southern speech is registered in the trivialization of *nefne* as *næfre* 'never' in the transmitted version of the following passage:

Næfre ic māran geseah
eorla ofer eorþan   ðonne is ēower sum,
secg on searwum;   nis þæt seldguma,
wæpnum geweorðad,   næf*ne* him his wlite lēoge,
ænlic ansȳn.

247b–251a

---

[23] See *HOEM*:§361; *KB:Lang.* §27; Flasdieck 1950.

I have never in the world seen a larger man than is one of you, a champion
in his equipment; ennobled by weapons, that is no mere hall-man, unless
his look play him false, his unique appearance.

Editors emend the transmitted *næfre* to *næfne*, though the emended form,
which is also attested in 1353a, might reasonably be regarded as a scribal
error as well (Flasdieck 1950:135–136). Elsewhere in *Beowulf* and in the
corpus of Old English, the word in question is spelt *nefne* or *nemne*. The
presence of the *æ* in *næfne* (1353a) and the transmitted *næfre* (250b) is the
probable consequence of the mechanical and erroneous scribal conversion of
Anglian *e* to LWS *æ*, which generated a number of textual anomalies, in the
form of unetymological spellings that reflected the phonology of no Anglo-
Saxon's spoken language (*KB:Lang.* §2.1). The process of hypercorrection
through misguided Saxonization—and its consequent generation of many
implausible forms—is exemplified in many cases discussed below.

§62. The transmitted form *siexbennum* provides a clear instance of
trivialization combined with the incorrect Saxonization of an Anglian form
(Fulk 2007a:269–270). The Geatish messenger notes that his lord is dead,
and then says of the slain dragon:

> him on efn ligeð   ealdorgewinna
> sexbennum sēoc;

2903–2904a

Beside him [i.e., Beowulf] lies his life's enemy, sickened by knife-wounds

Since the dragon was slain by a *wællseax* 'long knife' (2703b), there can be
little doubt that the transmitted *siex-* stands for the word spelled *seax* elsewhere in the *Beowulf* manuscript (e.g., 1545b). Evidently, the scribe was
confused by a form in the exemplar that evinced the Anglian smoothing of *ea*
into *e* (*KB:Lang.* §13.2). Encountering the spelling *sex*, the scribe presumed
it stood for the numeral "six" and converted it into *siex*. The correct application of the principles of Saxonization would have resulted, however, in the
conversion of *sex* into *seax* 'knife'. As can be seen, the accurate Saxonization
of the exemplar is contingent upon the scribal identification of the lexeme
signified by a given sequence of graphemes. The trivializing assumption that
a non-Saxon spelling (*sex*) should stand for a mundane word (*siex*) rather
than a poetic one (*seax*) led the process of Saxonization astray here.

§63. The failure of the scribes to identify the lexeme signified by an
Anglian spelling led in several places to the transmission of an erroneous

word that incidentally preserved its original Anglian vocalism. The following passage yields a clear instance of trivialization induced by an Anglian spelling:

> Nū ys lēodum wēn
> orleghwīle,   syððan under[ne]
> Froncum ond Frȳsum   fyll cyninges
> wīde weorðeð.

2910b–2913a

Now a time of strife is to be expected for the nation, after the king's fall is widely bruited to the Franks and Frisians.

When the scribe encountered the spelling *underne* 'visible' in the exemplar, he evidently presumed it stood for the preposition *under* and consequently refrained from Saxonizing the word into *undyrne*—a LWS spelling transmitted four other times in the manuscript (127b, 150b, 410b, 2000a). The scribe's conviction that a preposition should occur at this place in the text may have been strengthened by the appearance of two nouns in the dative plural case (*Froncum ond Frȳsum*) immediately following the word in question. Several parallel cases of syntactic misapprehension are discussed below (§§71–75). In any event, the trivialized outcome of the scribe's reasoning preserves the Anglian *e* (= EWS *ie*, LWS *y*) that must have characterized the orthography of an antecedent copy of the poem (*KB:Lang.* §3.2). Similarly, the confusion of *c* and *t* (§55) that produced MS *secan* for *sētan* (1602b) resulted in the misidentification of the lexeme and the preservation of the exemplar's Anglian vocalism. In LWS, the preterite plural of *sittan* 'to sit' is *sǣton*, yet the form that lies behind the erroneous *secan* must have been Anglian *sētan*, with *ē* = WS *ǣ* (*KB:Lang.* §8.1). Because *under* and *secan* are genuine lexemes, the scribes did not suspect them to be errors that inadvertently preserved the Anglian vocalism of the exemplar.

§64. Lexical confusion is likewise the probable cause of the transmission of a non-WS spelling in the verse *fēa þingian* 'resolve with payment' (156b). Elsewhere in the manuscript, the noun is consistently rendered as the LWS form *feoh*, as in *fēo þingode* (470b) and *fēo lēanige* (1380b). The preservation of the Anglian (or Kentish) *fēa* spelling (*KB:Lang.* §15.1) is most likely due to confusion with the lexeme *fēa* 'few', spelled as such in the formulaic verse *fēa worda cwæð* (2246b, 2662b). The trivializing assumption that the exemplar's *fēa* represented the commoner word ("few") led the scribe to refrain from Saxonizing the spelling before him. Scribal misreading of a dialectal form is also evident in the transmitted verse *beorn wið blōde* 'burned against blood'

(1880a). The sense of the passage indicates that *beorn*—a spelling otherwise reserved for the lexeme *beorn* 'hero, warrior'—must stand here for the preterite singular of *byrnan* 'to burn'. The scribe evidently encountered the Anglian form of the preterite, spelled *born* (= WS *barn*), and presumed that *born* was a nonstandard spelling of *beorn* that required correction (*KB:Lang.* §12.2). Though intended to improve the legibility of the text for a contemporary readership, the process of Saxonization frequently rendered it implausible. The scribal indifference to the sense of the text made Saxonization particularly perilous when the exemplar contained a non-WS spelling that superficially resembled a different word in the scribe's own dialect.

§65. In the course of Saxonizing the non-WS vocalism of the exemplar, the scribes grew accustomed to the routine conversion of *e* to *æ* (*KB:Lang.* §2.1). The transmitted text contains at least five readings in which the mechanical alteration of *e* to *æ* has resulted in corruption: MS *wæs* for *wes* (407a), *þæs* for *þes* (411b), *spræc* for *sprec* (1171b), *hwæðre* for *hreðre* (2819b), and *fæder* for *feðer* (3119a). In each case, the transmitted form is a genuine lexeme, but it is contextually incorrect. *Wæs þū, Hrōðgar, hāl!* (407a) requires the imperative *wes*, but the preterite *wæs* has been erroneously substituted. The verse *þæt þæs sele stande* (411b) requires the nominative *þes*, but the scribe has mechanically altered it to genitive *þæs*. When Wealhþeo urges Hroðgar to celebrate and speak pleasing words to the Geats—*þū on sælum wes … tō Gēatum spræc* (1170b–1171b)—her command is obscured by the scribal substitution of preterite *spræc* for imperative *sprec*. In the preceding cases, the alteration of *e* to *æ* vitiates the grammar of the text, while in the following two cases vocalic hypercorrection combines with the alteration of a neighboring consonant to generate complete nonsense. The passing of Beowulf is signified in the following clause:

> him of hreðre gewāt
> sāwol sēcean   sōðfæstra dōm.

> 2819b–2820

His soul set out from his breast to seek the judgment of the righteous.

In place of *hreðre* 'breast', the transmitted text reads *hwæðre* 'however'.[24] The readiness of the scribe to alter *e* to *æ* appears to have induced him to mistake

---

[24] The editors of *KB* conservatively print *hræðre* instead of *hreðre* here, but scribal alteration of an antecedent *hreðre* is nevertheless probable, since the word is spelled with an *e* in its root syllable in its ten other occurrences in the transmitted text.

hreðer for an entirely different word. The same mechanism underlies a corruption in the following passage, spoken by Wiglaf at Beowulf's funeral:

> Nū sceal glēd fretan,
> —weaxan wonna lēg—   wigena strengel,
> þone ðe oft gebād   īsernscūre,
> þonne strǣla storm   strengum gebǣded
> scōc ofer scildweall,   sceft nytte hēold,
> feðergearwum fūs   flāne fullēode.

3114b–3119

Now the blaze shall consume—the pale flame rise up—the prince of warriors, who often lived through a tempest of iron, when a downpour of missiles launched by bowstrings shot over the wall of shields; the shaft did its duty, readily followed the barb with its feather-gear.

In place of *feðer* 'feather', the transmitted text reads *fæder* 'father', which yields obvious nonsense in the present context. The transmitted form might constitute an additional indication that the exemplar made frequent use of archaic *d* to represent the dental fricative (§54). If the exemplar read *feder* (for *feðer*), it would have been natural for the scribe to presume that it stood for WS *fæder*. Since the Mercian equivalent of *fæder* is *feder*, due to second fronting (Hogg 1992:§§5.87–92), the scribe had probably encountered and altered the identical sequence of graphemes into *fæder* on several previous occasions. Diachronic and dialectal change might therefore have conspired to produce the transmitted reading.

§66. The preceding cases (§§60–65) illustrate how the mechanical application of the principles of Saxonization resulted in numerous corruptions of the poem's sense. The following paragraphs deal with cases where Saxonization has introduced metrical defects into the transmitted text. Meter indicates that in the Anglian dialect of the *Beowulf* poet, short medial vowels in open syllables were regularly syncopated when preceded by a long stem syllable (e.g. *ǣngum*). In the LWS dialect, however, paradigm regularization resulted often in the analogical restoration of syncopated medial syllables (e.g., *ǣnigum*). Consequently, the scribes felt impelled to Saxonize the exemplar by inserting medial syllables into various words.[25] The process sometimes had no effect on the meter, but there are at least eight cases where the additional syllable produces an unmetrical verse:

---

[25] On syncopation, analogical restoration, and its scribal consequences, see *KB:T.C.* §12; *HOEM*:§§215–220; Sievers 1893:§76.1; Amos 1980:27–28; Suzuki 1996:105–106; Fulk 2010b; Campbell 1959:§343.

cwæð þæt se ælmihtiga (92a)
ōþres dōgores (219b, 605b)
Ne seah ic elþēodige (336b)
secga ænegum (842b)
gumena ænigum (2416b)
endedōgores (2896a)
meltan mid þām mōdigan (3011b)

The metrical indication of the syllabic discrepancy between the poet's speech and the scribes' is corroborated by the occasional transmission of syncopated spellings: for example *mōdges merefaran* (502a), *mōdgan mægnes* (670a), *dōgra gehwylce* (1090a), and *manna ængum* (1461a). Furthermore, the process of Saxonization is exposed in a case of scribal self-correction: Scribe A committed *lēoda ængum* (793b) to parchment, but Scribe B inserted an *i* in superscript between *n* and *g* to produce *ænigum* (see figure 5). This combination of metrical and orthographical evidence confirms that syncopated forms characterized the poem's archetype, and that forms evincing analogical restoration are the products of linguistically motivated scribal alteration. In these cases, the scribes plainly Saxonized the text without regard for metrical consequences.

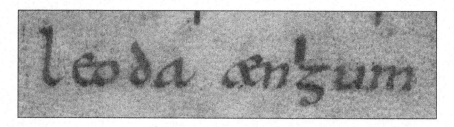

Figure 5. Scribal insertion of *i* into *ængum*, line 793b (fol. 150r).

§67. In many Old English poems, the Saxonization of the Anglian poetic form *dēdon* resulted in metrically defective verses.[26] *Beowulf* is no exception. The transmitted text of the poem consistently yields LWS *dydon* as the preterite plural form of *dōn* 'to do'. In most cases, this verb appears in type C verses where clashing stress permits the suspension of resolution,[27] thereby rendering both *dēdon* and *dydon* metrically acceptable (e.g., *þā þæt þær dydon*, 3070b). Yet in the verse *hwīlum dydon* (1828b), the meter

---

[26] See *KB:Lang.* §25.6, *T.C.* §27; Sievers 1885:498; *HOEM*:§355.4; Fulk 1996b:3.

[27] On this phenomenon, see Cable 1974:71–73 and Tolkien 1950:xxxn2.

indicates that *dēdon* is the authorial form: the short vowel in LWS *dydon* would here undergo resolution and result in an improbable three-position verse. The evidence of 1828b, combined with the fact that the meter never requires the short vowel of *dydon*, suggests that *dēdon* was the standard form in the archetype of *Beowulf*, which the scribes mechanically altered in every instance to LWS *dydon*.

§68. The scribes were less consistent in their treatment of *nēosan* 'to seek out', a weak verb of class I, which appears in the transmitted text alongside *nēosian*, a weak verb of class II. A curious consequence of the inconsistent treatment of these forms is that the text contains, for example, both *wīca nēosan* (125b) and *wīca nēosian* (1125b). While there is no difference in meaning between the two verbs, the class II form has an additional syllable, which spoils the meter on three occasions:

> wīca nēosian (1125b)
> fīonda nīos(i)an (2671b)
> dennes nīosian (3045a)

In each verse, the metrical defect is repaired upon restoration of disyllabic *nēosan*.[28] Accordingly, it is clear that the *Beowulf* poet used *nēosan* to the complete exclusion of *nēosian*, which is never required by the meter and must therefore be considered a scribal form whenever it appears. *Nēosan* and *nēosian* are not regarded as indicators of date or dialect, though the first form is prevalent in archaic, Anglian poetry, whereas the second form is more common in LWS prose. Although *nēosan* was not restricted to Anglian dialects, the probable motivation for the scribes' occasional substitution of *nēosian* was that this form was the more common one in their speech.

§69. When the scribes analogically restore syncopated medial vowels, alter *dēdon* to *dydon*, or substitute *nēosian* for *nēosan*, metrical considerations render the identification of the authorial form a simple matter. The long-standing crux *lissa gelong* (2150a) presents a more complicated case of probable scribal substitution.[29] As it stands, *lissa gelong* would appear to be the

---

[28] See *KB:T.C.* §§18, 31. Another relevant verse where an original *nēosan* has probably been altered is *Gewāt ðā nēosian* (115a). This verse can be accommodated to type C scansion as it stands, but the weight of the other verses suggests that the poet intended it to be a type A3 verse with *nēosan*—a classification supported by the tendency for nonalliterating finite verbs to appear in such verses. A historical connection between nonalliterating finite verbs and the development of type A3 verses is proposed in Pascual 2016.

[29] See *KB*:234; Pope 1966:320; Bliss 1967:§84; Russom 1987:117–118; *HOEM*:§209; Hutcheson 1995:31n113; Suzuki 1996:33–34.

only genuine verse in *Beowulf* that consists of three metrical positions (SxxS), a type of verse that the poet took considerable pains to avoid (Pascual 2013–2014). Because of the improbability that the poet should have composed a verse like *lissa gelong* (*KB:T.C.* §33), accidental corruption or deliberate alteration appears likely here. The existence of the comparably problematic verse *lēofes gelong* in *Guthlac A* (313a) suggests that scribal substitution has affected both verses. Since it would be a stunning coincidence for *gelong* to be present in two verses that suffer from the same rare metrical defect, this word is probably a scribal substitute for an unidentified dialectal form. In both verses, the meter would be repaired if a trochaic word were restored in the place of the iambic *gelong*. A fourth metrical position could also be supplied by a form of *gelong* that originally contained a suffix (**gelongen?*). In his study of the Saxonization of the *Old English Bede*, J. J. Campbell noted that suffix preference constituted one clear distinction between the Mercian and WS dialects (1951:367–368). Because *Beowulf* and *Guthlac A* share strong claims to archaic Mercian composition (*HOEM*:399–400), it is likely that they contained the same dialectal form that late, southern scribes altered to *gelong*.

§70. The numerous corruptions of the sense or meter of *Beowulf* that stem from the effort of the scribes to Saxonize the text confirm that the changes were made largely on a mechanical basis. In this respect, the Saxonizing changes resemble the various alterations intended to reverse the effects of diachronic change. Both types of alteration exhibit a preoccupation with form and an indifference to sense. The incomplete and inconsistent nature of these changes in the transmitted text suggests that the scribes worked erratically and opportunistically. When transcribing a form from the exemplar, if a form that accorded better with the LWS written standard came to mind, they would commit that form to parchment. If no such form came to mind— perhaps due to indifference, inattention, or insufficient knowledge—the scribes would more or less mechanically reproduce the antecedent form. Though they understood the basics of dialect conversion well, the scribes were not historical linguists. It is therefore not surprising that a verse like *rēþe renweardas* 'fierce hall-guardians' (770a), should be transmitted with a form that preserves both archaic and dialectal features (*KB:Lang.* §20.7). The scribe could not have known to convert *ren* 'hall' to LWS *ærn*, since the intervening process of metathesis, which must have taken effect in the language before the tenth century (Fulk 2007a:270n10), obscured the etymological parity of the two forms. The archaic absence of metathesis in *ren* made the form unfamiliar, and consequently ensured the preservation of the word's originally Anglian vocalism, with *e* for LWS *æ* (*KB:Lang.* §3.1). The places where the scribes failed to modernize or Saxonize the text remind us that the distance in time and space that separated the scribes from the *Beowulf* poet was often insurmountable.

3. Syntactic Misconstruction

§71. Misapprehensions of syntax, stemming from the scribes' superficial engagement with the text, played a role in the genesis of many errors and anomalies. The scribes frequently assumed an incorrect grammatical relationship between a particular word and the word that immediately preceded or followed it. The aforementioned corruption of *āþumswēoran* 'father-in-law and son-in-law' into *āþum swerian* 'to swear oaths' reveals that a scribe misconstrued the lexical identity of the first element of the compound and then altered the compound's second element in the belief that it should relate to the preceding word (§42). Similarly, the corrupt rendering of *underne* 'visible' into the preposition *under* was probably facilitated by the scribe's assumption that two nouns in the dative plural case (*Froncum ond Frȳsum*) should be preceded by a preposition (§63). These two errors merited discussion above due to their salient diachronic and dialectal significance, whereas the present section deals with errors that are purely syntactical. These errors reveal a great deal about the methods and motives of the scribes who transmitted *Beowulf*. They might also possess general diachronic significance, insofar as they pertain to the history of English syntax and illustrate the movement of the language from a more synthetic state to a more analytic one.

§72. Prepositions, or words that were misconstrued as prepositions, are the source of several corrupt readings. The *Beowulf* poet and the scribes plainly differed in their conception of prepositional phrases: the poet felt capable of having several words intervene between the preposition and its complement, and he felt licensed to use prepositions postpositionally, whereas the scribes worked under the assumption that the word immediately following a preposition must be its complement. This assumption is responsible for the corruption of the following passage:

> Gewāt him on naca
> drēfan dēop wæter,   Dena land ofgeaf.
>
> 1903b–1904

The ship set out onward, stirring up the deep water, left behind the land of the Danes.

Naca 'ship' must be the subject of the clause, yet the word is erroneously written in the manuscript as oblique *nacan*, having been misconstrued as the complement of *on* (*KB*:221). The participation of *on* in vocalic alliteration (with *yrfeláfe*, 1903a) guarantees that the scribe has erred, since verse grammar indicates that *on* functions here as an ictic adverb, not a preposition (Orchard 2003a:49). Nevertheless, the scribe's linguistic sensibility led him to regard the uninflected *naca* as a grammatical error that required correction through the addition of an inflection. A similar corruption entered the text due to the intervention of several words between the preposition and its complement:

> wēlhwylc gecwæð
> þæt hē fram Sigemunde[s]   secgan hȳrde
> ellendǣdum   uncūþes fela,
> Wælsinges gewin   wīde sīðas

> 874b–877

He related everything that he had heard said about Sigemund's feats of courage, a great deal unfamiliar, the struggles of the son of Wæls, wide travels

The transmitted text reads dative *sige munde* in place of genitive *Sigemundes*, a corruption induced by the scribal assumption that this proper name should be the complement of *fram* 'concerning'. The transmitted *fram Sigemunde* might seem to make respectable sense, but the inauthenticity of the phrase becomes apparent when one recognizes that it places *Sigemund* into apposition with *ellendǣd* 'feat of courage', and that human beings and abstract nouns are never apposed in Old English poetry.[30] The improbability of such apposition here indicates that the authorial reading must have been *Sigemundes*, since that is the only form of the noun that makes adequate sense in the present context. The scribal alteration of the original inflection was motivated, once again, by the belief that the syntax of the exemplar was in error and required correction.

§73. Meter provides the decisive indication that a scribe altered authorial syntax in the following passage:

---

[30] See *KB*:168; *OES*:§1175; Mitchell 1989:314–315.

Ic on Higelāc wāt,
Gēata dryhten,   þēah ðe hē geong sȳ,
folces hyrde,   þæt hē mec fremman wile
wordum ond worcum

1830b–1833a

I am confident of Hygelac, lord of Geats, though he is young, the people's
keeper, that he will offer me furtherance in word and deed

Because the manuscript reads dative *hige lace* in place of accusative *Higelāc*,
there is a problematic absence of concord between the dative proper name
and accusative *dryhten*, to which it is apposed. Some editors have resolved
the problem by emending *dryhten* to dative *dryhtne*, but the defective meter
of the transmitted *Ic on Higelāce wāt* (xxSsxS) indicates that it must be this
this verse that contains the corruption.[31] The scribe expected a word in the
dative case to follow *on*, so he added the *-e* inflection, thereby converting a
standard type B verse into an improbable five-position verse. The use of the
accusative case after *on* in this construction was strange to the scribe, though
not to the poet, who made use of the same construction in 2650b *God wāt
on mec*. Scribal expectations concerning the proper use of prepositional *on*
resulted elsewhere in a case of lexical confusion:

nǣnig þæt dorste   dēor genēþan
swǣsra gesīða,   nefne sinfrēa,
þæt hire an dæges   ēagum starede

1933–1935

None so bold of her own intimates, excepting her great lord, dared venture
to set eyes on her by day

This postpositional use of *on*, whose complement is the preceding *hire*,
evidently led a scribe to construe it as the numeral *ān* 'one' taken with
the subsequent word to form the compound *āndæges* 'for one day'. In one
other instance, *on* is spelled *an* (677a), yet in the hundreds of other occurrences of the word in *Beowulf*, it is consistently *on*. In the above passage, the
spelling *an* registers a scribal misunderstanding of the passage's syntax probably induced by diachronic change. For a speaker of late Old English, *hire on*
'on her' would have seemed unnatural.[32] The scribe's expectations led the
preposition to be misconstrued and miswritten as the numeral.

---

[31] See *KB*:218–219; *HOEM*:§238.

[32] On the chronological significance of the postpositioning of prepositions, see Lapidge 2006.

§74. The demonstrative pronoun *sē* figures into several corrupt readings caused by syntactic misconstruction. Two cases are particularly interesting for their illustration of the scribal tendency to assume false grammatical relationships between neighboring words—a tendency that has been evident in each of the syntactic corruptions discussed above. In the first case, the subject of a clause is corrupted into a dative noun due to the scribe's assumption that it must agree with the preceding demonstrative pronoun:

Swylce hē siomian geseah   segn eallgylden
hēah ofer horde,   hondwundra mǣst,
gelocen leoðocrǣftum;   of ðām lēoma stōd,
þæt hē þone grundwong   ongitan meahte,
wrǣtte giondwlītan.

2767–2771a

Likewise he saw an ensign all of gold hanging high over the hoard, the greatest piece of workmanship, woven by skillful hands; light glinted from it, so that he could make out the ground, look over the treasures.

Lēoma 'light' must be the agent of the verb *stōd* in order for the subsequent clause to make sense, yet the transmitted text reads oblique *leoman* in place of the nominative form. The scribe, not realizing that *ðām* refers back to *segn* 'ensign', assumed that this pronoun was a demonstrative adjective in concord with the subsequent word, *lēoma*, and therefore added the erroneous *-n* inflection. To a scribe concerned with the superficial dimensions of the text, the phrase *of ðām lēoman* looked like correct Old English and was therefore transmitted, though it deprived the passage of sense. In the next instance, the scribe altered the case of the pronoun because he misunderstood its relationship to surrounding words:

hīold hēahlufan   wið hæleþa brego,
ealles moncynnes   mīne gefrǣge
þone sēlestan   bī sǣm twēonum,
eormencynnes

1954–1957a

[Offa's queen] held deep affection for the lord of heroes, the best, I have heard, of all mankind, of the human race, between the oceans

In place of accusative *þone*, the manuscript reads genitive *þæs*. The accusative pronoun is required, however, since it and the adjective *sēlestan* refer back to *brego* 'lord', the accusative complement of *wið* (*KB*:227). The scribal

alteration of *þone* to *þæs* was plainly induced by the series of neighboring
words in the genitive case (*ealles moncynnes ... eormencynnes*). The scribe
expected the pronoun to refer to the more immediate genitive nouns rather
than to *brego*, from which it was separated by two verses. The transmitted
þæs sēlestan might have looked grammatically correct, but it destroys the
import of the passage, since it forces *sēlest* 'best' to modify *moncynn* rather
than King Offa.

§75. The syntactic errors lend powerful support to the hypothesis that
the final scribes of *Beowulf* did not comprehend the continuous narrative
of the poem as they copied. These errors confirm, rather, that the scribes
superficially scanned the text in order to standardize its orthography and
correct supposed errors committed by antecedent copyists. When a word
seemed incorrect in the immediate context of the words that precede or
follow it, the scribe imagined that it was necessary to intervene and correct
it. Had the scribe genuinely understood the text, however, such intervention
would never have occurred. These conclusions are illustrated again in the
corruption of the following passage:

> Þonne hē gyd wrece,
> sārigne sang,   þonne his sunu hangað
> hrefne tō hrōðre,   ond hē him helpe ne mæg
> eald ond infrōd   ænige gefremman

2446b–2449

Then he may tell a tale, a song full of pain, when his son hangs to the
raven's delight, and he, old and decrepit, cannot offer him any help

The manuscript reads *helpan* in place of the accusative noun *helpe* for a fairly
obvious reason: the scribe expected an infinitive to occur in close proximity
to the auxiliary verb *magan*. There can be little doubt that the transmitted
helpan is a scribal error, since *ænige* in the subsequent line must agree with
another noun (*helpe*) for *gefremman* to have a logical direct object (*KB*:246).
For a scribe inspecting the superficial dimensions of the text, the sequence
helpe ne mæg would have appeared to be a straightforward grammatical error,
reflecting the transmission of a finite verb in place of the infinitive form. Had
the scribe sought to comprehend the syntax of the entire sentence, rather
than of a few words in isolation, he would have realized that his impression
was erroneous and that *helpe* was the required form. Syntactical errors of
this sort demonstrate that the fluency of the scribes in Old English could,
in fact, imperil the accurate transmission of the text and generate varieties

of corruption that would not be present in the text if foreign scribes had transmitted it.

4. Trivialization

§76. No form of corruption connected to the fluency of the scribes in Old English is more common in the transmitted text of *Beowulf* than trivialization. Because the scribes' command of late Old English was not matched by a command of the archaic language and content of *Beowulf*, they frequently trivialized the text, corrupting unfamiliar words into words of similar appearance that were more familiar to them. Many of the errors analyzed above for their diachronic or dialectal significance can also be considered forms of trivialization, such as the corruption of *lǣn* into *lēan* (§50), *wǣrc* into *weorc* (§60), *nefne* into *nǣfre* (§61), and *feðer* into *fǣder* (§65). Similarly, much of the corruption of proper names, discussed in the following chapter, takes the form of trivialization, as unfamiliar names are miswritten as common words (e.g., *Ēomēr* corrupted into *geōmor*, §23) or as more familiar names (e.g., *Bēow* corrupted into *Bēowulf*, §24). The present section discusses cases of trivialization that possess no particular diachronic or dialectal significance, but cumulatively offer a general corroboration of the hypothesis that a wide linguistic and cultural gap separated the poem from the scribes who reproduced it. An overview of the various manifestations of trivialization also conveys a strong impression of the poor condition of the transmitted text and the consequent necessity of editorial intervention.

§77. Trivialization often resulted in corruptions that deprive the text of sense. The following passage furnishes a clear illustration of the process:

> gūðdēað fornam,
> (*f*)eorhbeal(*o*) frēcne,   fȳra ge(*h*)wylcne
> lēoda mīnra

2249b–2251a

war-death, fearful and deadly peril snatched away every person of my nation

The transmitted text reads *fyrena* 'sins' in place of *fȳra* 'people'. This substitution, which results in obvious nonsense in the present context, can easily be explained: *fīras* 'people' is a rare word restricted to poetry, whereas *fyren* is common in the homiletic and didactic discourses that were familiar to every eleventh-century scribe. The same considerations of relative frequency account for the trivialization of *eafoð* 'strength' into *earfoð* 'misery', which affected the transmission of two passages:

Sōð ic talige,
þæt ic merestrengo   māran āhte,
e*afe*þo on ȳþum,   ðonne ænig ōþer man.

532b–534

I consider it the truth that I had greater sea-strength, sturdiness on the waves, than any other person.

siððan Heremōdes   hild sweðrode,
e*afoð* ond ellen

901–902a

after Heremod's fighting subsided, his strength and his heroism

In the transmitted versions of both passages, *eafoð* has been corrupted into *earfoð*, which produces various difficulties (*KB*:153; *HOEM*:§241). Regularities of apposition confirm that *eafoð* was the authorial reading in each instance, since it is implausible that *earfoð* should be placed into apposition with *merestrengo* 'sea-strength' and *ellen* 'heroism'. The trivialization of these passages can surely be attributed to the fact that *eafoð* occurs only in poetry, where it is attested eleven times and is restricted to three works (*Beowulf, Andreas*, and *Juliana*), whereas *earfoð* is attested hundreds of times in texts that reflect a wide variety of literary discourses.

§78. Another case of trivialization due to scribal unfamiliarity with poetic diction resulted in a notable absurdity. Beowulf's final speech is preceded by a description of the king, *gomel on giohðe* 'the old man in a state of sorrow' (2793a), examining the treasures he has obtained. In the manuscript, however, *giohðo* 'sorrow' has been trivialized to *geogoð* 'youth', producing the remarkable corruption *gomel on giogoðe* 'the old man in a state of youth'. Once again, a scribe has substituted a word that is widespread in the corpus of Old English (*geogoð*) for a word that is confined to poetry (*giohðo*). The same phenomenon is evident in the transmitted version of the following passage:

ēode weorð Denum
æþeling tō yppan,   þær se ōþer wæs,
hæle hildedēor   Hrōðgar grētte.

(1814b–1816)

the prince cherished by the Danes went to the dais where the other was, the hero brave in battle approached Hrothgar.

Hæle 'hero', a characteristic element of the poetic vocabulary, is not present in the manuscript because a scribe trivialized the word into *helle* 'hell'. The transmitted *helle hildedēor* is another ludicrous corruption, which turns the pious Beowulf into a "battle-bold man from hell." A similar effect is produced by the trivialization of *hæleð* (= *hæle*) into *hæðen* 'heathen'. Queen Hygd distributes cups of mead *hæleðum tō handa* 'into the hands of heroes' (1983a), yet the transmitted text has her serving *hæðnum*—a startling appellation for the Geats, who are never elsewhere labeled heathens.[33] The trivialization of the vocabulary of heroic poetry (*fīras, eafoð, hæle, hæleð*) into words prevalent in theological discourse (*fyren, earfoð, helle, hæðen*) reflects the immersion of the scribes in religious literature and probably exposes some of their subconscious biases.[34] Engaging superficially with a text about pagans and monsters, the scribes expected words pertaining to sin, misery, hell, and heathenism to appear. Such words are present in *Beowulf*, but the poet placed restrictions upon their use, establishing subtle regularities of diction that the scribes did not apprehend.[35]

§79. Nominal compounds, a distinctive feature of Old English poetic diction, suffered trivialization on several occasions. The verse *in nīðgripe* 'in a malicious grip' (976a), was corrupted into the senseless *in mid gripe*, due to the misconstruction of the first element of the compound as the preposition *mid* (Fulk 2007d:162–164). At Hnæf's funeral, the smoke from the pyre that ascends to the heavens—the *gūðrēc* 'war-smoke' (1118b)—is trivialized into *gūðrinc* 'warrior', a common expression found in four other places in the poem (838b, 1501b, 1881a, 2648a).[36] The rules governing the formation of poetic compounds indicate that the authorial compounds *hildfrecan* (2205a) and *sibgedriht* (387a, 729a) received scribal expansion of their first element, resulting in the transmission of *hilde frecan* and *sibbe gedriht*, which would need to be improbably construed as genitival phrases

---

[33] It should be noted, however, that the MS reading *hæðnū* was subsequently altered by a scribe to *hæ nū*. The motivation for this alteration, which converted a genuine (but erroneous) lexeme into a meaningless sequence of letters, is unclear.

[34] For other examples, see Sisam 1953b:29–30 and Orchard 2003–2004:54.

[35] This is most apparent in the phenomenon known as "the two levels of knowledge": the poem's narrator uses theologically charged vocabulary, but such words are kept out of the mouths of the pagan characters. On this regularity, see Osborn 1978; Robinson 1985:32–34; Pascual 2014.

[36] See *KB*:186, where the corruption of *-rēc* into *-rinc* is presented as the paradigmatic example of trivialization.

rather than true compounds.[37] The corruption of *hererinc* 'warrior' (1176a), into *hereric* converts an epithet of Beowulf into a new proper name, since *-ric* 'powerful' is used in *Beowulf* to form personal names, but not nominal compounds. The *hildecumbor* 'battle banner' (1022a) that Hrothgar gives Beowulf is rendered peculiar through the trivialization of *hilde* into *hilte* 'hilt'. A striking term for Grendel—*scynscaþa* 'spectral enemy' (707a)—is trivialized into *synscaþa* 'sinful enemy', a corruption that may once again reflect the theological preconceptions of the scribes. The scribal alteration of *scyn-* to *syn-* is signaled by the defective alliteration that results, since the off-verse (*under sceadu bregdan*) requires alliteration on *sc.*

§80. Defective alliteration exposes the trivialization of authorial lexemes in no fewer than ten other lines. In seven cases, the scribal insertion of *h* alters the identity of a word and spoils the alliteration. Four lines are problematic for the same reason:

> Hēo him eft hraþe   andlēan forgeald (1541)
> yfla gehwylces   ondlēan forgeald (2094)
> eald ond egesfull,   ondslyht āgeaf (2929)
> ealdum ceorle   ondslyht giofan (2972)

The vocalic alliteration required in each of these lines is marred in the transmitted text due to the repeated trivialization of the *ond-* prefix into *hond* 'hand'." Consistent deletion of the *h* restores *ondlēan* 'requital' and *ondslyht* 'counter-blow', which improve the sense of the text and provide alliteration for each line (*KB:Lang.* §20.2). The following line presents a similar case:

> Ārīs, rīces weard,   uton raþe fēran (1390)

The manuscript reads *hraþe* for the etymologically equivalent *raþe* 'quickly', yet the form without *h* is plainly required. There are structural indications that the *Beowulf* poet made use of both *hraþe* and *raþe* (*KB:T.C.* §24); the alternation between them probably led a scribe to insert the *h* here in the belief that it generated the correct spelling, unaware of the alliterative defect it produced. In two other verses, the scribal insertion of *h* results in more alliteration than was permitted in classical Old English poetry:

> forhabban in hreþre.   Đā wæs heal roden (1151)
> þær hyne Hetware   hilde genǣgdon (2916)

---

[37] See Fulk 2007b:305, 312–314; Terasawa 1994; Weyhe 1905:79–83.

In the transmitted text, *roden* 'reddened' and *genǣgdon* 'assailed' are corrupted into *hroden* 'adorned' and *gehnǣgdon* 'humbled'." The two resulting lines suffer from the same problem: the trivialization of the authorial lexeme causes the final lift of the line to participate in alliteration, thereby violating a metrical constraint respected throughout the corpus of classical verse.[38] Scribal disregard for the alliterative regularities of *Beowulf* is most evident, however, in the transmitted versions of the following three lines:

> þæt hē for *mu*ndgripe   mīnum scolde (965)
> beloren lēofum   æt þām *l*indplegan (1073)
> on þ(ām) wēstenne;   hwæðre *wī̆ges* gefeh (2298)

These three lines were corrupted through the replacement of an authorial word with a more familiar synonym that begins with a different consonant: the manuscript reads *hand-* in place of *mund-* (965a), *hild-* in place of *lind-* (1073b), and *hilde* in place of *wī̆ges* (2298b). Since these alterations do not affect the sense of the text—indeed, since their sole consequence, besides the loss of alliteration, is to turn *mundgripe* and *lindplegan* into more prosaic compounds—it is doubtful whether the cases of synonym substitution reflect the deliberate intervention of the scribes. Considering their detrimental and obvious quality, these substitutions are probably best regarded as unconscious accidents that stem from a scribe's mental association of a word in the exemplar with a more familiar synonym.

§81. Metrical aberrations also result from minor changes that can be considered forms of trivialization. The scribes, accustomed to the expanded forms of certain words, increased the number of syllables they possess and consequently produced verses of anomalous scansion. The verse constituted by the transmitted *ungedēfelīce* (2435b) lacks authentic parallels as it stands (*KB*:245). It is probable that a scribe inserted *-līce*, since the removal of that suffix results in a standard type A verse (*ungedēfe*, SxSx). The transmitted verse *snūde eft cuman* (1869b) might also be anomalous due to the insertion of an adverbial suffix: as it stands, it must be categorized as an expanded type D*, though such verses are confined to the on-verse and require double alliteration (*KB:T.C.* §31). The problem is removed by perceiving a rare instance of elision in this verse, but if that solution were eschewed, it would appear to be necessary to regard *snūde* as a scribal alteration of an antecedent *snūd*. An inauthentic *-e* generates a clearer defect in the transmitted verse

---

[38] On these particular cases, see *KB:T.C.* §42; for the constraint violated in the transmitted text, see Sievers 1893:§21(c).

word wǣron wynsume (612a), where the final word appears to exhibit a late, analogical neuter plural inflection (*KB:Lang.* §22, *T.C.* §30). Restoration of authorial *wynsum* brings the verse back into line, accommodating it to type A scansion. The scribal substitution of *ymbe-* for *ymb-* produced the corrupt verse *ymbesittendra* (2734a), which possesses an improbable fifth metrical position on account of the additional syllable in *ymbe-* (*KB:T.C.* §22). It is also likely that the scribes replaced an original *ymb-* with *ymbe-* in the verses *hlǣw oft ymbehwearf* (2296b) and *heals ealne ymbeféng* (2691b).[39] Nuanced metrical considerations constrained the poet's lexical selection, but the scribal inclination to transmit the more familiar form was free of such constraints.

§82. To facilitate apprehension of the extent to which trivialization pervades the transmitted text of *Beowulf*, a brief survey of instances not mentioned above is provided here. Considerations of space do not permit full discussion of the context and consequences of these cases, but such discussion is hardly necessary, since much of what has been said above can be extended to the following examples: the trivialized outcomes produce defects of sense, meter, or alliteration that permit the straightforward restoration of the authorial lexeme. Some instances are notable for the outrageous distortions of sense they effect, including: MS *mǣgenes* 'power' for *mǣges* 'kinsman' (2628b, 2698b), MS *earme* 'wretched' for *éame* 'uncle' (1117a), MS *déore* 'precious' for *dréore* 'bloody' (447a), MS *oftost* 'most often' for *ofost* 'haste' (1663b),[40] MS *fealh* 'underwent' for *fléah* 'fled' (1200b), MS *fela* 'many' for *féola* 'file' (1032a), and MS *séoc* 'sick' for *sceóc* 'depart' (2254b). Other trivializations have less egregious consequences, but still result in palpable corruptions of the text: MS *gimme* 'gem' for *ginne* 'expansive' (466b), MS *inne* 'within' for *hine* 'him' (1868a), MS *hæleþum* 'hero' for *æþelum* 'nobility' (332b), MS *hnǣgde* 'subdued' for *nǣgde* 'addressed' (1318b), MS *gefraegnod* 'made famous (?)' for *gefrécnod* 'made bold' (1333a), and MS *eaxle* 'shoulder' for *feaxe* 'hair' (1537a). Many trivializations were induced by the visual similarity of letterforms, a factor that plainly informed the following corruptions: MS *fela ðā* 'much then' for *se lāða* 'the hateful one' (2305a), MS *hard* 'courageous' for *hord* 'hoard' (2245b), MS *wat* 'know' for *þæt* 'that' (2534a), and MS *hū* 'how' for *nū* 'now' (2884a). To be sure, the phenomenon of trivialization is overdetermined: a combination of linguistic,

---

[39] See Sievers 1885:258–620; Pope 1966:364, 369; Bliss 1967:§82.

[40] There is less editorial unanimity surrounding this corruption than the others mentioned in this paragraph, but there is a strong probability of trivialization here; see Fulk 2007d:167–168.

cultural, and paleographical factors is responsible for the remarkable degree to which the text of the poem was trivialized during its transmission.

5. Interpolation

§83. The various forms of evidence bearing on the unity of *Beowulf* (discussed below, §§168–181), provide ample reason to believe that relatively few words in the transmitted text are scribal interpolations. Seven minor words, however, produce metrical aberrations that raise doubts about their authenticity. These seven words all conform to a recognizable pattern, in that they are precisely the sort of words that Anglo-Saxon scribes are known to have freely interpolated into the texts they transmitted: each word possesses low semantic value, typically receives no metrical stress, and serves a pronominal, adverbial, or intensifying function.[41] Since classical Old English poets plainly sought to reduce their use of such words, the scribal insertion of them can be regarded as another form of trivialization, which functions to obscure poetic economy and render the text more familiar and prosaic. It would also be fair to regard these interpolations as part of the effort to modernize the language of the text, since the increasingly analytic (as opposed to synthetic) nature of English syntax necessitated the regular use of more function words than were required for comprehension at the time of the poem's composition.[42] On the whole, though, interpolation must have been a sporadic rather than a systematic phenomenon, reflecting the occasional whim of a scribe, not a coherent plan to recompose the poem.

§84. The prohibition against anacrusis (i.e., extrametrical syllables before the first lift) in type D verses when placed in the off-verse brings two interpolations to light.[43] Each of the two exceptions to this rule in *Beowulf* involves a word that is inessential and perhaps detrimental to the sense of the text: *þāra ymbsittendra* 'the neighboring peoples' (9b) and *þā secg wīsode* 'when the man led the way' (402b). The case for regarding *þāra* and *þā* as scribal interpolations rather than genuine exceptions to the rule is strengthened by the fact that *þāra* would need to be construed here as an unemphatic definite article (Pope 1988:106). This construction conforms to later usage

---

[41] See Amos 1980:171–196; Horgan 1980; Fulk 2003:18–22.

[42] Russom (2002) identifies several reliable criteria for the relative chronology of Old English poetry related to this aspect of language change.

[43] See *KB:T.C.* §36; Sievers 1885:256; Pope 1966:237; Bliss 1967:§49; Hutcheson 1995:104.

and probably seemed natural to the scribe, but it contrasts sharply with the practice of the *Beowulf* poet, who treated *sē* as a demonstrative pronoun, not a definite article. Irregular anacrusis calls attention to another possible inter-polation in the verse *Tō lang ys tō reccenne* 'it is too long to recount' (2093a). Because verses of type A with anacrusis consistently exhibit double allitera-tion in *Beowulf*, the presence of the first *tō* produces an anomaly here.[44] The sense is neither vitiated nor improved by its presence, since the idea of the excessive length of the narration might be implied in an understated *lang*. The interpolation of *tō* could function to make the sense of the passage more explicit, though it may well have been an accidental dittography induced by the scribe's anticipation of *tō reccan*. Of the seven interpolations discussed here, *tō* is the least secure, since Hutcheson (1995: 106, n. 32) has argued that the requirement of double alliteration in type A verses with anacrusis is an epiphenomenon of the frequent occurrence of double alliteration in type A verses whenever they occupy the on-verse. If the rule is epiphenomenal, then there is no reason to doubt that *tō* is authorial.

§85. Other interpolations are easier to identify with conviction because of the more salient improbabilities that they generate. The following passage plainly contains an interpolation:

> Næs ðā long tō ðon
> þæt ðā āglǣcean   hȳ eft gemētton.

2591b–2592

It was not long then till the troublemakers met again.

The presence of the superfluous reflexive pronoun *hȳ* produces a verse that is exceptional in several respects. Because of its position in the verse clause, the pronoun needs to receive ictus, though this is an improbable arrangement, since it does not alliterate. If *hȳ* were construed as a nonictic syllable, it would still be exceptional, since pronouns are not placed in posi-tions of anacrusis in *Beowulf* (*KB*:251). Syntactic considerations appear to have motivated the interpolation of *hȳ*: a scribe felt that *gemētton* required a reflexive pronominal object, not recognizing that the poet used *gemētton* as an intransitive verb. An interpolation even more obvious than *hȳ* appears in the transmitted version of the following passage:

> Eard gīt ne const,
> frēcne stōwe,   ðǣr þū findan miht

---

[44] See *KB:T.C.* §35; Bliss 1967:§§46–47.

sinnigne secg;   sēc gif þū dyrre!

1377b–1379

You are not yet acquainted with the region, that dangerous place where you can find the one who is the offender; go look if you dare!

The transmitted text contains the word *fela* before *sinnigne*, which results in the verse *felasinnigne secg*. The interpolation of this intensifier introduces transparent metrical and alliterative defects into an otherwise standard type E verse. The transmitted verse contains more than four metrical positions and cannot be accommodated to any of the five regular verse types. Furthermore, the inability of *fela-* to participate in alliteration signals its inauthenticity, since compounds with *fela-* always alliterate on *f* in adherence to Krackow's law (*KB*:202). A scribe evidently inserted *fela* into the text under the mistaken impression that 1379a was the off-verse for 1378b, and therefore required an additional word to provide *f*-alliteration.[45]

§86. The first-person singular pronoun *ic* creates metrical problems in two verses where it is inessential to the sense of the text. The first is *sceaðona ic nāt hwylc* 'an enemy I know not which' (274b). The verse stands out for two reasons: (1) type A verses rarely end in a monosyllabic word, and (2) type A2b verses with a heavy second drop require double alliteration and are consequently confined to the on-verse (*KB:T.C.* §27). There is a clear motive for the interpolation of *ic* into this passage: a scribe misconstrued the indefinite pronoun *nāthwylc* as a phrase consisting of a verb and an object that required a subject, which was supplied by *ic* (Bliss 1967:§79). The removal of the interpolation yields *sceaðona nāthwylc* 'a certain enemy', a verse paralleled by *niðða nāthwylc* (2215a) and *gumena nāthwylc* (2233b). The scribal belief that an unexpressed subject should require pronominal expression might also have given impetus to an interpolation of *ic* in the concluding statement of Hygelac's speech to the returning Beowulf:

Gode ic þanc secge
þæs ðe ic ðē gesundne   gesēon mōste.

1997b–1998

I give thanks to God that I have been permitted to see you again safe and sound.

---

[45] The interpolation of *fela* and its implications for the scribal understanding of meter are comprehensively analyzed in Pascual 2015.

The transmitted verse *Gode ic þanc secge* is an aberration, since it would appear to be an expanded type D* verse, yet genuine verses of this sort require double alliteration and are confined to the on-verse.[46] The defect can be remedied by positing that a combination of elision and resolution reduced the first three syllables of the verse into a single metrical position (*KB:T.C.* §31), but considering the rarity of such compression, the hypothesis that *ic* was interpolated might possess stronger claims to probability. If the authorial verse left the subject unexpressed, a scribe might have felt compelled to supply the pronoun. Furthermore, the presence of *ic* in the subsequent verse renders it possible that the problematic *ic* is an anticipatory dittography. Syntactic and paleographical inducements might therefore have conspired to prompt an interpolation.

§87. The seven words of dubious authenticity in the transmitted text of *Beowulf*—*þāra, þā, tō, hȳ, fela,* and *ic* (x2)—share several important features. One is that their presence hardly affects the sense of the text. The trivial character of these words suggests that although the scribes actively altered the superficial dimensions of the text, they did not feel licensed to alter its meaning by adding semantically consequential lexemes. Another noteworthy quality of these interpolations is that they tend to result in the violation of subtle metrical constraints rather than salient regularities. This feature suggests that the scribes possessed only a basic understanding of the rules of metrical composition, but that even this rudimentary awareness prevented them from interpolating words that would generate egregiously unmetrical verses. Finally, it is significant that each interpolation could easily have been added by a scribe paying little attention to the sense of the text he was copying. A scribe preoccupied with form and indifferent to sense is precisely the sort of scribe who would add *þāra* to *ymbsittendra* or insert *ic* before *nāthwylc*. The interpolations thus lend support to the findings about scribal behavior that have emerged throughout this chapter. The scribes responsible for the transmission of *Beowulf* analyzed individual lexemes or isolated stretches of text as they copied from their exemplar. The scribes then sought to make superficial changes to the text—of the sort that would not severely disrupt its sense or meter—in order to minimize diachronic and dialectal variation. Their aim was to generate an intelligible text in linguistic conformity with the LWS written standard, but the archaic and Anglian qualities of the poem often led the scribes to transmit palpable corruptions of its sense or meter.

---

[46] On this constraint, see note 8 above.

3

CULTURAL CHANGE

1. Obliteration of Personal Names

§88. Culture, like language, cannot be expected to persist in undisturbed stasis for several centuries. Heroes widely celebrated in one century often fall into oblivion within a century or two. As new heroes come to dominate the imagination of a people, their fame eclipses that of their predecessors, who gradually come to be forgotten. The *Beowulf* manuscript bears extraordinary witness to a process of cultural change that took place during the Anglo-Saxon period. Heroic-legendary traditions known to the *Beowulf* poet and the early audience for whom he composed were evidently unknown to the late scribes responsible for the poem's transmission. Scribal unfamiliarity with the traditions informing *Beowulf* led to the obliteration of dozens of proper names and the obfuscation of many others. Obliteration and obfuscation, to be clear, are two discrete consequences of the scribal inability to transmit proper names accurately: some names have effectively been eliminated from the text through the corruption of the name into common words of similar appearance; while other names, more or less present in the transmitted text, are accompanied by signs of confusion and difficulty. The present chapter deals first with the obliterated proper names and then analyzes the various paleographical curiosities that attend transmitted names. The evidence indicates that traditions familiar to Anglo-Saxons during the seventh and eighth centuries (§§120–124) were obscure to the late scribes who produced the extant manuscript, and perhaps to antecedent copyists as well.

§89. Readers of editions or translations of *Beowulf* may be surprised to learn that, among others, the name of the son of Scyld Scefing is not attested in the poem's extant manuscript. As emended by the editors of *KB*, the pertinent passages read as follows:

Bēow wæs brēme   —blǣd wīde sprang—
Scyldes eafera   Scedelandum in.

18–19

Beow was renowned—his fame sprang wide—the heir of Scyld, in Scania.

Đā wæs on burgum   Bēow Scyldinga,
lēof lēodcyning   longe þrāge
folcum gefrǣge   —fæder ellor hwearf,
aldor of earde—   oþ þæt him eft onwōc
hēah Healfdene;

53–57a

Then among the strongholds Beow of the Scyldings, beloved king of that folk, was celebrated by peoples for long years—his father had passed elsewhere, that elder, from the earth—until to him in turn high Healfdene awoke.

Every iteration of the West Saxon royal genealogy gives Beow (variously spelt) as the name of the son of Scyld (*KB:Par.* §1)—a striking consistency, considering the manifold discrepancies between the several versions—yet the transmitted text of *Beowulf* stands in marked disagreement with this tradition. On both occasions where Scyld's son is referenced, his name is transmitted as *Bēowulf*, not *Bēow*. Some scholars have defended the manuscript reading on the grounds that the poet could have known an alternative tradition or, indeed, could have invented details of Danish history extemporaneously.[1] Metrical considerations render such defenses untenable, however, and confirm that Beow was the name of Scyld's son in the poem's archetype. The verse *Bēowulf Scyldinga* represents a marked deviation from the poet's metrical practice. As it stands, this verse consists of five metrical positions (SxSsx) and can be accommodated only to an expanded type D* scansion, yet genuine verses of that sort are confined to the on-verse and require double alliteration (*KB:T.C.* §31). The metrical consequences of the scribal *-ulf* thus expose its inauthenticity. Because the restoration of *Bēow* repairs a glaring metrical defect and brings the poem into agreement with the West Saxon genealogies, it is clear that *Bēow* is the authorial reading and that *Bēowulf* is a scribal corruption.[2]

[1]   See, for example, the arguments presented in Whitelock 1951:69–70 and Earl 1994:22–25, the latter of which is discussed in this book's introduction (§§26–27).

[2]   For additional discussion of this emendation, see Child 1906 and Björkman 1918. Tolkien's trenchant remarks on the matter (2014:146–148) are presented in this book's appendix.

§90. There is a transparent reason for the effacement of *Bēow* from the transmitted text. A scribe in the course of the poem's transmission presumed that *Bēow* was an erroneous or abbreviated form of *Bēowulf*, the name that appears throughout the text being copied, and expanded the form accordingly. The scribe's reasoning betrays ignorance of Beow the Scylding and the mythical tradition from which he descends, while also suggesting that the scribe was unfamiliar with Beowulf the Geat and the legendry associated with him.[3] By inserting Beowulf into the Danish genealogy and making him the father of Healfdene, the scribe produced a notable absurdity: the error turns the poem's young protagonist into the grandfather of Hrothgar. Beow the Scylding and Beowulf the Geat were meaningful figures to the poet and his audience, but their names plainly meant little to the late scribes. The two corruptions of *Bēow* into *Bēowulf* are, moreover, products of the same scribal preoccupation with form that generated many of the errors discussed in the previous chapter. The scribes felt obliged to correct forms that they believed to be erroneous, but they lacked the linguistic and cultural knowledge required to distinguish genuine copyist's errors from authorial readings that were simply foreign to them. Consequently, the scribes introduced many corruptions into the transmitted text in the apparent belief that they were correcting the work of their errant predecessors.

§91. The name of Offa's son was also obliterated from the text of *Beowulf* during the course of its transmission (*KB*:227). The Mercian royal genealogy gives Eomer as the name of the son of Offa (Dumville 1976:33), yet in the extant manuscript of *Beowulf*, this name is not to be found. A scribe corrupted *Ēomēr* into the adjective *geōmor* 'mournful', for the same reason that a scribe corrupted *Bēow* into *Bēowulf*. Unfamiliar with the legendary traditions known to the *Beowulf* poet and the Mercian genealogist, the scribe saw no proper name in the sequence of graphemes comprising *Ēomēr*. Scribal error is here apparent not only because of the analogous genealogy, but also because of the salient alliterative defect that it introduces into the text. The poet placed *Ēomēr* into a line that exhibited vocalic alliteration:

> wīsdōme hēold
> ēðel sīnne;   þonon Ēomēr wōc
> hæleðum tō helpe

                                        1959b–1961a

---

[3] The probability that Beowulf existed in legendary tradition prior to the composition of *Beowulf*, and is therefore not an invention of the poet, is established in Neidorf 2013a.

[Offa] ruled in wisdom his native land; from him arose Eomer as a help to
heroes

The corruption of *Ēomēr* into *geōmor* thus disturbs both the formal structure
of the poem and the sense of the passage. The introduction of an anonymous
mournful individual at this point in the poem must have appeared perplexing
to anyone who conscientiously read the extant manuscript. The implausi-
bility of the continuous text was not apparent to the scribes, however, since
they scrutinized the formal accuracy of the text independent of considerations of sense, meter, or alliteration. To them, *Ēomēr* was the erroneous
form and *geōmor* was the obvious solution.

§92. Another name obliterated from the text of *Beowulf* during the
course of its transmission is that of Unferð, the counselor of Hroðgar. His
name is not attested in the poem's extant manuscript, where it has been seri-
ally corrupted into *Hūnferð*. Although no external sources provide a name
for Hroðgar's *þyle* (1456b), there can be little doubt that the *Beowulf* poet
referred to the man in question as *Ūnferð* rather than *Hūnferð*. The decisive
consideration pointing to the authorial form is that three of the four lines
containing this name link their constituent verses through vocalic alliteration, and use this name to provide a structurally required alliterating lift:

Ūnferð maþelode,   Ecglāfes bearn (499)
Hwæt, þū worn fela,   wine mīn Ūnferð (530)
æghwylc ōðrum trȳwe.   Swylce þǣr Ūnferþ þyle (1165)
Ond þū Ūnferð lǣt   ealde lāfe (1488)

Since the *Beowulf* poet treated *h* as a consonant that could alliterate only
with *h*—the name *Hūnlafing*, for example, alliterates with *hildelēoman*
(1143)—editors have strong grounds for emending the counselor's name to
Ūnferð (*KB*:149–511). There is a simple reason for the scribal insertion of
the inauthentic *h* before each instance of this name: *hūn-* was a productive element in the Old English onomasticon, whereas *ūn-* was never used
to form personal names in the British Isles. The scribes naturally regarded
Ūnferð as an implausible form that required correction, since none of their
contemporaries could bear such a name. In earlier name-giving traditions on
the continent, however, the *ūn-* element was used to form personal names
(Fulk 1987:121–124). The *Beowulf* poet's decision to retain the foreign name
Ūnferð must be attributed to the strength of the heroic-legendary tradition
at the time of composition. The poet expected his audience to know that
the man was named *Ūnferð*, so he refrained from converting the name into

the more familiar *Hūnferð*. The poet did not expect contemporary copyists to regard the form as an anomaly merely because Anglo-Saxon names do not contain the *ūn-* element. Communal knowledge of legends involving Ūnferð is implied, moreover, in the poem's terse allusions to his slaying of his kinsmen and his role in Scylding turmoil (Fulk 1987:127).

§93. A scribe's accidental omission of an indefinite stretch of the poem's words resulted in the complete loss of one proper name and the incomplete transmission of a second. The omission falls in the text's account of the four offspring of Healfdene:

> Ðǣm fēower bearn   forð gerīmed
> in worold wōcun,   weoroda rǣswa[n],
> Heorogār ond Hrōðgār   ond Hālga til;
> hȳrde ic þæt [......   wæs On]elan cwēn,
> Heaðoscilfingas   healsgebedda.

>   59–63

> To him four children in sum awoke in the world, to that leader of armies,
> Heorogar and Hrothgar and Halga the good; I have heard that [......] was
> Onela's queen, cherished bedfellow of the War-Scylfing.

The name of Healfdene's daughter, which is conjectured to be Yrse,[4] was entirely obliterated, whereas the name of his son-in-law, Onela, was transmitted as the corrupt *elan* (*KB*:117–118). Because there is no damage in the manuscript where this omission is located, it appears that the scribe inattentively skipped over some text and resumed copying in the middle of a proper name. The name of the Swedish king Onela must have meant nothing to this scribe, who was able to transcribe half of the name (in the vicinity of the *Scilfing* ethnonym) without realizing that the form was incomplete and preceded by a more substantial omission. The error constitutes yet another sign of the mechanical engagement the scribes had with the text they were transmitting. If they were reading it carefully—and scrutinizing it with the linguistic and cultural knowledge that circulated during the period of the poem's composition—this omission and many other corruptions would not stand uncorrected in the transmitted text.

§94. The name of Hreðric, son of Hrōðgar, occurs twice in *Beowulf* (1189a, 1836a), but only once in the poem's extant manuscript. On the second occasion where the poet referenced *Hrēðrīc*, a scribe corrupted his name into *hrēðrinc*, a compound that would mean "glory-warrior." The

---

4   See Clarke 1911:82 and Malone 1929.

corrupt rendering of the second element effectively turns this proper name into a common noun, since -*rinc* was not used to form personal names in *Beowulf* or in Anglo-Saxon England, whereas -*rīc* was an extremely productive element in the onomasticon. The factor that probably induced this corruption is the frequency with which *rinc* is used as the second element in the poem's nominal compounds, such as *beadorinc*, *gūðrinc*, *heaðorinc*, *hererinc*, *hilderinc*, *magorinc*, and *sǣrinc*. Not expecting a proper name, a scribe accustomed to -*rinc* compounds understandably altered the second half of *Hrēðrīc*. Errors involving -*rinc* and -*rīc* could, however, proceed in the opposite direction. As noted above (§79), the scribal corruption of *hererinc* 'warrior' (1176a), into *hererīc* converts an epithet referring to Beowulf into a discrete proper name, since the poet never uses *rīc* to form nominal compounds unless they are proper names (*Eormenrīc*, *Hererīc*, *Hrēðrīc*, *Swīorīce*).[5] Because there is an actual Hereric in heroic-legendary tradition— he is mentioned once in the poem as the uncle of Heardred (2206b)—the appearance of his name as a noun referring to Beowulf is yet another absurd feature of the transmitted text.

§95. Heardred, son of Hygelac, appears three times in *Beowulf* (2202a, 2375a, 2388b), but a mechanical error eliminated the first occurrence of his name from the transmitted text. In place of *Heardrēde* (2202a), the scribe wrote *hea rede*, thereby corrupting the first element of the name (*heard* 'courageous') into a different lexeme (*hēah* 'high'). The omission of one *d* and one *r* from the name is the probable consequence of haplography (*KB:Lang.* §20.6), since both of these consonants appear a second time in *Heardrēde*. The corruption is thus the outcome of an unconscious accident, but it remains noteworthy in the present context, since mechanical errors of this sort are likelier to occur with words that scribes find unfamiliar (Orchard 2003a:24). Scribal awareness of the correct rendering of a particular form also increases the likelihood that a scribe will detect and correct errors that he mechanically introduced into the transmitted text. Indeed, most of the alterations that the final scribes made to their work serve the purpose of correcting errors of a purely mechanical nature, such as haplography, dittography, or metathesis (Orchard 2003–2004:52). Scribal ignorance of the legendary Heardred explains why this haplography went undetected and uncorrected.

§96. There are reasons to believe that, in addition to *Ēomēr*, as many as three other proper names were obliterated from the Offa digression

---

[5] Consequently, Malone's insistent defense of the manuscript reading (1939, 1951) cannot be credited, since it pays no heed to the improbabilities it generates (i.e. that -*ric* should be used in compounds only in rare instances where there are independent reasons to suspect corruption).

(1931b–1962) during the course of the poem's transmission. The name of Hemming, kinsman to Offa and Eomer, occurs twice in the poem, but it was never successfully transmitted: it appears in the manuscript first as *hem ninges* and then as *hem inges*. The etymologically correct form of this name is structurally required in the poem, since the geminated consonant is essential to the scansion of the verse *Hemminges mæg* (1944b, 1961b). Without the consonant cluster, the first lift would be resolved and the verse would contain only three metrical positions (Sievers 1885:501). Meter thus confirms that both of the transmitted forms of Hemming's name are scribal errors. Corruption is less certain with regard to the name transmitted in the following line:

nefa Gārmundes,   nīða cræftig.

1962

Garmund's grandson, strong in strife

With few exceptions, the legendary tradition pertaining to Offa of Angeln holds that Offa's father (and hence Eomer's grandfather) was named Wermund, not Garmund. Wermund is the name of Offa's father in a wide range of works, including the Mercian royal genealogy, Saxo Grammaticus's *Gesta Danorum*, Sven Aageson's *Brevis Historia Regum Daniae*, the *Vitae Duarum Offarum*, and the *Annales Ryenses*.[6] Because the name in question is not bound to the structure of *Beowulf*—it does not participate in alliteration and the competing forms are metrically equivalent—editors do not emend *Gārmundes* to *Wērmundes*. The weight of the legendary analogues nevertheless establishes a decent probability of scribal corruption. Considering the fact that *Beowulf* and the Mercian royal genealogy are the only works in the tradition to name Eomer as the son of Offa, it is reasonable to expect them to have originally concurred with regard to Wermund as well. Finally, scholars have long suspected that an accidental omission obliterated the name of Offa's queen from the text.[7] For a variety of compelling reasons, her name cannot be Þryð or Modþryð, as many have believed, though it may be Fremu (1932a), a word traditionally construed as an adjective (Fulk 2004). If her name is not Fremu, then either the poet refrained from naming Offa's queen or a scribe accidentally omitted the name due to eye-skip. The relative probability of the competing hypotheses is difficult to gauge.

§97. One interesting error in the transmitted text affected the identity of Dæghrefn, the Frankish warrior killed by Beowulf during Hygelac's raid

---

[6] The analogous texts are edited and translated in Swanton 2010:133–184.

[7] See Grundtvig 1820:173; Craigie 1923:16–18; Whitelock 1951:58–59; and Sisam 1953b:41.

in Frisia. The following passage appears in a long, retrospective speech from the poem's protagonist:

> syððan ic for dugeðum   Dæghrefne wearð
> tō handbonan,   Hūga cempan—
> nalles hē ðā frætwe   Frēscyning[e],
> brēostweorðunge   bringan mōste,
> ac in campe gecrong   cumbles hyrde,
> æþeling on elne;

2501–2506a

> After I came to be, in the presence of the armies, hand-killer of Dæghrefn, champion of the Hugas—he was by no means permitted to bring those trappings, that breast-ornament, to the Frisian king, but the keeper of the ensign succumbed on the battlefield, a prince in a show of bravery

The poet evidently regarded Dæghrefn as a Frankish warrior (*Hūga cempa*) keen to serve the allied king of the Frisians by presenting loot plundered from the corpse of Hygelac. A scribe in the course of transmission, however, omitted the inflection in *Frēscyninge*, thereby converting it from a dative to a nominative form. The transmitted *frēscyning* stands in apposition to *hē* and consequently turns Dæghrefn into the king of Frisia. Dæghrefn is otherwise unknown in Germanic legendary tradition, but the transmitted text contains one decisive indication that he served the Frisian king and was not the king himself: as a verse, *frēscyning* would contain only three metrical positions. The syllable generated by the inflection renders the verse metrically viable and improves the sense of the passage. Onomastic considerations elevate the probability that Dæghrefn was a historical Frank rather than a Frisian: *dæg* and *hrefn*, though rare in English name-giving, were characteristic elements of the Frankish onomasticon (Shippey 2014:65–68). The authentic character of Dæghrefn's name, like that of Unferð, testifies to the vigor and accuracy of legendary tradition in the *Beowulf* poet's day.

2. Obliteration of Ethnic Names

§98. The frequent corruption of ethnonyms in the transmitted text of *Beowulf* reveals that late scribes were unfamiliar not only with particular heroes, but also with the peoples and dynasties who had inhabited the migration-era world of the poem. Ethnonyms suffered fates similar to those of personal names. Proper names were corrupted into common nouns, for example, in two of the three occurrences of the *Heaðobeard* ethnonym. This name, which appears only in its genitive plural form, is first rendered correctly as *Heaðobeardna* (2032b), then incorrectly as *heaða bearna* (2037b) and *heaðo bearna* (2067a). The corruption of *beard* into *bearn* is consequential because it turns the aptly named "battle-beards" into the improbable "battle-children." The error also converts an ethnonym into a noun phrase, since *bearn* was not used to form ethnonyms, whereas *beard* was a traditional element used for the naming of peoples (e.g. the Langobards). A phonological explanation for the loss of *d* in the genitive plural form cannot be credited: the ubiquity of forms such as *heardne* in the extant corpus and the corresponding rarity of those such as **hearne*, for example, confirm that there is no principled reason to expect *d* to be lost in this environment (*KB:Lang.* §20.6n1). Consequently, it is probable that a scribe unfamiliar with the *Heaðobeard* ethnonym presumed *beard* to stand for the more common *bearn* and altered it accordingly.

§99. The corruption of an ethnonym into a common noun also affected the transmission of the following passage, in which the poet contrasts Beowulf's unpromising youth with his later achievements:

> næs him hrēoh sefa,
> ac hē mancynnes   mæste cræfte
> ginfæstan gife   þe him God sealde,
> hēold hildedēor.   Hēan wæs lange,
> swā hyne Gēata bearn   gōdne ne tealdon,
> nē hyne on medobence   micles wyrðne
> dryhten Wedera   gedōn wolde;
> swȳðe wēndon   þæt hē slēac wære,
> æðeling unfrom.
>
> 2180b–2188a

He did not have a fierce temperament, but, brave in battle, with the greatest of human skill he managed the abundant gifts that God had granted him. For a long time he had been lowly, as the sons of the Geats had not thought him good, nor had the lord of the Weders cared to put him in possession of much on the mead-bench; they had rather thought that he was shiftless, a slack lordling.

In the transmitted text, the sense of this passage is disturbed in several respects due to the corruption of *dryhten Wedera* 'lord of the Geats' into *dryhten wereda* 'lord of hosts'. The error obliterates both the ethnonym and the reference to the Geatish king Hreðel, since the resulting phrase is a

standard description for a divine rather than a human ruler.[8] The transposi-
tion of *d* and *r* would seem to be a purely mechanical error (metathesis), but
the appearance of a reference to God (2182b) shortly before the reference to
Hreðel (2186a) might have conditioned a scribe to expect a phrase describing
the deity. Of course, since the passage is intended to contrast God's enduring
support for Beowulf with the Geats' low opinion of him, the scribal replacement of Hreðel with God is particularly nonsensical. This error, like several
discussed in the previous chapter (§§77–78), may reflect the immersion of
later scribes in religious literature and their consequent expectation that texts
should more frequently allude to spiritual matters.

§100. For reasons that remain unclear, a scribe also obliterated the
Geatish *Weder* ethnonym from the brief account of Ecgþeo's feud with the
Wulfings. Hroðgar explains to Beowulf that Ecgþeo sought out the Danes as
an exile and was received hospitably:

> Geslōh þīn fæder   fæhðe mæste;
> wearþ hē Heaþolāfe   tō handbonan
> mid Wilfingum;   ðā hine *Wede*ra cyn
> for herebrōgan   habban ne mihte.
> Þanon hē gesōhte   Sūð-Dena folc
> ofer ȳða gewealc,   Ārscyldinga;
>
> 459–464

> Your father caused the greatest vendetta; he came to be the killer of
> Heatholaf among the Wylfings; then for fear of war the nation of Weders
> could not keep him. From there he came to see the people of the South-
> Danes over the tumult of waves, the Honor-Scyldings

In place of *Wedera*, the transmitted text displays *gara*. The reading is a rather
puzzling one, since there is no straightforward manual or visual explanation
for the resultant form, which shares only its final two letters with the authorial form. That *Wedera* is to be regarded as the authorial form in this instance
cannot reasonably be doubted, since the transmitted form yields a line
without alliteration, and the other proposed emendations, such as *Wulgara*
(Malone 1940) or *Wīg-gara* (Kiernan 1981:183), render the verse unmetrical
(*KB*:146). The sense of the passage also demands the presence of *Wedera*
here: the reason Ecgþeo petitioned the Danes to intercede on his behalf is
that the Geats, fearful of a war with the Wulfings, were unwilling to protect

---

[8]   The formulaic expression *weroda dryhten* 'lord of hosts' is a common phrase for God, attested in
Genesis A (1362a, 1411b), *Genesis B* (255b, 386b), *Exodus* (8b, 92a), and *Judith* (342a), among other
places.

him. Accordingly, the scribe who corrupted *Wedera* into *gara* destroyed the logic of the narrative. Since *gara cyn* must be construed as a reference to the (Gar-)Danes, the transmitted text incoherently states that the Danes were unwilling to protect Ecgþeo, who then received protection from the Danes. Whatever the motivation behind the corruption may be, it is clear that the scribe who introduced *gara* into the text worked without making an effort to comprehend the material he copied. To this scribe, the various peoples in *Beowulf* were evidently indistinguishable from one another. The intricate knowledge of migration-era geopolitical history that the poet expected his contemporary audience to possess plainly could not be expected of the later scribes.

§101. Just as the Geats were corrupted into the Danes in the previous example, the Swedes were corrupted into the Danes in the transmitted version of the following passage. After Beowulf dies, a Geatish messenger predicts that his vulnerable people will suffer various disasters, including invasion from the Swedes, who will retaliate for Hygelac's aggression. The messenger relates a history of warfare between the Swedish and Geatish peoples—*sīo swāt-swaðu Swēona ond Gēata* 'the bloody track of Swedes and Geats' (2946)—then concludes with an ominous recapitulation:

Þæt ys sīo fæhðo   ond se feondscipe,
wælnīð wera,   ðæs ðe ic [wēn] hafo,
þē ūs sēceað tō   Swēona lēoda,
syððan hīe gefricgeað   frēan ūserne
ealdorlēasne,   þone ðe ær gehēold
wið hettendum   hord ond rīce
æfter hæleða hryre,   hwate Scil*f*ingas,
folcrēd fremede   oððe furður gēn
eorlscipe efnde.

                                        2999–3007a

That is the feud and the enmity, deadly hostility of men, as I expect, for which the Swedish people will come in search of us, the keen Scylfings, after they discover that our lord is no longer living, who guarded the hoard and kingdom against opponents after the fall of champions, furthered the people's interests, or what is more, accomplished heroic acts.

The messenger's final reference to the Swedes is obliterated, however, in the transmitted text, which reads *scildingas* in place of *Scilfingas* (KB:262).[9]

---

[9]   Hoops (1932a:78–88) proposed that *scildingas* should be emended to *scildwigan*, but this proposal cannot be correct, since true compounds must participate in the line's alliteration, in accordance

This corruption generated another notable absurdity for readers of the extant manuscript: after more than eighty lines concerning the enmity between the Swedes and the Geats (2922–3005), the messenger implausibly tells his people to prepare for an attack by the Danes, who have hardly been mentioned in the thousand lines preceding their spurious reintroduction into the text. The motivation behind the corruption of *Scilfingas* into *Scildingas* at this point in the text is difficult to discern. It seems necessary to imagine that a scribe who mechanically transmitted the *Scylfing* ethnonym on several previous occasions decided on this one occasion to scrutinize the text critically and deem the authorial form to be an erroneous spelling of the more common *Scylding* ethnonym. To be sure, the behavior envisioned is incoherent, but the transmitted text contains many inconsistencies that must be attributed to the "passing moods" (*KB:Lang.* §28n7) of whimsical scribes, who unsystematically altered perceived errors without regard for the nonsense that their alterations generated.

§102. The curious manuscript reading *Gēatena* (443b) also appears to owe its origin to the scribal conflation of two discrete ethnic names (Rieger 1871:400). Elsewhere in the poem, in approximately forty instances, the genitive plural form of the Geatish ethnonym is *Gēata*. The presence of the analogical weak *-ena* desinence thus renders the form transmitted in 443b a singularity requiring explanation. A paleographical observation from Kemp Malone (1963) may point us toward the probable reason for the anomaly: the scribe originally committed *geotena* to parchment before altering it to *Gēatena* (Fulk 2005a:194). The initially transmitted form suggests that an antecedent scribe had confused the Geats with the Jutes, since the genitive plural form of the latter is spelt *Ēotena* throughout the text of *Beowulf*. The final scribe partially corrected the work of his predecessor by converting *o* to *a*. The correction was simple enough to make, since the Geatish name appears dozens of times in the text, and the Jutish name was probably unfamiliar to this scribe, as errors discussed in the following paragraph indicate. The antecedent scribe's confusion of Jutes and Geats is paralleled in the *Old English Bede*, where the *Iutae* are erroneously converted into the *Gēatas* (*KB:Lang.* §16.2). The parallel is worth bearing in mind, as it constitutes one of many external signs (surveyed in §§120–124 below) that the scribes who transmitted *Beowulf* were not unique in their ignorance of the heroes and peoples who flourished during the migration period.

---

with Krackow's law; see Krackow 1903 and *KB:T.C.* §39. Syntactic objections to the *Scilfingas* emendation are answered in Campbell 1962:22n1.

§103. The Jutish ethnonym (*Ēotan*), meanwhile, was twice obliterated from the transmitted text because the scribes mistook it for *eoten* 'giant', an altogether unrelated word. The first passage that exhibits the corruption is located in the Sigemund-Heremod digression and concerns the latter's demise:

> Hē mid Ēotenum wearð
> on fēonda geweald   forð forlācen,
> snūde forsended.

902b–904a

Among the Jutes he was betrayed into the hands of enemies, quickly dispatched.

The second passage to feature the corruption of Jutes into giants falls in the Finnsburh episode, in the description of the sword that would inspire Hengest to resume the conflict with Finn:

> þonne him Hūnlāfing   hildelēoman,
> billa sēlest,   on bearm dyde,
> þæs wǣron mid Ēotenum   ecge cūðe.

1143–1145

when Hunlafing should place in his lap a battle-light, the best of blades, whose edges were familiar to the Jutes.

The problem with both passages is that the manuscript reading *eotenum* is not the expected dative plural form of *Ēotan*, which is properly *Ēotum*, whereas *eotenum* is the correct dative plural form of *eoten* 'giant'. Since there is no reason to believe that a process of analogy resulted in a genuine *Ēotenum* form, it appears necessary to explain the transmitted reading as the product of scribal confusion (*KB*:171; Hogg and Fulk 2011:§2.70n5). A scribe, unfamiliar with the Jutes, presumed that the authorial *Ēotum* was an error for *eotenum* and altered it accordingly. A factor that might have conditioned this error is that elsewhere in the poem, the Jutish name appears only in the genitive plural form, *Ēotena* (1072a, 1088a, 1141a), which is graphically identical to the genitive plural form of *eoten*. If a scribe preoccupied with form and indifferent to sense construed the three occurrences of *Ēotena* as references to giants, this would explain his conviction that *Ēotum* must be altered to *eotenum*. To this scribe, there simply were no Jutes in *Beowulf*, only giants.

§104. The corruption of the Jutes into giants has proved to be one of the more consequential obliterations of a proper name from the transmitted text of *Beowulf*. A substantial number of scholars have contended that *eotenum* is an authorial form rather than a scribal error and that there are genuinely no Jutes in *Beowulf*.[10] Scholars who maintain this belief evidently do not apprehend the considerable improbabilities that it generates, which I have expounded at length elsewhere (Neidorf 2015a). To mention just one of the most salient problems with belief in the authenticity of *eotenum*: there are many independent reasons to expect Jutes to appear in both of the passages cited above. Analogues concerning the Danish king Lotherus, whose story parallels Heremod's in many respects, recount his demise as an exile among the Jutes.[11] Even more compelling are the external sources related to the participants of the Finnsburh episode. A principal agent in the *Beowulf* account, Hengest, is identified in a variety of sources as the legendary leader of the Jutes (Aurner 1921). Furthermore, a passage in *Widsið* (26b–29a) establishes a connection in legend between the Jutes, the Frisians, and the Danes; the poet's specific allusion to Finn and Hnæf indicates that his collocation of these peoples reflects their participation in the momentous battle at Finnsburh. Consequently, to believe that there are no Jutes in *Beowulf* is to lend credence to a massively improbable coincidence: one must believe that although five words (*eotena* x3, *eotenum* x2) bearing an uncanny resemblance to the Jutish ethnonym occur in the text precisely where Jutes are to be expected, these words must be construed as references to giants, not Jutes. Plainly, belief in the authenticity of *eotenum* is less rational than belief in its being a scribal corruption of *Ēotum*.[12]

§105. Credence in the hypothesis that a scribe corrupted Jutes into giants is supported by the fact that such a corruption is entirely consistent with the picture of scribal behavior that has emerged throughout the present chapter. The scribes, confronting unfamiliar personal and ethnic names, frequently changed them into common words of similar appearance, in the evident belief that they were correcting errors committed by antecedent copyists. Most of the errors discussed above involve the corruption of a proper name into a common noun or a different proper name, yet the difficulties that the scribes experienced with names are also indicated in some minor errors that obliterate or obscure ethnonyms in the transmitted text. For example, the

---

[10] For examples of recent scholarship adhering to the "giants" interpretation, see the references provided in Neidorf 2015a:616n60; the currency of the idea in earlier scholarship is illustrated in *KB*:171n1. For one of the most influential defenses of this position, see Kaske 1967.

[11] See Chambers 1959:89–97, 262; and Tolkien 2006:54–60.

[12] The epistemological considerations informing the argumentation of this paragraph are presented at greater length in this book's introduction (§§29–32) and in Neidorf 2015b.

erroneous vocalism of the transmitted *swona*, which must stand for *Swēona* (2946b), may signal confusion about the correct form of the Swedish name. Similarly, the transmitted *scyldenda*, which must stand for *Scyldinga* (148a), seems to have resulted from a scribe mistaking an ethnonym with an *-ing* suffix for a present participle with an *-end* suffix. Finally, the transmitted *de ninga*, which must stand for *Deniga* (465b), reflects unfamiliarity with the original *-iga* genitive plural desinence of this *i*-stem ethnonym (§§48–49). The scribe conflated the authorial desinence with the *-ing* suffix and produced an altogether improbable form (*KB*:146). The loss of proper names from the transmitted text is not, however, the only sign of scribal unfamiliarity with the poem's heroes and peoples. Names more or less successfully transmitted can also bear signs of scribal confusion.

3. Erroneous Spacing

§106. Several names in the *Beowulf* manuscript are spaced in aberrant ways that reflect the inability of the scribes to comprehend the text in their exemplar. Because conventions of spacing and word division in manuscripts containing Old English poetry differ so considerably from the conventions employed in other manuscript and print cultures, some scholars have mistakenly judged these conventions to be entirely unpredictable and chaotic. For example, Kiernan rejected the claim of Sisam (1953b:37) that the manuscript's *mid finnel* (discussed in §109 below) is a genuine corruption on the grounds that "strange combinations and divisions of words are characteristic of Old English MSS" (Kiernan 1981:181). Of course, if there were no discernable regularities of manuscript spacing and word division, then apparent anomalies would convey no meaningful information about scribal comprehension. Yet studies from Robert D. Stevick (1968, 1975) and Megan E. Hartman (2007) have demonstrated that the conventions of spacing in the manuscript of *Beowulf* are surprisingly regular. Anomalies and inconsistencies exist, but judgments about what is normal or abnormal practice for the scribes can readily be formed. The spacing of dithematic names is similar to the spacing of compounds: the scribes tend to divide dithematic names and compounds into two sense-bearing units. The names of Hroðgar and Hygelac are thus normally written as *hroð gar* and *hyge lac*. The scribes rarely spaced compounds into units devoid of meaning when construed individually. Hartman (2007:207–214) illustrates this tendency by observing that the *-lēas* suffix tends to be spaced, whereas a space rarely separates the *-ing* suffix from the word to which it belongs. The discrepancy is principled, since the significance of *-ing* depends on the preceding morpheme, whereas *-lēas* possesses meaning when construed individually. Normally, moreover, the scribes did not space words into senseless units: nowhere in the manuscript is the name Hroðgar spaced into *hro ðg ar*.

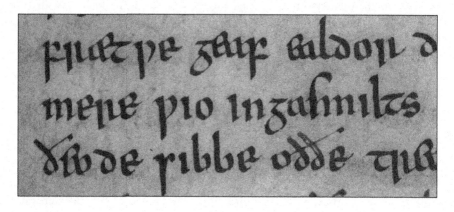

Figure 6. Anomalous spacing in *mere wio ingasmilts*, line 2921b (fol. 197r).

§107. A marked aberration is thus apparent in the stretch of the text in the manuscript that reads *mere wio ingasmilts* (see figure 6). Properly edited, the passage containing this sequence reads as follows:

> Ūs wæs ā syððan
> Merewīoingas   milts ungyfeðe.

2920b–2921

> The good will of the Merovingian was ever afterward unobtainable for us.

The spacing in the manuscript indicates that the scribe, who probably never heard the Merovingian name uttered, was unable to identify a proper name in the letters comprising *Merewīoingas*. Spacing of that name into *mere wio ingas* is unusual, since a space rarely separates the *-ing* suffix from the preceding morpheme, as noted above. Yet the absence of a space between *ingas* and *milts*, entirely uncharacteristic of the manuscript's spacing, is the firmest sign of misunderstanding. Commenting on *mere wio ingasmilts*, Stevick remarked: "The 0-space at the boundary between forms of these types is contrary to the scribe's writing habits; it is also contrary to the principle of leaving space between verse halflines; and it produces a string of ten letters unusual in both its length and structure" (1975:xxxiv). An additional sign of the scribe's confusion is that he originally committed *ingannilts* to parchment before converting the first minim after *a* into *s*. It is worth noting that even though the scribe did not understand the text he copied, there can be no doubt that he successfully transmitted the authorial reading: *merewioing* is, in fact, the only etymologically correct rendering of the Merovingian name in a medieval document (Shippey 2005:398–400). The form indicates that this name must have circulated orally in the period when *Beowulf* was composed. The poet's knowledge derives from native vernacular tradition, not written Latin sources, where the Merovingian name is uniformly mangled.[13]

§108. Scribal confusion is likewise evident in the spacing of *Ongenþeoes* (1968b) into *on gen þeo es*. In general, proper names are not divided in this manner, and elsewhere in the manuscript this particular name is never subjected to such curious spacing. There is a straightforward explanation for the unusual treatment of the name in this instance: it is the first appearance of Ongenþeo in the text of the poem. Confronting the letters comprising this name for the first time, the scribe saw no proper name in them and consequently divided the sequence into a few recognizable morphemes. The regular word divisions discernible in the later appearances of the name, meanwhile, indicate that the scribe remembered this perplexing sequence of letters and realized that it was a proper name the second time he encountered it. It makes sense that scribal unfamiliarity with this proper name and that of the Merovingians should manifest itself in aberrant spacing rather than obliteration. A scribe could regard *Ēomēr* as a mistaken form of *geōmor* and *Ēotum* as a mistaken form of *eotenum*, but no common noun of similar appearance could come to the scribe's mind when scrutinizing *Ongenþeoes* or *Merewīoingas*. Puzzled, the scribe mechanically transcribed the letters he encountered in the exemplar, successfully transmitting the authorial readings in graphic sequences that betray his inability to comprehend them.

§109. A defective passage in the Finnsburh episode concerns the winter that Hengest spent with Finn in Frisia. The transmitted text states that Hengest *wunode mid finnel un hlitme*. Emended and lineated, the passage reads as follows:

---

[13] Contrary to those who have contended that the *Beowulf* poet's knowledge of legend derives from later Scandinavian or Latin sources (proponents of this view are listed in Neidorf 2014b:40n13), the etymologically correct character of the poem's proper names confirms that they derive from native oral tradition. Just as *Merewioing* and *Hygelac* could not plausibly have been reconstructed from Latin sources, where their names are rendered in forms such as *Meroweching* and *Chochilaichus*, the names of Hroðgar and Hroðulf could not have been reconstructed from their Scandinavian forms, *Roarr* and *Rolf*. See Fulk 1982:343–345 and the comments on the authenticity of proper names scattered throughout Neidorf 2014b.

Hengest ðā gȳt
wælfāgne winter   wunode mid Finne;
h[ē] unhlitme   eard gemunde,
þēah þe *ne* meahte   on mere drīfan
hringedstefnan

1127b–1131b

Hengest still remained with Finn a slaughter-stained winter; he fondly remembered his homeland, though he could not drive a ring-prow on the sea

The transmitted *finnel* is a product of erroneous spacing. The first ascender of the subsequent word, which is not present in the transmitted text perhaps because of damage to the scribe's exemplar, has been added to the authorial *Finne*, resulting in the nonsensical *finnel*. There has been considerable variation among editors in the identification of the lost word: many have conjectured that it was *eal* or *ealles*, though there are advantages to *hē*, the reading adopted above (*KB*:187–188). Regardless of the particular word, the scribe's decision to append its ascender to *Finne* must be construed as a sign of misunderstanding, since the scribe would not deliberately join the first letter of a new word to the preceding word. For a scribe preoccupied with form, indifferent to sense, and unfamiliar with legendary tradition, the transmitted *finnel* probably seemed adequate and plausible, because there is a productive -*el* suffix in Old English, which is used in one of the poem's most prominent personal names (Grendel). The scribe was satisfied with the authentic appearance of the transmitted form, which could be interpreted as another proper name, Finnel. Kiernan's claim that "there is no good evidence here that the scribe did not know that Hengest stayed with a man named Finn" (1981:181) is thus mistaken. Had the scribe known that Finn was the name of a character in this episode, word divisions would reflect this knowledge, and *finnel* would not be present in the transmitted text.

§110. Scribal difficulty with the text of *Beowulf* is also apparent in the anomalous spacing of *in Frēswæle* 'in the Frisian slaughter' (1070a), which is written in the manuscript as *infr es wæle*. The resultant form is exceptional both in its joining of *in* to the following word and in its spacing of the phrase into senseless units. An erasure beneath *es* bears additional witness to the scribe's struggle to comprehend the text: he initially wrote a different letter after *r*, then erased it, and proceeded to write *es wæle*. A faint line connecting *r* and *e* suggests that before committing the error he corrected, the scribe intended to space the letters encountered in the exemplar into *infres wæle*—a division that still betrays the scribe's inability to discern the correct lexemes in this sequence of graphemes. Unfamiliarity with the Frisian ethnonym might have been the source of the scribe's confusion.

§111. Erroneous spacing is combined with syntactic misconstruction in the transmitted text's *hea þo ræmes* for authorial *Heaþorǽmas*. The passage containing the anomaly is located in Beowulf's speech about his swimming exploit with Breca:

> Þā hine on morgentīd
> on Heaþo-Rǽmes   holm up ætbær

> 518b–519

> Then in the morning hours the breakers brought him up among the Heatho-Reams

Since the syntax of the passage requires an accusative plural complement to follow the preposition *on*—the idea being that the sea thrust Breca into the midst of a foreign people—the form of the ethnonym to be expected is *Heaþorǽmas*. Some editors, including those of *KB*, have retained the transmitted *-es* desinence by construing it as an instance of the leveling of inflectional endings that is evident elsewhere in the manuscript.[14] Yet while the genitive *-es* desinence is leveled into *-as* on a few occasions—for example *Heaðoscilfingas* (63a), *yrfeweardas* (2453a), *Merewioingas* (2921a)— the reverse process is without precedent in the text and confined to this particular example (*KB:Lang.* §19.5). The consistent decision of the scribes to avoid using *-es* for the nominative and accusative plural *-as* suggests that the exceptional *Heaþorǽmes* is the product of grammatical misunderstanding rather than phonological leveling. The spacing of the name into units devoid of sense (*hea þo ræmes*) raises the possibility that the scribe saw no proper name here. He divided the sequence into three separate morphemes and altered *ræmas* to *ræmes* in the belief that this final element was a genitive noun modifying *holm* 'sea'. That the scribe should misconstrue the syntax of the text by wrongly presuming a word to accord with its neighbor is consistent with behavior observed in the previous chapter (§§71–75).

---

[14] The judgment is grounded in the argument of Malone, who contended that the leveling of inflectional endings characteristic of Middle English is already evident in the four Old English poetic codices from ca. 1000 (1930). Yet some of the evidence adduced by Malone is surely the product of scribal error rather than phonological change; see *KB:Lang.* §19.3 and Kitson 1997.

4. Scribal Self-Correction

§112. Similar to erroneous spacing, cases of scribal self-correction constitute another category of paleographical evidence capable of registering
some of the difficulties that the scribes experienced while transmitting
the poem's proper names. In the estimate of Orchard (2003–2004:52), the
scribes altered approximately 145 transmitted readings after they had been
committed to parchment. In most cases, a scribe corrected his own mechanical error immediately after committing it (e.g., *wlocn* corrected to *wlonc*,
331b), though in some cases, it is clear that a scribe skimmed his collaborator's work and made superficial *ex post facto* alterations. Proper names
fell among the altered words for two reasons: some were initially corrupted
and then corrected, whereas others were altered in order to modernize their
spellings. The process of modernization, discussed in the previous chapter
(§56), accounts for various changes made to proper names, including the
insertion of *g* in *Ecþēow* (263b) following the *c* (see figure 2), the addition
of a concluding *p* to *Wealhþēo* (612b) and *Ongenðīo* (2961a) (see figures 3–4,
chapter 2), the substitution of *a* for *æ* in *Hetware* (2916a), and the alteration
of *-ung* to *-ing* in *Sige-Scyldingum* (2004a). These alterations bear witness
to aspects of language change that took place between the composition and
reproduction of *Beowulf*, whereas the correction of initially corrupted names
yields some additional evidence for the process of cultural change indicated
in the errors and anomalies discussed throughout the present chapter.

§113. A straightforward case of scribal self-correction is evident in
Healfdenes (189b). The scribe originally committed *healfdes* to parchment
before altering *s* to *n* and adding *es*. The authorial form is successfully transmitted, but the initial corruption might reflect unfamiliarity with Healfdene
or with dithematic personal names consisting of such elements. Correction is
also evident in *Scyldunga* (2159a). The scribe had committed the nonsensical
scyinunga to parchment, then altered *in* to *ld* through the imposition of two
crude ascenders upon the original minims. Two transliteration errors initially
resulted in the corruption of proper names. When transmitting the name
Bēowulf (1024b), the scribe originally wrote *feo-* or *weo-* (i.e., *peo-*) as the
first element of the name before imposing *b* upon the consonant that had
preceded it. Similarly, *Hrōþgār* (1236a) was originally written as *broþgar*—a
form that suggests misapprehension of the name as *brōðor*—before an erasure
effected the conversion of *b* to *h*. These cases of self-correction reveal that the
scribes' mechanical fidelity to the exemplar prevented numerous corruptions

of unfamiliar names from being introduced into the transmitted text. The scribes were ignorant of the traditions informing the poem, but they were not careless. When conflation of forms did not induce them to corrupt an unfamiliar form to a more familiar one, the scribes faithfully reproduced the substance of the text before them.

§114. One scribal self-correction is distinguished by its chronological significance. The poet's use of the archaic toponym *Scedenig* (cf. *Scedeland*)—corresponding to Pliny's *Scadinavia*—has long been regarded as a sign of the poem's relative antiquity.[15] This toponym is not found in works composed during or after the reign of King Alfred, which instead refer to the same entity as *Sconeg*, a term that reflects the ninth-century borrowing of Old Norse *Skáney*. The early obsolescence of the native term, *Scedenig*, is suggested in a paleographical indication of scribal misapprehension. For *Scedenigge* (1686a), the scribe originally committed *scedeninge* to parchment before correcting the reading by imposing *g* upon the second *n*. The initially transmitted form indicates that when the scribe analyzed the text in the exemplar, he expected an ethnonym with an *-ing* suffix here, not a toponym. He corrected his own error, but his prior misapprehension of *Scedenig* lends support to the hypothesis that this word is a notable archaism.

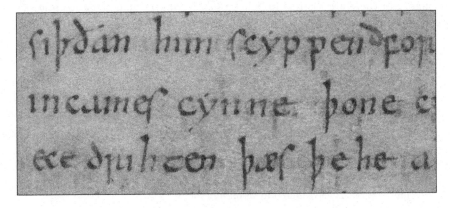

Figure 7. Scribal alteration of *cames* into *cāines*, line 107a (fol. 134r).

§115. The scribal alteration of *Cames* to *Cāines* (see figure 7) gener-ated a textual crux of exceptional complexity. In the passage concerning Grendel's descent, there is a verse edited as *in Cāines cynne* 'among the race of Cain' (107a). Before the manuscript read *Cāines*, it is clear that it

---

[15]   See Fulk 1982:343–344; *KB:Lang.* §27; Townend 2002:108.

read *Cames*, and that a scribe converted *m* to *in* through the erasure of a ligature. Metrically, the verse that results from the scribal alteration is an anomaly. Bliss (1967:§§46–47) observed that anacrusis is not permitted in type A verses that would otherwise consist of two trochaic words. Verses such as *nū hæleð ne mōstan* (2247b) thus conform to an allowable pattern, whereas verses such as **nu gomban gyldan* (or *in Cāines cynne*) were studiously avoided by the *Beowulf* poet (*KB:T.C.* §35). The fact that a scribal alteration is visible in the lone verse that deviates from the poet's metrical practice must raise suspicions about its authenticity. Restoration of the antecedent reading—*Cames*, with a short vowel, referring to Ham (or Cham), son of Noah—removes the metrical defect from the verse. *In Cames cynne* scans as a standard type C verse with resolution of the first lift, closely paralleled in verses such as *on grames grāpum* (765a), *on weres wæstmum* (1352a), and *on sefan sende* (1842a). If *Cames* is the authorial reading, then the scribal alteration of the name functioned not to correct an error, but to obliterate a proper name from the transmitted text.

§116. To gauge the relative merits of *Cames* and *Cāines*, it is necessary to consider which of the two scribes is responsible for the alteration. Kiernan (1981:196–197) understandably assumed that Scribe A corrected himself here, but there are reasons to believe that Scribe B altered the reading that his collaborator committed to parchment. Because a single erasure effected the alteration of *Cames* to *Cāines*, the scribe responsible for the erasure cannot be identified with assurance (Westphalen 1967:98–100). Alterations to transmitted readings can be confidently attributed to a particular scribe only when they involve the post hoc addition of a letter, since the formal characteristics of the letter indicate which of the two scribes is responsible for its insertion into the text. According to this criterion, thirteen alterations to the work of Scribe A have been attributed to Scribe B (Orchard 2003–2004:52):

> fol. 132r13: *scyppen* altered to *scyppend* (106a)
> fol. 133r20: *beortre* alt. to *beorhtre* (158a)
> fol. 140v14: *dol scaðan* alt. to *dolsceaðan* (479a)
> fol. 142r13: *o* alt. to *on* (537a)
> fol. 144r5: *wealhþeo* alt. to *wealhþeow* (612b)
> fol. 147r11: *ængum* alt. to *ænigum*(793b)
> fol. 158v15: *on* alt. to *in* (1302a)
> fol. 160r17: *hafelan* alt. to *hafelan* [*mark*](1372a)
> fol. 160v14: *gan* alt. to *gang* (1391b)
> fol. 167v10: *ferþe* alt. to *ferhþe* (1718b)

fol. 168v3: *feh* alt. to *fehð* (1755b)
fol. 169r19: *dogor* alt. to *dogore* (1797b)
fol. 171v20: *hreþe* alt. to *hraþe* (1914a)

The distribution of these alterations reveals that Scribe B did not comprehensively scrutinize his collaborator's efforts. To the contrary, it appears that he haphazardly scanned a fraction of the text in search of forms to modernize or standardize, skimming folios 132–133, 140–144, 147, 158–160, and 167–171. Significantly, the erasure of *Cames* is located on fol. 132r, one of the folios that Scribe B is known to have examined. More remarkable is its proximity to the one alteration that Scribe B made to that folio: on the thirteenth line, Scribe B added *d* to *scyppen*, and on the fourteenth line, a mere three words later, *Cames* was altered to *Cāines* (see figure 7). Evidently, the scribe's eye fell upon the stretch of text that included *Cames*, which he regarded as an error for *Cāines*, prompting him to alter the reading that his collaborator transmitted. The attribution of this alteration to Scribe B further depreciates the authority of *Cāines*, since it is clear that Scribe B did not consult the exemplar when altering his collaborator's work (*KB*:xxxiii). The linguistically modernized readings that result from his alterations—such as *ǣnigum* (§66), *Wealhþēow* (§56), and *dogore* (§44) (figures 1, 3, and 5, chapter 2)—must constitute deviations from the readings that had been present in the exemplar, for reasons explained in the previous chapter.

§117. Metrical and paleographical considerations thus align in support of the conclusion that *Cames* is the authorial reading in 107a. The tenability of this conclusion is complicated by the fact that disyllabic *Cāin* is metrically required in the verse *siþðan Cāin wearð* (1261b). In the latter instance, a scribe obliterated *Cāin* from the text by corrupting the name to *camp* 'struggle', but it is nevertheless clear that *Cāin* is the authorial reading there (see §§16–17). Can it be that the *Beowulf* poet referred to both Cam and Cain? He would not have been alone in doing so: a wide range of early insular texts, including eighth-century works from Alcuin, bear witness to an exegetical tradition that conflated Cain and Cam as the literal and spiritual progenitors of the world's reprobates.[16] A clear rationale for the statement that Grendel belongs to *Cames cynne* is provided, moreover, in the Irish *Sex Aetates Mundi* (Tristram 1985:221–222), which explains that because God eliminated Cain's monstrous progeny in the flood, the monsters that currently inhabit the world are descendants of Cam, who was present in Noah's ark. The *Beowulf* poet's maintenance of a lexical distinction (Mellinkoff 1980:184) between

---

[16] See Pulsiano 1985; Orchard 2003b:58–85; Anlezark 2006:298–304; Neidorf 2015a.

antediluvian monsters (*gīgantas*) and postdiluvian monsters (*eotenas ond ylfe ond orcnēas*) may reflect knowledge of the tradition attributing the latter to Cam. Awareness of this tradition is also manifest in the description of the sword-hilt that Beowulf discovers in the underwater dwelling of Grendel's mother (1687b–1693). This hilt, carved in runes that preserve antediluvian information, is paralleled in a tradition articulated by Cassian, which states that Cam transmitted evil arts to the postdiluvian world by carving them on metals that would survive under water, incapable of being destroyed by the flood.[17] The *Beowulf* poet's allusion to this tradition suggests that he regarded Cam, the inheritor of Cain's curse, as the progenitor of postdiluvian evil.

§118. Since it is probable that *Cames*, the antecedent reading, is also the authorial reading in 107a, the scribal alteration of this name to *Cāines* is a locus of considerable interest in the transmitted text. Most of the errors discussed in this chapter owe their origin to scribal ignorance of proper names from heroic-legendary tradition, whereas this error owes its origin to a scribe's knowledge of a proper name (*Cāin*) from biblical tradition. Scribe B, less tolerant of fanciful exegesis than the *Beowulf* poet, appears to have regarded *Cames* as a mistaken form of *Cāines*. Consequently, although this error is unique in certain respects, it remains the product of cultural change: different theological traditions distinguished the religious learning of the *Beowulf* poet and Alcuin, with its heterogeneous influences, from the learning of the scribes, who were educated after the Benedictine reform. Scribal ignorance of traditions known to the *Beowulf* poet and his original audience proves once again to have been a grave impediment to the accurate transmission of this centuries-old poem.

5. Chronological Significance

§119. The frequent obliteration and obfuscation of heroic-legendary names in the transmitted text of *Beowulf* is no mere accident. Carelessness might account for a few errors, but the serial corruption of proper names, extending from the beginning to the end of the text, must reflect a systematic problem that affected both of the final scribes, and perhaps antecedent copyists as well. The problem was chronological: a brief survey of the evidence for the circulation of heroic legend in Anglo-Saxon England, provided below, suggests that the traditions known to the *Beowulf* poet flourished during the

---

[17] See Pulsiano 1985:35–36 and Orchard 2003b:67–69.

seventh and eighth centuries, but ceased to be widely known during the ninth and tenth centuries. Before embarking upon this survey, the pervasiveness of the corruption of proper names in the *Beowulf* manuscript should be apprehended. Personal names obliterated, obscured, or confused in the transmitted text include Beowulf, Hroðgar, Unferð, Eomer, Finn, Beow, Ongenþeo, Onela (and Yrse?), Hreðric, Heardred, Wermund, Hemming, Hereric, Wonred,[18] the Frescyning, and the Merovingian. Ethnonyms that underwent corruption encompass the majority of those featured in the poem, including the Danes, Geats, Swedes, Jutes, Frisians, Heaðobeards, Heaðoreams, Weders, Scyldings, and Scylfings. The final scribes, responsible either for generating or preserving these myriad corruptions, were plainly ignorant of the legendary traditions required for the composition and comprehension of *Beowulf*. The chronological significance of the condition of the transmitted text emerges when the following question is answered: When did these traditions circulate in Anglo-Saxon England and when did they lose currency?

§120. Four categories of evidence testify to the circulation of Germanic legend: Anglo-Latin testimonia, Old English poetry, the onomastic record, and Anglo-Saxon royal genealogies.[19] Comprising the first category are three Latin texts that constitute independent witnesses to traditions known to the *Beowulf* poet. The *Liber Monstrorum*, probably composed at Malmesbury around 700 (Lapidge 1982:165–175), contains a reference to the wondrous bones of "King Hygelac, who ruled the Geats and was killed by the Franks" (*rex Higlacus, qui imperavit Getis et a Francis occisus est*) (Orchard 2003b:258–259). Felix of Crowland's *Vita Sancti Guthlaci*, composed ca. 730–740, presents Guthlac as a descendant of the legendary Icel, whom the Anglian genealogies identify as a descendent of Eomer and Offa (Dumville 1976:33). Consequently, when Guthlac's decision to become a war-band leader is motivated by his memory of "the valiant deeds of heroes of old" (*valida pristinorum heroum facta*), and when Guthlac becomes a hermit after contemplating the wretched deaths of "the ancient kings of his race" (*antiquorum regum stirpis suae*), it is clear that these phrases allude to the protagonist's immersion in continental Anglian legendry (Colgrave 1956:80–83). Alcuin's letter to his colleague pseudonymously known as Speratus, composed in 797, famously

---

[18] The corruption of *Wonrēding* (to *wonreðing*) was not cited in the present chapter because it has already been adduced in §54 as an instance of the *d/ð* transliteration error. To be sure, the transmitted form suggests that the scribe saw no proper name here, since -*rēd* is a standard name element, whereas -*reð* corresponds to no element used to form proper names.

[19] See Neidorf 2014b for a fuller treatment of the evidence surveyed in §§120–124.

chastised an ecclesiastical community for listening to "pagan songs" (*carmina gentilium*) by asking: "What has Ingeld to do with Christ?" (*Quid Hinieldus cum Christo?*) (Dümmler 1895:183). These three works confirm that legends known to the *Beowulf* poet, involving migration-era Geats, Franks, Angles, Heaðobeards, and Danes, circulated in England during the eighth century. Since there are dialectal indications that *Beowulf* is a Mercian composition, it is worth noting that each of the Anglo-Latin testimonia has ties to the midland regions: *Liber Monstrorum* is associated with Malmesbury, on the border of Wessex and Mercia; *Vita Sancti Guthlaci* concerns a Mercian saint and is dedicated to an East Anglian king; and Alcuin's letter is addressed to a Mercian bishop.[20]

§121. Besides *Beowulf*, five Old English poems draw on material from Germanic legendary tradition: *Widsið*, *Deor*, *Waldere*, *Finnsburh*, and *Wulf and Eadwacer*. With the exception of *Widsið*, these poems contain no conclusive signs of either early or late composition—a state of affairs to be expected, considering their brevity. For *Widsið*, however, there are compelling linguistic reasons to date the composition of this poem to the seventh or eighth century (Neidorf 2013c, 2015b). The relative antiquity of *Widsið* is important, since the poem exhibits knowledge of many of the heroes and peoples known to the *Beowulf* poet and his original audience. *Beowulf* and *Widsið* share reference to heroes such as Hroðgar, Hroðulf, Ingeld, Ongenþeo, Eormenric, Breca, Offa, Hama, Finn, and Hnæf; and to peoples such as the Danes, Swedes, Geats, Frisians, Hetware, Heaðobeards, and Wulfings. *Beowulf* and *Widsið* are, in fact, the only extant works that refer to Breca and give the name Heorot to the Danish royal hall (*KB*:clxxvii).[21] In short, *Widsið* provides perhaps the strongest indication that the traditions informing *Beowulf* were known and productive during the earlier Anglo-Saxon period. The Franks Casket, a fusion of visual and literary art, is also relevant in the present context as a vernacular rendering of heroic legend. Constructed in Northumbria around 700, the Franks Casket exhibits knowledge of the legendry concerning Weland in both its images and its inscription "*aegili*,"

---

[20] For the identification of Speratus with Bishop Unwona of Mercia, see Bullough 1993. There are other striking connections between *Beowulf* and early Mercia, such as the similarities between Grendel and the monster depicted on the Repton Stone from ca. 750 (following the dating of Biddle and Kjølbye-Biddle 1985). On their relationship, see Pascual 2014:216 and Clemoes 1995:65.

[21] Harris (2014) recently called attention to the existence of a monastery named Heorot in seventh-century England and contended that this datum might constitute additional evidence for the early circulation of Beowulfian legendry.

referring to Weland's brother.[22] Like *Beowulf*, this object was created for an early audience immersed in legendary tradition, capable of comprehending laconic allusions and recognizing the significance of a legendary proper name.

§122. The record of names borne by historical Anglo-Saxons during the seventh, eighth, ninth, and tenth centuries also sheds considerable light on the transmission and circulation of heroic legend. Chadwick (1912:42–44, 64–66) and Wormald (2006:71–81, 98–105) have observed that names from legend predominate in sources that reflect the name-giving practices of the seventh and eighth centuries, but are rare or absent in the onomastic record from the ninth and tenth centuries. Men born during the seventh and eighth centuries can be found bearing names prominent in *Beowulf* and its constituent traditions, including Beowulf, Hygelac, Wiglaf, Hroðulf, Ingeld, Heremod, Sigemund, Heardred, Offa, Hama, and Froda (Neidorf 2013a:571). Linguistic considerations indicate that the presence of these names in the early onomasticon is not mere coincidence, but is a genuine consequence of the circulation of heroic legend. Many legendary names borne by historical Anglo-Saxons contain elements that were foreign to or unproductive in English name-giving: Ætla and Widia derive from Gothic lexemes (Schönfeld 1911:263, 275); dithematic names such as Hroðulf, Beowulf, Ingeld, Theodric, Heremod, Widsið, and Wyrmhere contain elements (*hrōð-*, *bēow-*, *-geld*, *þēod-*, *-mōd*, *-sīð*, *wyrm-*) that were not commonly used to form personal names in England; and monothematic names such as Breca, Froda, Offa, Wada, and Hama derive from elements that were never individually productive in English name-giving. To account for the presence of these anomalous names in the Anglo-Saxon onomasticon, it is necessary to posit that they derive from familiarity with Germanic legend and reflect a custom of naming children after legendary heroes.[23] This custom prevailed during the seventh and eighth centuries, but it appears to have fallen out of fashion during the ninth and tenth centuries.

§123. Genealogies constructed for five Anglo-Saxon kings include figures from Germanic legend among the king's distant ancestors: Eomer, Offa, and

---

[22] On the dating and provenance of the Franks Casket, see Napier 1901 and the more recent works cited in Abels 2009:551n7.

[23] The use of heroic-legendary names during the seventh and eighth centuries provides a particularly decisive form of counterevidence against Frank's argument that Germanic legend originated during the Carolingian period (1991). Of course, the Anglo-Latin testimonia, *Widsið*, and the Anglian genealogies (inter alia) also provide firm indications that Germanic legend had been transmitted to England well before the age of Charlemagne.

Wermund appear in the genealogy of King Æðelred of Mercia (r. 675–704); Finn appears in the genealogy of King Aldfrið of Lindsey (r. 685–704/5); Hengest and Witta appear in the genealogy of King Æðelberht of Kent (r. 590–616); Hroðmund appears in the genealogy of King Ælfwald of East Anglia (r. 713–749); and Scyld(wa), Scef, Beow(i), and Heremod appear in the genealogy of King Æðelwulf of Wessex (r. 839–858).[24] The Anglian genealogies are preserved in a Mercian collection compiled ca. 787–796, which derived in turn from a Northumbrian collection compiled ca. 765–779 (Dumville 1976:45–49), but there is reason to believe that these genealogies were constructed during the reigns of the respective kings. Knowledge of the Anglian (and Kentish) genealogies exhibited in works by Bede and Felix of Crowland confirms that these genealogies existed during the first quarter of the eighth century (Newton 1993:62, 78). Comparable antiquity must be ascribed to the genealogical use of the legendary names in the West Saxon genealogy. Vestiges of ancient morphology preserved in spellings such as *Sceldwa* and *Beowi* reveal that Æðelwulf's genealogist acquired these names from an archaic, Anglian source (Fulk 2007e:128; Cronan 2014:121–213). The regular corruption of legendary names in later ninth- and tenth-century iterations of Æðelwulf's genealogy—for example, Asser's corruption of Scef into Seth and Æðelweard's confusion of Scyld with Scef—indicates that the currency of these names diminished after the reign of Æðelwulf.[25] The genealogies thus suggest that the political significance of descent from legendary heroes extended from the beginning of the seventh century to perhaps no later than the middle of the ninth century.

§124. The four principal categories of evidence for the circulation of Germanic legend in Anglo-Saxon England thus align in providing a coherent chronological framework for the literary history of this material. Legendary traditions orally transmitted to England by Germanic migrants during the sixth and seventh centuries circulated vigorously there throughout the eighth century, but ceased to be widely known during the ninth and tenth centuries. It is significant that the only figure from Germanic legend to be referred to in a work of indisputably late authorship is Weland, who appears in the *Old English Boethius* (Godden and Irvine 2009:1.283, 427), a work composed during or after the reign of King Alfred. Knowledge of Weland,

---

[24] For texts of the genealogies, see Dumville 1976 and *KB:Par.* §§1–3.

[25] Cf. Sisam: "The variant forms of Æthelwulf's pedigree could not have arisen or survived if consistent legends about the heroes or gods in its remoter part had been well known in the ninth century. Sometimes stereotyped spelling of names tells against a living tradition. And there are instances of surprising carelessness" (1953a:346).

a character absorbed into Arthurian tradition in the Middle English period (Wilson 1952:14), was uniquely perpetuated in independent traditions involving toponymic folklore rather than Germanic legend (Ellis Davidson 1958:149). Beyond this allusion of dubious significance, there is no evidence for the circulation of Germanic legend in Anglo-Saxon sources from the tenth and eleventh centuries. Late homilists, such as Ælfric and Wulfstan, express no disdain for tales of Ingeld. Learned compilers, such as Byrhtferth of Ramsey, do not think to impress readers with their encyclopedic knowledge of migration-era rulers and peoples. Late vernacular poems contain no allusions to the old heroes. Parents cease to name their children after Germanic heroes and ambitious kings no longer add legendary figures to their genealogies. By all appearances, the material became irrelevant. The old stories were forgotten, having been supplanted by new enthusiasms with the passage of time.

§125. The preceding survey demonstrates that the serial corruption of proper names in the transmitted text of *Beowulf* is neither an isolated phenomenon nor a meaningless accident that can be attributed to sloth or carelessness or to the exceptional ignorance of the final scribes. Rather, the vitiated condition of the transmitted text is a consequence of a process of cultural change as inexorable and impersonal as the process of language change documented in the previous chapter. Just as the scribes could make little sense of archaisms like *āþumswēoran* (§42) or Anglianisms like *wærc* (§60), because these words were absent from their lexicon, the scribes were naturally perplexed by names like *Ūnferð*, *Merewīoing*, and *Ongenþēo*, because they had never heard such names uttered in their lifetime. Through no fault of their own, the scribes did not possess the cultural and linguistic knowledge required for the accurate transmission of the text. In their effort to reproduce the text while standardizing and modernizing its spellings, the scribes were forced to scrutinize the words before them, extract lexemes from sequences of graphemes, and determine the correct Late West Saxon form of a given word. Scribal unfamiliarity with the poem's archaic language and content rendered this process perilous to the condition of the text and resulted in the frequent obliteration of words and names. The often implausible character of the transmitted text is a consequence of the passage of time: knowledge that was available to the *Beowulf* poet and the audience for whom he composed simply was not available to the scribes responsible for the poem's transmission.

4

SCRIBAL BEHAVIOR

1. The Lexemic Theory

§126. The preceding chapters have interpreted scribal errors in the extant manuscript of *Beowulf* as the textual consequences of processes of linguistic and cultural change that took place during the Anglo-Saxon period. The manifold alterations made to the text, discernible through probabilistic reasoning, were not merely the result of human fallibility, but were induced by historical changes that distinguished the period of the poem's composition from the period of its reproduction. The scribes responsible for the poem's transmission have emerged from these chapters not as the "monastic blockheads" lambasted in classical textual criticism (Willis 1972:12), but as earnest laborers who were charged with a task beyond their capabilities. They simply lacked the knowledge required for the transcription and simultaneous modernization of this centuries-old poem, the text of which was replete with archaic and dialectal spellings, rare words, artificial syntax, and unfamiliar proper names. It is imperative to recognize that the deficient knowledge of the scribes is evident in the transmitted text because of their particular approach to its reproduction, which forms the subject of the present chapter. The scribes were engaged in a mechanical task whose success was continuously predicated on one critical operation: the identification of the lexeme present in a sequence of graphemes in the exemplar. As they copied, the scribes focused their attention on the transcription and modernization of individual words, not on the continuous sense of the poem.

§127. When the scribes correctly identified the word before them, they altered the superficial characteristics of the antecedent reading in order to commit the word's standard Late West Saxon form to parchment. When the scribes erred in their identification, they would transmit a word of similar appearance that was intelligible and genuine, but manifestly erroneous in the present context. Because the need for orthographic regularity required the scribes to tinker with the antecedent text, rather than transcribe it *ad litteram*, gaps in their knowledge owing to linguistic and cultural change were able to be registered in the corruptions that pervade the *Beowulf* manuscript. The transmitted text is a valuable witness to diachronic change because of the liminal nature of the scribes' engagement with the work of their predecessors. Corruptions imbued with chronological significance would not be present in the text if, on the one hand, the scribes had turned off their critical faculties and painstakingly reproduced every letter of the antecedent text without making any alterations. On the other hand, if the scribes had actively comprehended the substance of the poem and continuously construed the words they copied as the constituents of a sense-bearing narrative, many obvious corruptions would not have been transmitted. Credence in the lexemic theory of scribal behavior is thus required to explain the peculiar condition of the transmitted text, which brims with implausible readings, yet is relatively devoid of the gibberish forms to be expected from careless copyists. The scribes were not careless, but they were preoccupied with form and indifferent to sense.

§128. The present chapter contends that the scribes responsible for the transmission of *Beowulf* were not uncommon or idiosyncratic. Rather, the lexemic approach to the transmission of earlier works appears to have been the dominant mode of textual reproduction for copyists of Old English poetry in general. Because of the archaic and Anglian features that characterize much of this poetry, late scribes charged with the task of modernization and dialect translation directed their scrutiny to the orthographical forms of the words before them, paying no sustained attention to the meter or sense of the texts they were transmitting. The major codices that preserve Old English poetry contain numerous indications that they were produced by scribes whose professional concerns were limited to the realm of the orthographic, not the literary or the intellectual. The conclusions about scribal behavior to be drawn from these codices corroborate the findings from *Beowulf*, and contradict several widespread beliefs about the participation of scribes in the transmission of Old English poetry. The lexemic theory of scribal behavior, to be sure, runs counter to some recent trends in Old English scholarship, where scribes are increasingly viewed as poets' collaborators, who apprehended the literary qualities of the texts they copied and even, in the view of a prominent minority, "felt free to reshape and adapt existing texts to meet their needs" (Muir 2005:189). The improbability of such views will become apparent before the end of the present chapter.

§129. The lexemic theory of scribal behavior is intended neither to deprive copyists of agency nor to restrict their activities to the introduction of corruptions into transmitted texts. To the contrary, the scribe under this theory is regarded as a trained craftsman, charged with a difficult task, who approached that task methodically. Contrary to the belief that scribes would arbitrarily alter antecedent readings for inscrutable reasons, the lexemic theory construes textual variation as the principled consequence of the scribal effort to process linguistic material in the exemplar. When diachronic or diatopic change rendered the antecedent reading too obscure for accurate modernization, scribes exercised their critical faculties in order to commit an intelligible form to parchment. Their responses, both ingenious and predictable, result in sporadic corruptions that conform to recognizable patterns. Furthermore, the considerable evidence for hypercorrection in the transmitted text of *Beowulf* indicates that scribes systematically corrected errors committed by antecedent copyists when they scrutinized lexemes in their exemplar. Many corruptions discussed above seem to have been generated by scribes who believed (erroneously) that they were correcting the errors of their predecessors. Accordingly, it is reasonable to assume that scribes also often restored authorial readings by correcting genuine errors—an assumption corroborated by the paleographical evidence for scribal self-correction (§116). In short, the scribal contribution to the transmission of Old English poetry was not limited to corruption, but encompassed emendation, modernization, and dialect translation. Textual critics concentrate on corruptions to restore authorial readings, but the more benign aspects of the scribal contribution must be borne in mind for a holistic understanding of scribal behavior to be achieved.

§130. Outside of *Beowulf*, the explanatory power of the lexemic theory of scribal behavior can be illustrated, for example, by its ability to resolve a dispute concerning the rhyming passage in the epilogue to Cynewulf's *Elene*. Several rhymes in the transmitted text appear to have been spoiled by the scribal substitution of Late West Saxon forms for authorial readings that were originally Anglian:

Þus ic frōd ond fūs   þurh þæt fæcne hūs
wordcræft[um] wæf   ond wundrum læs,
þrāgum þreodude   ond geþanc reodode
nihtes nearwe.   Nysse ic gearwe
be ðære [rōde] riht   ǣr mē rūmran geþeaht
þurh ðā mǣran miht   on mōdes þeaht
wīsdōm onwrēah.   Ic wæs weorcum fāh,
synnum asǣled,   sorgum gewǣled,
bitrum gebunden,   bisgum beþrungen,

ǣr mē lāre onlāg   þurh lēohtne hād
gamelum tō gēoce,   gife unscynde
mægencyning āmæt   ond on gemynd begeat,
torht ontȳnde,   tīdum gerȳmde,
bāncofan onband,   brēostlocan onwand,
lēoðucræft onlēac.   Þæs ic lustum brēac,
willum in worlde.

Elene 1236–1251a

Thus I, wise and ready to depart because of my old body, have woven and wondrously gathered my word-craft, at times have deliberated and sifted my thoughts in the closeness of night. I did not clearly know the truth about the cross before wisdom by its glorious power revealed to me a more spacious understanding in the thought of my mind. I was stained by my deeds, fettered by sins, afflicted by sorrows, bitterly bound, encircled by afflictions, before the mighty king gloriously bestowed on me his teaching as a comfort in my old age, meted out the noble gift and begot it in my mind, disclosed the brightness, extended it at times, unbound my bone-coffer, loosened my breast-hoard, unlocked the craft of poetry. I have used that with pleasure, with joy in the world.

Trans. Bjork 2013:229

Vowels rhyme in every line in this sequence, with the exception of *riht* : *geþeaht*, *miht* : *þeaht*, *onwrēah* : *fāh*, and *amæt* : *begeat*. Because the conversion of these transmitted readings into Anglian forms restores the rhyme to each of these lines, philologists from Sievers (1884) onward have regarded the rhyming passage as firm evidence for the Anglian origin of Cynewulf's poetry.[1] Some scholars, however, have questioned this conclusion, contending that the faulty rhymes could have originated with the poet rather than the scribe (Rogers 1971; Stanley 1993; Conner 1996). Their contention generates gross improbabilities, since independent signs of Anglian composition pervade the Cynewulf corpus, and it would be an extraordinary coincidence for a poet to have produced faulty rhymes that could be uniformly corrected by the substitution of Anglian forms (*HOEM*:§§389–393). Nevertheless, one advocate for the view that the faulty rhymes were deliberate and authorial has maintained this position by expressing disbelief at the notion that a scribe could have obliterated the passage's most salient feature:

[1]   To apprehend the consensus surrounding this view, see the references in Sisam 1953b:1–28 and Fulk 1996a.

If the Anglo-Saxon scribes valued pure rhymes ... would they not have refrained from messing them up? In the last sixty years competent scholars have moved away from the supercilious view that scribes are so incompetent that their texts cannot be trusted, and may be safely emended to bring readings into line with superior, scholarly knowledge. The scribes' eyes and ears may have been less offended by impure rhymes than those of the scholars. Are the scribes likely to have belonged to a class different from that to which the poets belonged?

Stanley 1993:181

Several beliefs about scribal behavior, common to dubious arguments in Old English textual criticism, inform this line of reasoning and merit reconsideration in the light of the lexemic theory. Stanley's statement is predicated upon three assumptions: (1) that the readings transmitted in extant manuscripts reflect the literary values of the scribes who produced them, (2) that belief in the incompetence of the scribe is a prerequisite for the emendation of transmitted readings, and (3) that poets and scribes shared the same literary interests and professional concerns. If there were compelling reasons to hold these assumptions, one might well hesitate before believing that a scribe should be responsible for the obliteration of rhymes in Cynewulf's *Elene*. The untenability of these assumptions, however, becomes apparent when it is recognized that Anglo-Saxon scribes employed a lexemic approach to textual transmission.

§131. The scribe who obscured the rhyme of Mercian *reht* and *geþeht* by converting these words into *riht* and *geþeaht* had professional reasons to be indifferent to the formal consequences of his treatment of the antecedent readings.[2] Scribes charged with the responsibility of imposing the Late West Saxon written standard upon texts of earlier Anglian poetry appear to have been trained to prioritize orthographical form over literary form. Even if the scribes responsible for the transmission of *Elene* appreciated rhyme as a literary device, it is doubtful whether they read the poem they transcribed and apprehended its formal qualities. And even if a scribe recognized that rhymes were structurally required in the epilogue, it is doubtful that he would have preserved or restored Anglian vocalism for the sake of poetic form. The scribal obliteration of the poet's rhymes is therefore not a sign of obtuseness, but of professional competence, since the scribe's job was to produce a legible text that conformed to the written standard in which he

---

[2]   On the dialectology informing the reconstruction of Cynewulf's rhymes, see Gradon 1958:13–14 and *HOEM*:§391.

was trained. This job did not require the scribe to care about the features of the work that poets cared most about. Poets imposed regularities of meter and alliteration (and rhyme) upon their works, whereas scribes sought to impose orthographic regularity upon the texts of those works. When their aims conflicted—if such a conflict was even apparent to a scribe who scrutinized lexemes on an individual basis—orthographic form took precedence over literary form. For insights into the textual history of Old English poetry to be obtained, it is necessary to recognize that the aims of scribes differed fundamentally from the aims of poets.

§132. The enormous chasm between the concerns of poets and scribes is exemplified in much of the evidence for the lexeme-centered transmission of *Beowulf*. The poet was concerned with meter, alliteration, sense, syntax, and narration; whereas the scribes concentrated on orthographic form to the exclusion of all other considerations. Metrical regularities that the poet imposed upon his work are corrupted through the scribal inflection of uninflected infinitives (§45), the analogical restoration of syncopated vowels (§66), and various lexical modifications including the substitution of *gehwǣre* for *gehwǣm* (§46), *dydon* for *dēdon* (§67), and *nēosian* for *nēosan* (§68). Alliteration is marred by the systematic corruption of *Ūnferð* into *Hūnferð* (§92), while both alliteration and sense are vitiated by the scribal addition of *h* to *ondlēan* and *ondslyht* (§80), not to mention the corruption of *oreðes ond āttres* into *rēðes ond hāttres* (§§19–20). Transliteration errors routinely deprive the text of sense, in egregious corruptions such as *hord* for *hond*, *unhār* for *anhār*, *þēod* for *dēoð*, and *wrǣce* for *wrǣtte* (§18). Syntax is obscured in several places by the scribal assumption that nominative, accusative, and genitive nouns following prepositions should be transmitted in their dative forms (§§71–75). Finally, the poem's narrative is rendered defective through the frequent obliteration of personal and ethnic names from the transmitted text (§§88–118). Convergent defects of both poetic form and narrative coherence were introduced into the text when scribes corrupted *Bēow* into *Bēowulf* (§§89–90), *Cāin* into *camp* (§16–17), *Ēomēr* into *geōmor* (§91), and *Wedera* into *gāra* (§100). A poet who scrutinized the sense and meter of his works could not have been responsible for generating these implausible readings. Only a scribe concentrating on the orthographic form of individual lexemes could have committed such corruptions to parchment.

§133. The lexemic theory of scribal behavior is not radically new. Much philological scholarship on Old English poetry has been predicated upon a set of assumptions about scribal behavior that more or less amount to the lexemic theory propounded in this book. For example, scholars who believed that southern scribes corrupted Cynewulf's Anglian rhymes must have believed that those scribes prioritized orthographic form over literary form. Likewise, metrical studies of every persuasion have presumed scribal indifference to meter in order to account for recurrent anomalies, such as the frequent correlation of inflected infinitives with unmetrical verses. Philologists have generally refrained, however, from articulating their assumptions about scribal behavior and combining them into a coherent theory. As a result, scholars with an inadequate grasp of the probabilistic considerations that justify credence in the postulates of philology have come to regard longstanding suppositions about scribal behavior as arbitrary and erroneous ideas. Because philologists have not enunciated their understanding of scribal behavior, theories that overstate the role of the scribe in textual transmission have been able to flourish in contemporary scholarship virtually unopposed. The proliferation of these theories and the increasing amount of credence lent them renders the articulation and defense of the lexemic theory of scribal behavior an urgent task for philological scholarship. The explanatory advantage of the lexemic theory over its competitors is illustrated in the subsequent sections of this chapter.

2. Competing Theories

§134. Competing theories of scribal behavior differ from the lexemic theory principally by maintaining the conviction that poets and scribes shared the same interests, concerns, and abilities. Under these theories, the scribe is not a mechanical laborer fixated on the text's orthography, but an active participant in literary creation, who took an informed interest in the sense, meter, and substance of the poems he transmitted. Textual reproduction is consequently envisioned not as a difficult or tedious task, where occupational requirements constrained scribal subjectivity, but as an opportunity for aesthetic experience and creative expression, where spontaneous intervention into the text was permitted and encouraged. Proponents of these theories thus reconceive the scribe as an editor, a performer, or the poet's collaborator; an individual sensitive to literary nuance, who cannot be expected to have introduced implausible readings into the text. Depending on the extent of intervention hypothesized, the scribe might even be said to be "effectively the poet of the final recorded version of the text" (Muir 2005:181). Crediting such theories has proved attractive to scholars suspicious of philological argumentation, since a scribe who commits no errors removes the need for textual criticism, and a scribe regarded as the author of his transmitted works reduces the dating of poetry to a question of paleography. Because competing theories of scribal behavior threaten to retard the advancement of knowledge in this way, it is imperative to subject them to critical scrutiny and gauge their relative probability.

§135. Katherine O'Brien O'Keeffe's contention (1990) that formulaic reading influenced the textual transmission of Old English poetry constitutes the most detailed theory of scribal behavior in competition with the lexemic theory. In her view, the variant readings in parallel texts of poetic works that survive in more than one manuscript, such as *Cædmon's Hymn* and *Solomon and Saturn I*,[3] were generated by scribes in touch with poetic tradition, who read formulaically and spontaneously replaced words in their exemplar with appropriate equivalents. Textual variation—for example the presence of *aelda bearnum* 'children of men' in some manuscripts of *Cædmon's Hymn* versus *eorðan bearnum* 'children of earth' in others (discussed below in §148)—is interpreted under this theory as a sign of transitional literacy and a product of the informed participation of scribes in the transmission of Old English poetry. O'Brien O'Keeffe's interpretation of textual variation is dubious, for reasons made clear below, yet it forms the basis for her generalizations about scribal behavior. She contends: "The presence of variant readings which are semantically, metrically, and syntactically appropriate suggests a strong overlay of oral habits of transmission in the copying of Old English formulaic verse" (1990:21). Scribal practice thus involved "the conflation of the two roles of language-producer and visual-reproducer" (1990:67). Her conclusion encapsulates her view: "Surviving Old English verse texts, whatever the circumstances of their composition, are collaborative products whose scribes have not merely transmitted the texts but have actually taken part in shaping them" (1990:193).

§136. Theories of scribal behavior similar to O'Brien O'Keeffe's were articulated in several works of scholarship contemporary with her monograph. A. N. Doane further developed the notion that oral tradition influenced textual transmission, and compared the scribe to an oral performer. In his view, "the Anglo-Saxon scribe copying vernacular texts, and particularly vernacular poetic texts, is in many cases a special kind of speaking performer and, as such, has a status analogous to that of traditional performers of oral verbal art" (1994:421). Doane regards the variant readings in parallel texts

---

[3] For a complete list of multiply attested poems and the manuscripts that preserve them, see O'Donnell 1996:435–438.

as evidence for the creative intervention expected of the scribal performer: "From what we can tell, they always varied the text, as if the mere copying of a text was bad form, or empty form" (1994:434). In another essay attributing textual variation in parallel texts to informed scribal intervention, Roy M. Liuzza criticized the aims of traditional textual criticism and, citing O'Brien O'Keeffe, articulated a conception of scribal behavior comparable to hers:

> An alternative model of manuscript transmission proposes that scribes were active participants in the process, mediating between the text and its readers, reconstituting the text in a performance on the manuscript page with sometimes scant regard for the precise reproduction of an authorial text; some of them, perhaps, even had a sense of the sound of a line of Old English poetry.
>
> 1995:291

The influence of O'Brien O'Keeffe is also pervasive in the work of Carol B. Pasternack (1995), who does not discuss specific variant readings, but presumes unfettered scribal intervention to be a demonstrated fact of textual transmission. Pasternack levels the distinction between poets and scribes by regarding them both as equal "participants" (1995:200) in poetic tradition. She imagines the intervention of scribes to have been so extensive, and to have formed such an essential part of their duties, that "the task of identifying the poet's work versus the scribe's work is impossible and anachronistic" (1995:193). As these remarks make clear, there is one salient difference between O'Brien O'Keeffe's theory and those that emerged in the years following its publication: whereas the original theory limited scribal intervention to the formulaic unit,[4] its later adherents place fewer limitations on the scribe, whose labors are increasingly conflated with those of poets or performers. The hypothesis of scribal intervention has drifted far away from the evidence it was formulated to explain, that is, the actual variant readings discernible in parallel texts of Old English poems.

§137. Kevin S. Kiernan's argument concerning the scribes who produced the *Beowulf* manuscript merits consideration in the present context, insofar as it constitutes the most extreme manifestation of the desire to elevate the

---

[4]   The limitations placed on scribal intervention under O'Brien O'Keeffe's theory were stated clearly: "We see a reading activity reflected in these scribal variants which is formula-dependent, in that the variants observe metrical and alliterative constraints, and which is context-defined, in that the variants arise within a field of possibilities generated by a context of expectation. The mode of reading I am proposing operates by suggestion, by 'guess' triggered by key-words in formulae" (1990:40). A serious impediment to the credibility of this theory, however, is that few of the pertinent variants occur in the context of known formulae; see Moffat 1992:812 and Orton 2000:203–205.

role of the scribe. Kiernan (1981:171–278) combined strained interpretations of various forms of paleographical and codicological evidence to argue that the scribes of the extant manuscript revised and augmented the poem they transcribed, and should therefore be considered its authors. Refutations of Kiernan's work have been so numerous and convincing that credence in his theory is more or less limited to the individual who propounded it.[5] Indeed, much of the evidence discussed in this book alerts observers to the extraordinary improbability of Kiernan's argument: it is difficult to believe, for example, that the author of *Beowulf* was unfamiliar with the names of his poem's characters and corrupted them into words of similar appearance. Kiernan's book is thus an outlier from the trend noted above, since it has been much less influential, and it is not based on textual variation in parallel texts of Old English poems. Nevertheless, scholars who reject the traditional understanding of scribal behavior have aligned their own work with Kiernan's. In a foreword to the reprinted edition of his monograph, O'Brien O'Keeffe wrote: "Kiernan's proposal makes the scribe a thoughtful and participatory editor/author or, in another way of thinking, displaces the hypothesized poet in favor of the actual scribe" (Kiernan 1996:xi). Though their arguments differ, the work of Kiernan and O'Brien O'Keeffe is united by the assumption that textual phenomena originate not with poets or antecedent copyists, but with the particular scribes who happened to produce the few extant manuscripts.

§138. An epistemological error that pervades and vitiates the competing theories of scribal behavior is apparent in O'Brien O'Keeffe's reference to "the hypothesized poet" and "the actual scribe." These tendentious terms reflect a failure to apprehend that the attribution of textual material to scribes is also a matter of hypothesis, not a self-evident fact. The theories of scribal behavior in competition with the lexemic theory have been erected upon the assumption that variant readings in parallel texts of Old English poems must be attributed to scribes. Taking the scribal origins of textual variation for granted, proponents of these theories have misrepresented their hypothetical character and obscured the amount of conjecture required to invest credence in them. Comparison of the parallel texts of the *Leiden Riddle* and *Riddle 35* brings these issues into focus:

---

[5]   Expositions of the improbability of Kiernan's claims are available in Amos 1982; Bately 1985; Dumville 1988; Dumville 1998; Fulk 1982; Fulk 2003:9–16; Gerritsen 1989b; Gerritsen 1998; Neidorf 2013b. Many other publications (e.g., Lapidge 2000 and Cronan 2004) indirectly falsify Kiernan's work.

Mec sē uēta uong, uundrum frēorig,
ob his innaðae āerest cændæ.

Ni uāat ic mec biuorthæ uullan
flīusum,

hērum ðerh hēhcraeft, hygiðonc...

Uundnae mē ni bīað ueflæ, ni ic
uarp hafæ,

ni ðerih ðrēatun giðraec ðrēt mē
hlimmith,

ne mē hrūtendu hrīsil scelfath,

ni mec ōuana āam sceal cnyssa.

Uyrmas mec ni āuēfun uyrdi
craeftum,

ðā ði geolu godueb geatum
fraetuath.

Uil mec huethrae suāeðēh uīdæ
ofaer eorðu

hātan mith hęliðum hyhtlic giuæde;

ni anōegun ic mē aerigfaerae egsan
brōgum,

ðēh ði n... ...n sīæ nīudlicae ob
cocrum.

Mec sē wǣta wong, wundrum frēorig,
of his innaþe ǣrist cende.

Ne wāt ic mec beworhtne wulle
flȳsum,

hǣrum þurh hēahcræft, hygeþoncum
mīn.

Wundene mē ne bēoð wefle, ne ic
wearp hafu,

ne þurh þrēata geþrǣcu þrǣd mē ne
hlimmeð,

ne æt mē hrūtende hrīsil scrīþeð,

ne mec ōhwonan sceal ām cnyssan.

Wyrmas mec ne āwǣfan wyrda
cræftum,

þā þe geolo godwebb geatwum
frætwað.

Wile mec mon hwæþre se þēah wīde
ofer eorþan

hātan for hæleþum hyhtlic gewǣde.

Saga sōðcwidum, searoþoncum
glēaw,

wordum wīsfæst, hwæt þis gewǣd[e]
sȳ.

The first twelve lines of *Riddle 35* are nearly identical to those of the *Leiden Riddle*, with differences in orthography reflecting the modernization and Saxonization of a Northumbrian original. Substantial variation is limited to the final two lines, in regard to which the two versions differ entirely from each other. How is such variation to be explained? One possibility is that a scribe, after mechanically transcribing twelve lines of poetry, spontaneously decided to omit two lines in his exemplar and compose two new lines to replace them. Another possibility is that the text was modified not by a copyist, but by an anthologist who compiled texts of sundry riddles and altered their concluding lines to give his collection the impression of unity. This anthologist might also have been a copyist, but he might have been an intermediate figure not involved in textual reproduction—perhaps he was even the poet who composed the *Leiden Riddle*, adapting his own work for a new literary context. If any of the latter hypotheses is correct, then the variation in the final two lines of the *Leiden Riddle* and *Riddle 35* has nothing to do with scribal behavior, and provides no basis for generalizations about textual transmission.

§139. The competition among hypotheses that emerges upon consideration of the *Leiden Riddle* and *Riddle 35* is not unique to this particular case. Whenever a scholar wishes to account for the genesis of variant readings in parallel texts, the attribution of variants to scribes is one hypothesis to be considered, but it is not necessarily the most probable one. The theories of scribal behavior advanced by O'Brien O'Keeffe, Doane, Liuzza, and Pasternack take the scribal origin of textual variation as a self-evident fact, but it is a hypothesis whose explanatory superiority over its competitors must be demonstrated. An additional element of conjecture inheres in these theories because textual variation, having been attributed to scribes, is then presumed to reflect the creative and informed participation of those scribes. Alternative hypotheses that might account for scribal intervention during transmission—for example, the need to repair lacunae in a damaged exemplar—are not entertained. An additional possibility discounted in these theories is that textual variants might owe their origin to a scribe's alienation from poetic tradition, not his competence in versification. In sum, the theory of the participatory poet-scribe represents a sweeping and highly conjectural interpretation of the evidence for textual variation in parallel texts of Old English poems. Closer examinations of the evidence, which respect the different circumstances of transmission affecting the parallel texts, indicate that this theory has little to recommend it.

3. Variation in Parallel Texts

§140. None of the studies of scribal behavior cited in the preceding paragraphs was based on a comprehensive treatment of the parallel texts. Rather, the method employed in these studies has been to adduce select passages from a few poems and use them to produce generalizations about scribal behavior. Since their publication, there have been two comprehensive studies of the variant readings in parallel texts, both of which questioned the validity of theories of formulaic reading and unrestrained scribal intervention. Daniel P. O'Donnell, whose dissertation constitutes the most comprehensive study, rejected O'Brien O'Keeffe's attempt to infer a mode of literacy from the variant readings and contended that a more accurate assessment of the evidence must "explicate the full range of habits, techniques, and motivations influencing the way Anglo-Saxon scribes worked" (1996:11). O'Donnell observed, for example, that the many parallel texts amounting to more or less *verbatim* reproductions of other poems indicate "that Anglo-Saxon scribes were able to copy Old English poetry to an extremely high standard of substantive accuracy whenever they chose or were required to do so" (1996:81). The overarching conclusion of his study is that substantive textual variation was not an inevitable feature of Anglo-Saxon scribal practice, but a possibility contingent on the manuscript's context and the particular scribe. Compelling evidence for this view emerged in O'Donnell's demonstration (1996:87–222) that poems transmitted alongside prose works—for example *Cædmon's Hymn* and the *Chronicle* poems—exhibit a degree of variation corresponding to the amount of alteration in the accompanying prose text. In other words, when an entire work was subject to the critical scrutiny of a reviser, variation resulted, but the mechanical reproduction of an exemplar generated few variants in poetic texts.

§141. The other comprehensive study, Peter Orton's (2000) monograph, significantly advanced the effort to identify the particular causes and motives that gave impetus to the generation of variant readings in parallel texts. Orton demonstrated that many variants are the consequence of scribal misunderstandings, mechanical errors, and unfamiliarity with poetic tradition. Some variants represent a scribe's attempt to repair corruptions committed by antecedent copyists, while others function to trivialize a poem's text by increasing the clarity of its syntax or replacing poetic words with prosaic alternatives. Orton argues that the corpus of textual variants lends no firm support to the theories of formulaic reading and scribal participation (2000:189–208). After surveying the cases of lexical variation in parallel texts, for instance, Orton writes:

> Most are satisfactorily explained on the assumption that a scribe has mistaken a legitimate but unfamiliar form in his exemplar for an error and has changed it into a word he knows.... [A]gainst the idea that these represent informed editorial decisions on the part of transcribers is the fact that the new readings do not, generally speaking, suit the general context at all well; there seems to have been a concern to produce a recognizable word, but the substitutions show only a very local (i.e. word-bounded) awareness of the sense.

> 2000:28

Like the scribes who transmitted *Beowulf*, the scribes responsible for these variants were concentrating on the form of the individual lexeme, not the continuous sense of the text. Orton's view of the scribe as a mechanical laborer concerned with committing plausible forms to parchment plainly aligns with the view advanced throughout the present book. The trenchant conclusion of his study is that "there is really no need to think of scribes as alternating in, combining or confusing the roles of 'language-producer' (performer, poet) and that of 'visual-reproducer' (or copyist)" (2000:202). Drawing attention to the nonsense frequently transmitted in extant manuscripts, Orton observes: "The scribe, unlike the reader or hearer, had a specific job to do, a technical job which did not actually require him to read his exemplar with understanding; all he had to do was reproduce it" (2000:203).

§142. Perhaps the most significant insight to emerge with clarity from Orton's study, anticipated in some brief remarks in O'Donnell's conclusion (1996:429–430), is that the parallel texts regarded as the most secure evidence for extensive scribal intervention probably do not owe much of their variation to scribes who spontaneously recomposed the works they transmitted. The parallel passages in *Soul and Body I* and *II* have long been adduced as straightforward evidence for scribal practice, yet it is now clear that a separate poet, who composed the 40-line address of the blessed soul (*SBI* 127–166, not present in *SBII*), was involved in the transmission of this work. Because a variety of metrical, phonological, and literary features distinguish *SBI* 127–166 from the first 126 lines of the poem (shared with *SBII*), it is probable that a different poet, who did not compose the shared passages, revised and expanded an earlier composition to produce the poem transmitted in the Vercelli Book (*SBI*).[6] Meanwhile, the poem transmitted in the Exeter Book (*SBII*) appears to represent the earlier work, which prompted another poet to compose an expanded version with an additional address from the soul. Some variants in the parallel passages were doubtless introduced into the respective texts by copyists, but the extraordinary quality and quantity of variation between these texts must be attributed to the critical intervention of a poet, who comprehended and revised an earlier *Soul and Body* poem to compose a new work. In the light of Orton's findings (2000:155–159), the assumption that the variation in these texts must be attributed to scribes appears both naive and untenable.

§143. Paul G. Remley's exhaustive study (2002) of the variant readings in the parallel passages from *Daniel* (lines 279–439) and *Azarias* superseded earlier treatments of these texts by reaching a conclusion about their textual

---

[6]   For the evidence that supports this view see Orton 1979, whose arguments are corroborated in Moffat 1990:41–44.

variation similar to Orton's conclusion about *SBI* and *SBII*. Remley observed that the parallel texts in *Daniel* and *Azarias* progressively diverge, with early passages resembling one another closely and later passages exhibiting considerable differences. An example from the beginning of their shared text illustrates their initial similarity:

Metod alwihta, hwæt! þū eart
   mihtum swīð
	Meotud allwihta, þū eart meahtum
	   swīð

nīðas tō nergenne. Is þīn nama
   mǣre,
	nīþas tō nerganne. Is þīn noma
	   mǣre,

wlitig and wuldorfæst ofer
   werðēode.
	wlitig ond wuldorfæst ofer
	   werþēode.

Daniel 283–285   *Azarias* 5–7

As the works proceed, however, variants that go beyond the occasional corruption or interpolation begin to materialize in each text.[7] Remley's brilliant explanation for this progressive textual divergence is that it represents the disparate responses of individuals wrestling with "the decreasing legibility of a defective [*Daniel*] exemplar" (2002:137). The explanatory power of this codicological hypothesis is demonstrated in its ability to account for the graphemic overlap in certain passages that diverge considerably from one another, such as the following:

þæt ēower fela geseah,			þæt ic geare wiste,	
þēoden mīne,	þæt wē þrȳ syndon,		þæt wē *III* hæfdon, wīsan, ...	þēoda
geboden tō bǣle	in byrnende		gebunden to bǣle	in byrnendes
fȳres lēoman. fēower men	Nū ic þǣr		fȳres lēoman. men	Nū ic þǣr *IIII*
gesēo tō sōðe, lēogeð.	nales mē selfa		sende tō sīðe, gerād.	nales mē sylfa

Daniel 411b–415   *Azarias* 170b–171, 173–175

Since it is unreasonable to regard the recurrent graphemic overlap in lexically distinct variants—*gesēo tō sōðe* vs. *sende to sīðe*—as an extraordinary coincidence, the most plausible explanation for these divergences is that they derive from lacunae in an earlier exemplar of *Daniel*. A lacunous text that read *geb...den*, for example, is the probable source of the divergence between

---

[7] Regarding the parallel passages cited above, it might be noted that in the case of the one substantial difference between them—the presence of *hwæt* in *Daniel* 243a—the unmetrical character of the verse indicates that *hwæt* was interpolated into the text by a scribe paying no attention to meter.

geboden and *gebunden*. Similar lacunae might account for other curious divergences, such as *woruldcræfta wlite* (*Daniel* 363a) versus *woruldsceafta wuldor* (*Azarias* 74a) and *witig wuldorcyning* (*Daniel* 426a) vs. *wlitigne wuldorhoman* (*Azarias* 179a). Complicating the relationship between these texts further are the interventions of the poet responsible for *Azarias*, who excerpted and programmatically revised material from a *Daniel* exemplar to create an independent work. Remley's demonstration of the systematic nature of this poet's labors combines with his identification of the codicological source of textual divergence to generate the firm conclusion that the variant readings in *Daniel* and *Azarias* "can no longer be regarded as evidence for the standard practice of Anglo-Saxon scribes" (2002:136).

§144. Variants in the parallel passages from *The Dream of the Rood* and the fragmentary verses inscribed on the Ruthwell Cross (Swanton 1987) also furnish unreliable evidence for scribal practice. A common textual source, to be sure, must account for some of the close correspondences between them, such as those in the following passage:

Krīst wæs on rōdi.			Crīst wæs on rōde.	
Hweþræ þēr fūsæ kwōmu	fearran		Hwæðere þēr fūse cwōman	feorran
æþþilæ til ānum. bi*h*[ēald]	Ic þæt al		tō þām æðelinge. behēld.	Ic þæt eall
Sār[æ] ic wæs mi[þ] sorgu*m* gidræ [fi]d,			Sāre ic wæs mid [sorgum] gedrēfed,	
h[n]āg [ic] ...			hnāg ic hwæðre þām secgum to handa	
Ruthwell Cross			*DrR* 56b–60	

The occasional discrepancies evident in the parallel passages might be attributed to scribes who understood the text and substituted plausible alternatives, but the scribal origin of these variants cannot be assumed, since it is clear that a different poet was involved in the transmission of this work. Salient differences between the first and second halves of *The Dream of the Rood* indicate that a later poet revised and expanded an earlier work, part of which was preserved on the Ruthwell Cross. Orton identified compelling metrical evidence to support this conclusion: the first seventy-eight lines of *The Dream of the Rood*, which contain all of the passages shared with the Ruthwell Cross, frequently include hypermetric clusters and consistently exhibit double alliteration in verses of type 1A or 1A*; the remaining portion of the poem, which shares no text with the Ruthwell Cross, contains no genuine hypermetric lines and fails to consistently exhibit double alliteration in 1A/1A* verses (2000:159–161). In the light of this evidence for the composite authorship of *The Dream of the Rood*, it appears doubtful that its variant readings should be attributed to copyists, rather than to the poet who comprehended and expanded an earlier work.[8] Like the case of the *Leiden Riddle* and *Riddle 35*, the parallel texts pertaining to *The Dream of the Rood* might shed light on the activities of poets and anthologists critically reusing earlier works, but they probably tell us little about the regular practice of scribes charged with the task of textual reproduction.

§145. The conventional practices of Anglo-Saxon scribes are thus more likely to be illuminated through comparison of parallel texts of poems that never underwent processes of revision or expansion, such as *Solomon and Saturn I*, *Cædmon's Hymn*, *Gloria I*, the *Chronicle* poems, and the *Prologue* and *Epilogue* to the *Pastoral Care*. The parallel texts of these works contain significant variants that merit scrutiny in the present context, but the kind and number of their variants differ markedly from those found in *Soul and Body*, *Daniel* and *Azarias*, and *The Dream of the Rood*. The distinction reflects the difference between the labors of individuals who read texts critically to put them to new use, and the labors of scribes who mechanically reproduced texts without reading them critically. Mechanical reproduction still generates discrepancies in parallel texts, but these discrepancies tend to involve the corruption, omission, interpolation, or modification of individual words. Many of the alterations introduced by scribes would, in fact, be apparent to editors without the existence of a parallel text preserved in another manuscript. These variant readings support the lexemic theory of scribal behavior and indicate that standard scribal practice did not involve the careful comprehension or spontaneous recomposition of earlier poems. The scribe emerges from the following survey not as a poet or performer, but as a methodical laborer prone to commit certain errors and alter texts in predictable ways.

§146. The sixty-four lines from *Solomon and Saturn I* transmitted in both CCCC 422 (MS A) and CCCC 41 (MS B) illustrate well the kinds of textual variants that are engendered through the mechanical concentration of copyists on individual lexemes.[9] As the following example demonstrates, the parallel texts are often substantially identical:

---

[8] For a fuller account of the reasons to regard *The Dream of the Rood* as a poem of composite authorship, see Neidorf forthcoming.

[9] Semidiplomatic transcriptions of the two texts are printed in Anlezark 2009, the edition cited here.

Forðon hafað sē cantic	ofer		Forðan hafað sē cantic	ofer
ealle Crīstes bēc			ealle Crīstes bēc	
wīdmǣrost word;	hē gewritu		wīdmǣrost word;	hē gewritu
lǣreð,			lǣreð,	
stefnum stēoreð,	and him stede		stefnum stēoreð,	and him stede
healdeð			healdeð	
heofona rīces,	heregeatewa		heofonrices,	heregeatowe
wigeð.			wegeð.	

SnS A 49–53

SnS B 49–53

The sole substantive variant in this sequence of text—*heofona rīces* (A) versus *heofonrīces* (B)—is a straightforward consequence of lexemic transcription. A scribe indifferent to meter corrupted the authorial *heofona rīces* into *heofonrīces*, an unmetrical verse on account of resolution, by converting a noun phrase into a familiar compound. Editors would be able to detect and emend this corruption even if no parallel text were extant. The same holds true for the omission of *oððe* in MS B: editors would have no difficulty restoring the line (*elnes oððe ǣhte oððe eorlscipes, SnS* 11) if MS A did not confirm the presence of the second *oððe*, since meter and sense require the word here. Related consequences of the lexemic approach to transmission are evident in the following passage:

Mec ðæs on worolde full oft			Mec ðæs on worulde full oft	
fyrwit frīneð,	fūs gewīteð,		fyrwit frīneð,	fūs gewīteð,
mōd gemengeð.	Næ[nig]		mōd geondmengeð.	Nænig
manna wāt,			manna wāt,	
hæleða under hefenum,	hū		hæleða under heofnum,	hū
mīn hige drēoseð,			mīn hige drēogeð,	
bysig æfter bōcum;	hwīlum mē		bisi æfter bōcum;	hwȳlum mē
bryne stīgeð,			bryne stīgeð,	
hige heortan nēah hǣdre wealleð.			hige heortan [nēah] hearde wealleð.	

SnS A 57b–62

SnS B 57b–62

Without the existence of a parallel text, meter would render the omission of *nēah* in MS B apparent to editors, who might well be able to restore the authorial reading through conjectural emendation. Comparison of the parallel texts, however, reveals three cases of lexical change due to trivialization: the hapax legomenon *geondmengeð* (MS B) was reduced to *gemengeð* (MS A); the poetic verb *drēogeð* (MS B) was corrupted into *drēoseð* (MS A); and the rare word *hǣdre* (MS A) was metathesized into the common *hearde* (MS B). O'Brien O'Keeffe adduced these three sets of variants as evidence for "participatory copying and formulaic reading" (1990:61), but Orton exposed the improbability of her interpretation (2000:203–205). A grave problem with the theory of formulaic reading here is that the variants are not located within known formulae. The scribal alterations function not to convert one formula into another formula, but to trivialize an uncommon word into a more familiar one.[10] Furthermore, if genuine participation and recomposition were evident here, the graphemic overlap in the transmitted readings would need to be regarded as an extraordinary coincidence. That is to say, if a participating scribe sought to replace *drēogeð* (a word not bound to the line's alliteration) with a suitable alternative, it is incredible that such a scribe should choose *drēoseð*, a verb consisting of six of the same graphemes. Clearly, there is a visual basis for each of these trivializations: a scribe concentrating on the orthographic form of the individual lexeme corrupted it (probably unconsciously) into a genuine, but less appropriate, word of similar appearance.

§147. Comparison of the parallel texts of *Solomon and Saturn I* also calls attention to the presence of two minor interpolations:

mid īrenum æpplum (*SnS* A 28a)	īrenum aplum (*SnS* B 28a)
on wēstenne weard (*SnS* A 83a)	wēstenes weard (*SnS* B 83a)

In each case, the verse transmitted in the A text contains an additional word and exhibits a conspicuous metrical defect. The constraint against anacrusis in type A verses like *īrenum aplum* (Bliss 1967:§§46–47; *KB:T.C.* §35) exposes the interpolated status of *mid*. Likewise, the stricture against the presence of anacrusis before verses of type E (Bliss 1967:§§50, 59) reveals the scribal origins of *on* in *on wēstenne weard*. By preserving the authorial rendering of these verses, MS B confirms the inauthenticity of each additional word in the A text, but metrical probabilities are independently sufficient for an editor to regard *mid* and *on* as interpolations. Nevertheless, the attestation of the metrically correct authorial verses is worth noting for the corroboration

---

[10] This analysis holds for most of the variants in *Solomon and Saturn I* that O'Brien O'Keeffe regarded as "truly alternate readings" (1990:64) generated by informed scribal participation. For example, *smēalīce* (B 85a) is less common and more appropriate contextually than the variant *sōðlīce* (A 85a). Likewise, the hapax *fyrngestrēona* (B 32a) is rarer than the variant *feohgestrēona* (A 32b). *Dumbra* (B 78b) is far superior to *dēadra* (A 78b) in the context of a passage concerned with the human senses; it is difficult to see how this pair of variants could be regarded as "truly alternate readings" of equal validity. On these passages see Moffat 1992:812; O'Donnell 1996:278; Orton 2000:107, 110.

it provides of the reliability of meter as a tool for textual criticism.[11] These two interpolations are notably similar to the seven interpolations identified in the transmitted text of *Beowulf*. In every case, the word is semantically insignificant and results in the violation of one of the subtler rules of metrical composition. Close attention to the continuous sense of the work, moreover, is not required for the introduction of these interpolations into the text. The minor and predictable character of these interpolations suggests that scribes intended to avoid altering the sense or meter of the works they transmitted, though they occasionally interpolated function words they believed to be semantically and metrically inconsequential.

§148. Textual divergences in the numerous manuscripts that preserve *Cædmon's Hymn* produce findings about scribal behavior in line with those that emerged from *Solomon and Saturn I*. Apprehension of changes to the text introduced by scribes is facilitated through comparison with the poem's earliest Northumbrian recension, preserved in two eighth-century manuscripts:

Nū scylun hergan   hefaenrīcaes uard,
metudæs maecti   end his mōdgidanc,
uerc uuldurfadur,   suē hē uundra gihuaes,
ēci dryctin,   ōr āstelidæ.
He āerist scōp   aelda barnum
heben til hrōfe,   hāleg scepen;
thā middungeard   moncynnæs uard,
ēci dryctin,   æfter tīadæ
fīrum foldu,   frēa allmectig.[12]

There is one case of lexical substitution comparable to those observed in *Solomon and Saturn I*: *eorðan* (or *eorðe*) replaces *aelda* in some West Saxon renderings of the poem, and *eordu* replaces *aelda* in a distinct Northumbrian recension.[13] This variation has been adduced as evidence for informed scribal

---

[11] Because unmetrical verses in one parallel text nearly always possess metrical counterparts in other witnesses, the parallel texts furnish strong evidence against the notion that Old English poets might have deliberately composed unmetrical verses. It is clear that the unmetrical verses consistently represent scribal corruptions of verses that had originally complied with the rules of metrical composition. The argument that the parallel texts of Old English poetry confirm the reliability of metrical criteria for emendation is propounded at greater length in Neidorf 2016a.

[12] The poem is cited here from the edition of Krapp and Dobbie (1931-1953). Diplomatic transcriptions of every witness to *Cædmon's Hymn* are conveniently printed in O'Donnell 2005:215–230.

[13] The stemmatic rationale for regarding *aelda* as the authorial reading (and *eordu* as a scribal substitute) is summarized in Dobbie 1937:43–48. Most scholars have shared Dobbie's view, but

participation (O'Brien O'Keeffe 1990:23–46), but the graphemic overlap involved exposes the visual origin of the divergence. A Northumbrian scribe trivialized the poetic word *aelda* by converting it into the more familiar *eordu*, a genuine word of similar appearance. The prior corruption of *aelda* into *aeldu* (induced by the open-headed *a* letterform), which is attested in one early Northumbrian manuscript (St. Petersburg, National Library of Russia, MS lat. Q. v. I. 18), might have facilitated the word's decay into *eordu*. Another lexical variant is doubtless the product of a scribe's mechanical concentration on orthographic form: in most West Saxon texts, *tīadæ* is correctly Saxonized into *tēode*, but in a few texts it appears as *tīda*, a form that must be construed as an accusative plural of *tīd* 'time' (Dobbie 1937:39–40; O'Donnell 2005:151–152; Orton 2000:45–46). Because the obliteration of the verb from the final clause introduces grave defects of sense and syntax into the text, it is clear that the scribe responsible for this corruption was indifferent to the continuous sense of the poem and was not an active participant in its transmission.

§149. The two interpolations that appear in several texts of *Cædmon's Hymn* confirm the conclusions about the constrained nature of interpolation reached above. In many texts, the pronoun *wē* has been inserted into the poem's first verse, converting *Nū scylun hergan* into *Nū wē scylun hergan*. The introduction of the pronoun is nugatory, serving merely to clarify the syntax of the first clause without altering it. The metrical insignificance of the pronoun probably licensed its interpolation: it appears in the first drop of the verse, where syllabic protraction is permitted (Sievers 1893:§§10.1, 82.6). Similar observations hold true for the interpolation of *on* into the poem's penultimate verse, which turns *fīrum foldu* into *fīrum on foldu*. Depending on whether *foldu* represents an accusative or a dative form, the preposition serves either to clarify the poem's syntax or to distort it slightly. Regardless of the poet's intention, the interpolation trivializes the text by

---

O'Donnell (2005:132–168) argued for the anteriority of the *eordu* reading. His contention makes inferior sense of the stemmatic evidence and is predicated upon a questionable interpretation of the *lectio difficilior* principle. O'Donnell regards *eordu* as the *difficilior* reading because *aelda bearnum* is a widespread formula in Germanic poetic tradition (see Dobbie 1937:48n69), whereas *eordu bearnum* is rare and unexpected. This argument would be more credible if there were compelling reasons to believe that scribes actually practiced formulaic reading and were consequently inclined to trivialize nonformulae into formulae. Since scribes appear to have concentrated on individual words while copying, the principle of *lectio difficilior* should apply to the relative rarity of the individual words in question, not to the rarity of the verses they would generate. The poetic status of *aelda*, in contrast to the colloquial status of *eordu*, surely renders it the *difficilior* reading. The presence of *aelda* in the two earliest manuscripts of *Cædmon's Hymn*, combined with the fact that Bede translated the verse as *filiis hominum*, confirms the antiquity and supports the authority of *aelda*.

removing the syntactic ambiguities inherent in *fīrum foldu*. Metrically, the preposition is insignificant, since it is once again located in the first drop of the verse, where protraction is permitted. The two interpolations in the parallel texts of *Cædmon's Hymn* support the conclusion drawn from *Beowulf* and *Solomon and Saturn I*: scribes did not feel licensed to alter drastically the sense or meter of the texts they transmitted. The only words that scribes were permitted or encouraged to introduce into poems while copying were particles (i.e., pronouns, prepositions, and adverbs) believed to be metrically and semantically inconsequential.

§150. Variant readings in the poems transmitted in manuscripts of the *Anglo-Saxon Chronicle* lend further support to the lexemic theory of scribal behavior.[14] There are numerous signs of scribal preoccupation with form and indifference to sense in the various transmitted texts, including corruptions of proper names comparable to those found in the *Beowulf* manuscript. The toponym representing the city of Dublin (*difelin*) was corrupted into an obscure adjectival form, *dyflig*, in the D text of *Brunanburh* (55b). Meanwhile, in the poem's A text, the Irish ethnonym was trivialized into a third-person plural pronoun when the scribe rendered *eft Īra land* (56b) as *eft hira land*. Scribal unfamiliarity with the *Brunanburh* poet's diction resulted in two egregious corruptions that are also reminiscent of aberrations in the *Beowulf* manuscript. The hapax legomenon *cumbolgehnāstes* 'clashing of standards' (49b) was reduced in the A text to the nonsensical *cul bod ge hna des*, with anomalous spacing intimating the scribe's desperation. More remarkable is the D text's infamous corruption of *nægledcnearrum* 'with nailed ships' into *dæg glēd on gārum*, a sequence of words that deprives the text of both sense and alliteration. This corruption is a quintessential by-product of the lexemic approach to transmission. When the scribe attempted to discern the lexical identity of the word in his exemplar, unfamiliarity with the Norse loanword *cnear* (Campbell 1938:114) evidently led him to believe that an antecedent copyist had transmitted nonexistent lexemes that required correction. The scribe then tried to ascertain the genuine words that were preserved in the perceived corruption, *nægledcnearrum*. The outcome of this lexical scrutiny—*dæg glēd on gārum*—was transmitted because it satisfied the scribe's desire to transmit plausible forms regardless of the contextual nonsense they might generate.

---

[14]   For semidiplomatic renderings of these texts, see the pertinent volumes of Dumville and Keynes's (1983–) collaborative edition of *The Anglo-Saxon Chronicle*.

§151. The parallel texts of the *Chronicle* poems also corroborate the reliability of meter as a tool for textual criticism. Metrical aberrations that would attract editorial suspicion in poems preserved in a single manuscript are here confirmed to be corruptions by the attestation of metrically correct authorial readings in parallel texts. For example, an apparent exception to the requirement for double alliteration to be present in verses of expanded type D* scansion (Bliss 1967:§§64–65) is *wīse sōðboran*, a verse transmitted in the A text of *Death of Edgar*. The B/C texts of the poem, however, preserve the authorial reading, *wīse wōðboran* (33a). The presence of double alliteration in the genuine verse should strengthen the editorial conviction that poets maintained strict adherence to this inflexible rule of verse composition. The readiness of editors to emend unmetrical verses is justified by the confirmation that *þæs þe þearf wæs*—an apparent three-position verse (xxSS) transmitted in the C text of *Death of Edward*—represents a corruption of *þæs þe þearfe wæs* (34a), the reading preserved in the D text.[15] The attestation of *and dēorabȳ* (8a) in the B/C/D texts of *Capture of the Five Boroughs* confirms that the unmetrical appearance of the verse comprised by *dēorabȳ* in the A text is a consequence of the scribal omission of the copulative conjunction, not authorial deliberation. The inauthenticity of *secgas hwate*, an unmetrical verse in the A text of *Brunanburh*, is confirmed by the attestation of the authorial verse, *secga swāte* (13a), in all other texts of the poem. Meter thus emerges from the comparison of parallel texts as a trustworthy indicator of scribal corruption.

§152. The variant readings that can reasonably be attributed to scribes provide little reason to believe that scribes ever substantially recomposed the poems they transmitted. Most of the parallel texts are nearly identical aside from sporadic and insignificant variants that are the transparent consequences of mechanical reproduction. There are a few exceptional variants, however, that might appear to reflect deliberate scribal intervention. In the B text of *Brunanburh*, for example, *agēted* 'destroyed' has been replaced by the synonymous *forgrunden*; and in the T text of the *Metrical Preface to Pastoral Care*, the *īegbūendum* 'island-dwellers' whom Augustine converted appear instead as the *eorðbūendum* 'earth-dwellers'.[16] These variants are outliers because the minimal graphemic overlap between the authorial reading and

---

[15] On the improbability that three-position verses ever represented an acceptable metrical type to Old English poets, see *HOEM*:§208 and Pascual 2013–2014.

[16] On the variation in these passages see O'Brien O'Keeffe 1990:93, 121–122; O'Donnell 1996:102–103, 197–198; and Orton 2000:100, 103.

the scribal substitute suggests no mechanical source for the divergence. One might therefore regard these variant readings as the genuine traces of participatory scribes who practiced formulaic reading. Yet even *forgrunden* and *eorðbūendum* cannot be regarded as unambiguous evidence for the existence of these spectral figures. It is possible that the variants represent competent responses to lacunous exemplars, rather than spontaneous revisions of antecedent forms. Saxonization, moreover, is a probable motive for the replacement of *agēted* with *forgrunden*, since the poetic verb *agǣtan* exhibits Anglian vocalism in all of its attestations (Campbell 1938:103). The replacement of *īegbūendum* with *eorðbūendum* can be explained as an unconscious trivialization: *īegbūendum* is the more suitable label for the insular recipients of Christianity, but the vague *eorðbūendum* is a much commoner word. Saxonization and trivialization are intimately linked to the lexemic approach to transmission. In short, these few substantial variants form an insecure basis for credence in the hypothesis that formulaic reading influenced the reproduction of poetic texts.

4. The Four Poetic Codices

§153. The explanatory superiority of the lexemic theory over its competitors is most clearly demonstrated by its ability to account for a wide array of textual phenomena in the four codices that preserve the majority of the extant poetic corpus. Since evidence from the *Beowulf* manuscript was adduced in the preceding chapters, the present section focuses on the Exeter Book, the Junius Manuscript, and the Vercelli Book. The occurrence in these codices of numerous corruptions comparable to those found in the manuscript of *Beowulf* suggests that Anglo-Saxon scribes maintained a relatively uniform approach to textual transmission. Charged with the task of reproducing and modernizing Anglian works composed one to three centuries earlier, these trained professionals concentrated on the orthographic form of individual lexemes and paid little attention to the continuous sense of the texts they transmitted. Just as the parallel texts provide no compelling evidence for formulaic reading or scribal recomposition, the poetic codices contain firm indications that scribes maintained a mechanical relationship to the material in their exemplars. There are many extraordinary corruptions in these texts that could never have been generated or preserved if the scribes responsible for their transmission were concerned with sense, meter, or alliteration. Pervasive trivialization provides the clearest evidence for the scribal prioritization of orthographic form over all other considerations when copying.

§154. Indifference to sense is particularly apparent when an authorial word is corrupted into a word of similar appearance, but with antithetical meanings or connotations. This phenomenon is not uncommon in the poetic codices.[17] In the Exeter Book, *hǣþnum* 'heathens' (*Christ* 485a) is corrupted into the inappropriate *heofonum* 'heavens'. The adjective *egle,* meaning 'loathsome, troublesome, horrid', is twice corrupted to *engel* 'angel', when *eglum* (*Christ* 762a) is transmitted as *englum* and *egle* (*Guthlac* 962b) is transmitted as *engle.* The corruption of *fēond* 'enemy' (*Vainglory* 70b) into its antonym *frēond* 'friend' in the Exeter Book is paralleled in the Junius Manuscript, which contains the reverse corruption of *frēond* (*Exodus* 45b) into *fēond.* In the same text, *hēofung* 'lamentation' (*Exodus* 46b) is corrupted into the familiar *heofon*—a word that seems frequently to have been on the mind of scribes transmitting religious literature. The Exeter Book and the Vercelli Book exhibit three similar corruptions where reversals of sense are accompanied by defects of alliteration: twice *nīed* 'compulsion, servitude' (*Christ* 361a, *Andreas* 1377b) and once *nēod* 'desire' (*SBI* 48b) are corrupted into *mēd* 'reward' in lines linked by *n*-alliteration.[18] Violent distortions of sense, however, are particularly common in the Junius Manuscript, where one can find the corruption of *flōd* 'sea' to *fold* 'land' (*Genesis A* 150b), *fēran* 'journey' to *frēan* 'lord' (*Gen A* 1211b), *bearm* 'bosom' to *bearn* 'child' (*Gen A* 1664a), *sinces* 'treasure' to *synna* 'sins' (*Gen A* 2642a), and *ecgum* 'edges' to *ēagum* 'eyes' (*Exodus* 413b). Minimal attention to the sense of the text is all that would have been required for the prevention or correction of these obvious corruptions.

§155. Four particularly illuminating cases of trivialization involve the poetic noun *geofon* 'ocean'. Scribes alienated from the poetic tradition evidently regarded *geofon* as a nonexistent word that required correction to a genuine word of similar appearance when they encountered it in their exemplars. The word that invariably came to their minds, unsurprisingly,

---

[17] Several of the examples adduced in this section were noted in Sisam 1953b:29–44; Lucas 1994:24–27; and Orchard 2003–2004:54.

[18] Orton's perceptive comments concerning the case from *Soul and Body I* are worth citing, since they hold true for many comparable errors: "Mistakes involving the confusion of a letter in an exemplar with another of similar shape are simple errors of the eye; but their presence, if left uncorrected, indicates a copyist who is either taking no notice of the meaning of the text that is being reproduced, or does not understand it. SB1 48 *mēda* for *nīeda* is particularly revealing, for alliteration depends on the *n* of *nīeda....* The scribe responsible for such a mistake was probably working silently, with no sense of the text as a communicative utterance" (2000:23).

was *heofon*. The transmitted text of *Andreas*, preserved in the Vercelli Book, contains three corruptions of *geofon* into *heofon*, which are located in the following passages:

> Gārsecg hlymmeð,
> [g]eofon gēotende.

392b–393a

The sea is roaring, the surging ocean.

> Læt nū of þīnum staþole   strēamas weallan,
> ēa inflēde,   nū ðē ælmihtig
> hāteð, heofona cyning,   þæt ðū hrædlīce
> on þis fræte folc   forð onsende
> wæter wīdrynig   tō wera cwealme,
> [g]eofon gēotende.

1503–1508a

Let streams now surge from your foundation, a flowing river, now that the Almighty, the king of the heavens, commands that you immediately send forth onto this ignominious people water flowing far and wide for the destruction of these men, a surging ocean.

> Þā wæs forð cumen
> gēoc æfter gyrne.   [G]eofon swaðrode
> þurh hāliges hæs,   hlyst ȳst forgeaf,
> brimrād gebād.

1584b–1587a

Help was then forthcoming after grief. The ocean became still at the saint's command, the storm passed out of earshot, the sea-road obeyed.

The Junius Manuscript yields a fourth example of this corruption in the text of *Christ and Satan*:

> Hē selfa mæg   sǣ geondwlītan,
> grundas in [g]eofene,   godes āgen bearn,
> and hē ārīman mæg   rægnas scūran,
> dropena gehwelcne.

(9–12a)

He himself is able to see through the sea, the grounds in the ocean, God's own child, and he can count the showers of rain, every drop.

The four corruptions of *geofon* into *heofon* provide compelling support for the lexemic theory of textual transmission. The scribes responsible for the generation or preservation of these corruptions must have transcribed text from their exemplars on a word-by-word basis without concern for the continuous sense of the text. Considerations of narrative or poetic form plainly did not affect the labors of these scribes, since even the slightest interest in a word's place in the text would have rendered the corruption apparent. In every passage, *geofon* participates in the line's alliteration and is surrounded by synonymous words denoting bodies of water. In the first passage, it is preceded by *gārsecg*; in the next, it is preceded by *strēamas, ēa,* and *wæter*; then it is followed by *ȳst* and *brimrād*; and in the final case, it is preceded by *sǣ* and followed by *rægnas* and *scūran*. The two or more scribes who corrupted *geofon* into *heofon* did not treat the text in the exemplar as a poetic narrative to be understood and enjoyed as a coherent work. Rather, they regarded it as a sequence of independent words requiring mechanical reproduction and orthographic modernization. Transmitting *geofon* as *heofon* deprived texts of sense and alliteration, but it satisfied the scribe's need to commit what he believed to be genuine lexemes to parchment.

§156. The corruption of proper names into common nouns of similar appearance, perhaps the most revealing consequence of the lexemic approach to textual reproduction, is a common phenomenon in the transmitted text of *Genesis A*, preserved in the Junius Manuscript. The scribal obliteration of proper names in this text often results in nonsense, and thereby calls to mind comparable examples from the *Beowulf* manuscript surveyed in the previous chapter. For instance, Gōmor (*Gen A* 1610b), son of Japheth, suffered the same fate as Ēomēr, son of Offa: his name was corrupted into the adjective *geōmor* 'mournful'. The name of Loth, the nephew of Abraham, was twice corrupted into an implausible *lēoht* 'light': first *Loth* (*Gen A* 1938b) is transmitted as *lēoht*, then *Lothes* (*Gen A* 2402b) is transmitted as *lēohtes*. The name of Agar (*Gen A* 2252b), the handmaiden of Sarra, is corrupted into the verb *āgan* 'to own', again generating nonsense. Defects of meter joined defects of sense when the toponym *Sǣgor* (*Gen A* 2522a) was corrupted into *sigor* 'victory', since the long vowel of the proper name is required for the pertinent verse (*on Sǣgor up*) to possess four metrical positions. The genealogy of Abraham, meanwhile, is disrupted by the obliteration of his father's name from the transmitted text: *Þāre* (*Gen A* 1705a) was trivialized into a common noun *wer* 'man', due to the similarity of *þ* and *p*. Similar defects were introduced into the text through the corruption of the verse *fæder Nebroðes* 'the father of Nimrod' (*Gen A* 1628a) to *fæder nebrēðer* 'father nor brother (?)'.

Finally, *Wendelsǣ* (*Gen A* 2211a), the standard Anglo-Saxon name for the Mediterranean, is erroneously rendered *wendeð sǣ*, thereby obscuring the notion that Egypt is surrounded by three bodies of water, the Euphrates, the Nile, and the Mediterranean (2204b–2211).

§157. The Exeter Book, Vercelli Book, and Junius Manuscript contain numerous aberrations that would never have materialized if the scribes responsible for these codices had paid attention to the continuous sense of the words they transmitted. Consequently, it is difficult to believe that these scribes regarded themselves as active participants in the transmission process, who might read their exemplars formulaically and spontaneously recompose poetic texts. By all appearances, these scribes did not read *poems* when they copied; they read *words*. The lexemic theory, distinct from its competitors, is the only theory of scribal behavior capable of accounting for the striking textual pattern discernible in the four poetic codices: the serial corruption of authorial words into genuine but contextually implausible words of similar appearance. If such errors were the product of mere sloppiness or inattentiveness, we should expect them to materialize often as gibberish forms that correspond to no actual words in the Old English language. The surprising frequency with which corruptions take the form of genuine words becomes explicable only when it is understood as a consequence of the scribal concentration on the orthographic form of individual lexemes. Doubting the lexemic theory leaves this regularity unexplained—a regularity that embraces much evidence not mentioned above, including the corruption of *lēod* 'man' to *þēod* 'nation' (*Exodus* 277a), *frōd* 'wise' to *forð* 'forth' (*Gen A* 1642b), *bold* 'building' to *blōd* 'blood' (*Riddles* 15.9a), *frēfran* 'console' to *fēran* 'journey' (*Seafarer* 26b), *līg* 'flame' to *līf* 'life' (*Fortunes of Men* 44a), *segn* 'standard' to *þegn* 'servant' (*Phoenix* 288a), *wiht* 'creature' to *niht* 'night' (*Christ* 419b), and *wōð* 'speech' to *sōð* 'truth' (*Guthlac* 391b).

5. Theory and Evidence

§158. There is little merit and much peril in maintaining unwavering credence in theoretical generalizations about Anglo-Saxon scribes. When confronting textual problems, scholars must weigh the merits of competing readings on a case-by-case basis, without allowing a priori beliefs about scribal behavior to dictate their conclusions. The follies that characterize textual scholarship more concerned with enunciating theoretical dicta than analyzing the actual evidence were famously illustrated by Housman (1961), when he exhorted scholars to apply *thought* rather than *theory* to their assessments of the evidence. Theories erected upon a minuscule set of data (such as the theory of formulaic reading) that are then assumed to have significant implications for the transmission of all extant poetic works are bound to be impediments, rather than aids, to understanding. A promising trend in Old English textual scholarship is apparent in several recent critiques of the tendency to allow theoretical generalizations to replace detailed analyses. O'Donnell's comprehensive study demonstrated that variant readings cited from a small sample of parallel texts cannot reasonably be regarded as evidence for "the general reliability of Anglo-Saxon scribes" (1996:7). Peter S. Baker, in his study of variant readings in the Metrical Psalms, also rejected the notion that textual transmission should be a uniform process:

> If such texts as C's *Brunanburh* and the Corpus 12 *Preface* and *Epilogue* show how faithfully Old English scribes were capable of following their exemplars, such texts as D's *Brunanburh* and those cited by Sisam [1953b:29–44] show how many changes might be introduced into a text, whether as a result of memorial transmission, revision, or scribal incompetence. Thus it is impossible to generalize about "the authority of Old English poetical manuscripts": neither a conservative nor an adventurous editorial philosophy will be correct if applied indiscriminately.

> 1984:269

Similar critiques of the indiscriminate application of textual theory can be found throughout the methodological writings of Fulk (1996b; 1997; 2003; 2007f). Characteristic of his thought is the concluding statement of an essay that praises Klaeber's pragmatic approach to editing: "The temptation to develop larger editorial principles in a textual vacuum should be avoided: it is only in the act of editing that the issues which should determine those principles come into sharp focus" (2007f:153). Finally, a powerful critique of theoretical generalizations inheres in Orton's (2000) exposition of the many diverse causes of variation in parallel texts, which showed that few of these variants can be reconciled with coherent theories of scribal participation or spontaneous recomposition.

§159. A virtue of the lexemic theory is that it makes no theoretical predictions about the extent to which a given text might have been corrupted during its transmission. Scribal concentration on the orthographic form of individual lexemes could result in a text that is a substantially *verbatim* (not *literatim*) reproduction of its antecedent or it could result in a text riddled with egregious corruptions. The different outcomes depend entirely on factors incidental to the theory, such as the duration of transmission or the lexical knowledge of the scribe. Theories of scribal behavior in competition with the lexemic theory, on the other hand, force their adherents to expect texts to exhibit relatively few corruptions, since scribes who followed the sense and meter of the poems they copied are unlikely to transmit unmetrical nonsense. When adherents of these theories confront the implausible readings that pervade the extant poetic manuscripts, cognitive dissonance is bound to result, since awareness of these corruptions is not compatible with the belief that scribes were poets, performers, or literary collaborators. No such dissonance is produced under the lexemic theory, which makes predictions not about the amount of corruption, but about the types of corruption to be expected. Since the kinds of corruption it predicts are precisely those that are actually found in the extant manuscripts of Old English poetry, the internal coherence and explanatory power of this theory recommend it over its competitors. The lexemic theory should not dictate editorial conclusions, but it can help an editor decide between two readings, since a theory erected upon so much data distinguishes realistic textual developments from those that are farfetched.

§160. While it is prudent to acknowledge that the transmission of one text is likely to differ in certain respects from the transmission of any other text, it is imprudent to approach all texts in the belief that scribes might have substantially recomposed them for deliberate ideological or artistic reasons. The scribal alterations discernible in the parallel texts and the four poetic codices appear predominantly to be the accidental, expected, and reversible consequences of the lexemic approach to textual transmission. In certain cases, such as *Soul and Body* and *The Dream of the Rood*, earlier works were revised and expanded by later authors who left palpable traces of their labors. Yet when poetic texts bear no sign of disunity and appear to have been transmitted entirely by scribes, it is reasonable to assume that these texts retain most of the structural characteristics they possessed when they were first committed to parchment. Scribes modernized and Saxonized spellings, interpolated function words they believed to be semantically and metrically inconsequential, and occasionally corrupted authorial words into genuine words of similar appearance. There is little reason to believe, however, that the scribal contribution to a transmitted poetic text should have exceeded the spectrum of activity delimited by the lexemic theory. Corruptions and lacunae aside, an eighth-century work preserved in an eleventh-century manuscript should remain substantially intact. Scribes changed texts not as poets or performers, but as the inspectors and guardians of orthography.

5

CONCLUSION

1. The Unity of *Beowulf*

§161. Recent trends in textual theory have rendered it difficult for some scholars to credit a conclusion that many philologists have reached about *Beowulf*: namely, that the poem is substantially the work of a single poet who composed ca. 700, or roughly three centuries before the production of the sole extant manuscript. If Anglo-Saxon scribes were creative participants in the transmission process who thoroughly recomposed the poems they copied, then we should not expect a poem to retain the metrical, lexical, or syntactic characteristics it possessed when it was first committed to parchment. Indeed, if *Beowulf* had been reproduced multiple times by these participatory scribes during the three centuries of its transmission, then we should expect few traces of archaic composition or unitary authorship to be discernible in the extant manuscript. Rather, the transmitted text should contain an admixture of structural archaisms and innovations, among other signs of composite authorship. Subtle and pervasive regularities of rhythm, diction, and grammar—signs of unitary authorship—should not be found in the text. Of course, if such regularities actually are found in the transmitted text of *Beowulf*, then their presence casts grave doubt upon the validity of the theories of scribal behavior that predict their obliteration. The present chapter surveys linguistic regularities in *Beowulf* in order to gauge the extent to which the poem's text might have been altered during its transmission. If subtle regularities pervade *Beowulf* and distinguish it from the rest of the poetic corpus, then it is doubtful that libertine scribes substantially recomposed it.

§162. For the literary critics and cultural historians who constitute the majority of scholars interested in *Beowulf*, no question pertaining to textual transmission is more consequential than that of the poem's unity. Does *Beowulf* represent the unified work of an individual poet composing at a particular moment, whose controlling intelligence is evident in the subtle regularities of the text? If *Beowulf* is an integral product of the early Anglo-Saxon period, then historicist scholars must situate their interpretations of the poem long before the extant manuscript. Does *Beowulf* represent a collaboration between a poet and a series of scribes, who continuously recomposed the work, adapting it for new audiences and contexts? If this were the case, then both historicist and formalist studies would be undermined, since passages of the poem would belong to various times, places, and authors. If scribes deliberately wrote the poem anew, then interpretations of *Beowulf* would need to be situated in the manuscript context, since the work as we know it would never have existed before that moment. On the other hand, if the scribes responsible for the transmission of *Beowulf* took few compositional liberties with the text and preserved its structural characteristics, then scholars would be compelled to divorce the poem from its manuscript context and interpret it as an archaic composition reflecting an entirely different cultural milieu. Much is at stake in our understanding of what happened and what did not happen to *Beowulf* during its transmission.

§163. Earlier chapters of this book examined the remarkable array of corruptions that entered into the transmitted text of *Beowulf* on account of linguistic and cultural changes that took effect between the eighth and eleventh centuries. Scribal difficulty with archaic vocabulary, Anglian features, and earlier orthographical practices is registered in errors throughout the extant manuscript. Unfamiliarity with poetic tradition and Germanic legend is frequently evident in the corruption of rare words and proper names into common nouns of similar appearance. The strenuous effort of the scribes to Saxonize and modernize the orthography of the text often obscured its sense or vitiated its meter. In the light of so many alterations to the poem's text, it may seem paradoxical to maintain the conviction that *Beowulf* should be regarded as the coherent work of one archaic poet. This conviction is grounded, however, in the belief that probabilistic reasoning can enable textual critics to detect scribal errors and restore authorial readings to the text. Because the scribes who transmitted *Beowulf* worked at a vast remove in time and space from the poet, with no scholarly resources to aid their efforts, an editor equipped with concordances, legendary analogues, and historical grammars is often in a much better position to understand and recover the poem's text. John M. Kemble articulated this observation in one of the first critical editions of *Beowulf*:

> A modern edition, made by a person really conversant with the language which he illustrates, will in all probability be much more like the original

than the MS. copy, which, even in the earliest times, was made by an ignorant or indolent transcriber.

1835:xxiv

Confidence in the ability of textual critics to detect and extract the scribal
contribution to the transmitted text depends, of course, on our understanding of the probable extent and nature of that contribution.

§164. If the lexemic theory of scribal behavior is correct, as the previous
chapter argued, then there are firm grounds for confidence in the editorial
ability to recover the work of the *Beowulf* poet. According to this theory,
scribes concentrated on the orthographic form of individual lexemes while
copying in order to produce a text that conformed to the written standard in
which they were trained. Variants found their way into the text not because
scribes wished to express their literary sensibilities, but because they failed to
identify the lexemes embedded in sequences of graphemes in the exemplar.
Scribes did not recompose the antecedent text spontaneously, but they were
permitted to insert or modify function words they believed to be metrically
and semantically inconsequential. The evidence surveyed in the preceding
chapters of this book suggests that the lexemic theory accurately describes the
contribution of Anglo-Saxon scribes to the poetic texts they transmitted. The
structural characteristics of a poem are intended to remain intact, but when
they are accidentally corrupted, the corrupt form tends to bear a graphemic
resemblance to the authorial form. Consequently, it is often a simple matter
of probabilistic reasoning for an editor to detect and emend scribal errors.
Once these corruptions have been emended, readers have firmer justification
for regarding the poem as the integral work of one early poet than as anything
else. Minor changes might remain undetected and lacunae of unknowable
length will remain lost beyond recovery,[1] but what survives of *Beowulf* is
essentially the work of the *Beowulf* poet, not a union of scribal laborers.

§165. If competing theories of scribal behavior were correct, and Anglo-
Saxon scribes thoroughly recomposed the poetic texts they copied, then
Beowulf should be such a heterogeneous accretion that no amount of editorial intervention could restore the more or less unified work of one archaic
poet. An argument to this effect was in fact propounded by Liuzza (1995),
who contended that unconstrained scribal intervention should have fundamentally altered the structural characteristics of the poem. Interpreting
variant readings in parallel texts of Old English poetry as evidence for routine

---

[1] For discussion of suspected lacunae in *Beowulf*, see Gerritsen 1989a; Sisam 1953b:40–41n2;
Lehmann 1969; and Craigie 1923:16–18.

scribal recomposition—a dubious interpretation in the light of §§140–152 above—Liuzza argued that more than one-fifth of *Beowulf* should have been substantially altered during its transmission. Consequently, in his view, "it is therefore implausible to suppose that a poem might preserve for several centuries of written transmission the metrical shape of its first composition" (1995:294). An additional conclusion drawn from this argument is that "the only meaningful date for the 'effective composition' of *Beowulf* is that of the manuscript, since any version previously existing would be different to an unknowable degree from the surviving text" (1995:294–295). There are many reasons to doubt Liuzza's claims, but the fatal methodological flaw of his study is that it adduces no textual evidence from *Beowulf* in support of the poem's supposedly composite origins. Liuzza erected his argument on a purely theoretical plain, but the only principled way to determine whether *Beowulf* is the work of one poet or the work of numerous scribal contributors is to scrutinize the text in search of signs of unitary or composite authorship.

§166. A thorough linguistic investigation into the unity of *Beowulf* affords an opportunity to falsify, in addition to the arguments of Liuzza (1995), many similar attempts to regard *Beowulf* as a textual accretion of heterogeneous origins. Throughout the nineteenth century, scholars working under the influence of Homeric studies endeavored to dissect *Beowulf* into a collection of discrete compositions. Proponents of the *Liedertheorie*, such as Müllenhoff (1869) and ten Brink (1888), contended that Christian scribes had yoked together pagan lays of varying antiquity and authority. In their view, *Beowulf* was an incoherent work reflecting the involuntary collaboration of chronologically and ideologically disparate authors. In twentieth-century scholarship, the principal effort to dissect *Beowulf*, inaugurated by Levin Schücking (1905), has aimed to divide the poem into three compositions of discrete authorship: Beowulf's youthful adventures in Denmark (lines 1–1887), Beowulf's homecoming (1888–2199), and Beowulf's final days in Geatland (2200–3182). Francis P. Magoun, Jr. (1958, 1963) maintained Schücking's tripartite view of the poem's origins, arguing that two orally circulating poems were compiled by an anthologizing scribe, who composed a third poem (lines 2009b–2176) to link them together (cf. Palmer 1976). Kiernan similarly contended that *Beowulf* is "an amalgamation of two originally distinct poems which first came together in the MS that has come down to us" (1981:249). In his view, scribes responsible for the extant manuscript recomposed two independent works and freshly composed Beowulf's homecoming to serve as a narrative bridge between them.

§167. Credence in theories of composite authorship waned in the twentieth century in response to changing trends in *Beowulf* literary criticism. Linguistic and metrical arguments for the unity of *Beowulf* were adduced (for example by Chambers 1959:117–120), but by far the most influential cause for the abandonment of *Liedertheorie* and Schücking's tripartite theory was the formation of a critical consensus, following J. R. R. Tolkien's influential lecture (1936), that *Beowulf* was the masterwork of an individual poet, replete with signs of conscious artistry and thematic unity.[2] As this consensus weakens in turn with the rise of postmodern aesthetics and pervasive skepticism in Old English studies, scholars may well be prepared to credit once again the notion that *Beowulf* is a heterogeneous accretion. The theory of scribal recomposition is attractive to scholars who are skeptical of the philological enterprise, since it provides a rationale for obscurantist efforts to urge observers to refrain from emending *Beowulf* or dating its composition. The critical overview of linguistic evidence for the unity of *Beowulf* presented below is intended to halt the spread of credence in the theory of scribal recomposition by making its improbability more apparent to observers. Literary-critical arguments for the unity of *Beowulf*, such as those propounded by Arthur G. Brodeur (1953, 1970), have been persuasive, but the linguistic evidence carries much weightier probabilistic force. The presence of subtle linguistic regularities throughout the poem lend firm support to the hypothesis that *Beowulf* is the work of one archaic poet. The preservation of these regularities through three centuries of written transmission collaterally confirms that scribes refrained from altering the structural characteristics of the poem they copied.

2. Linguistic Regularities

§168. The same metrical features that establish *Beowulf* as an archaic composition also provide firm indications that the poem is a unitary composition transmitted with minimal scribal interference. As a criterion for relative chronology, the incidence of verses requiring noncontraction for scansion suggests that *Beowulf* is one of the earliest extant poems, since such verses are most common in *Beowulf*, *Genesis A*, *Exodus*, and *Daniel*, less common in Cynewulfian and Alfredian poetry, and virtually unknown in poems dating to the tenth or eleventh century (*HOEM*:§§104–106).[3] Earlier poets

---

[2]   For a critical history of *Liedertheorie* and its gradual abandonment, see Shippey 1997.

[3]   For prior discussion of non-contraction in this book, see above, §§4–6 (chap. 1) and 51 (chap. 2).

felt licensed to compose verses in which words that underwent contraction during the seventh century must assume their precontracted forms, whereas later poets were evidently less aware of the syllabic variability of these words (see Fulk 2007b). An indication that the entirety of *Beowulf* is an archaic work inheres in the fact that verses exhibiting noncontraction are distributed throughout the poem, as the following selection makes clear:

> man geþeon (25b)
> hean hūses (116a)
> nean bīdan (528b)
> feorhsēoc fleon (820a)
> on flet teon (1036b)
> dēaþwīc seon (1275b)
> swā sceal man don (1534b)
> on flett gæð (2034b)
> swā sceal mæg don (2166b)
> egesan ðeon (2736a)
> swā hē nū gēn deð (2859b)
> beorh þone hean (3097b)

The distribution of these verses strengthens conviction in the unity of *Beowulf* by exposing the improbability of the alternative hypotheses. It is doubtful that such a distribution would be found if *Beowulf* consisted of three or more poems of various ages, since noncontraction is rare in later poetry. Similarly, it is improbable that these metrical archaisms would have been preserved throughout the transmitted text if scribes operating during the ninth and tenth centuries had thoroughly recomposed the *Beowulf* poet's work. To these scribes, who allegedly understood metrical composition (Liuzza 1995:291), most of the verses cited above should have appeared unmetrical, unless our scribes are conjectured to have possessed more insight into poetic tradition than the authors responsible for late Old English poetry, who demonstrate limited awareness of the possibility of treating contracted monosyllables as if they remained disyllabic. Surely, if participatory scribes read *Beowulf* carefully and paid attention to its meter, they would have corrected ostensibly defective verses such as *hean hūses* (116a) by interpolating function words that would render them metrically acceptable. Had a scribe inserted a proclitic into the verse, we would have something like **þæs hean hūses*, an acceptable type C verse with *hean* assuming its contracted form. It was well within the power of the scribes to obliterate this metrical archaism, but its frequent preservation in the transmitted text confirms that this did not happen.

§169. What has been said of contraction can also be said of parasiting. As a chronological criterion, verses requiring nonparasiting for scansion identify *Beowulf* as a relatively early composition, since this feature is most common in poems abounding with metrical archaisms (*Beowulf, Genesis A, Exodus*, and *Daniel*) and less common in poems exhibiting various innovations that are known or conjectured to be relatively late compositions (*HOEM*:§§88–92). The declining incidence of this archaism reflects a gradual decay in knowledge of poetic tradition: earlier poets were aware that etymologically monosyllabic words that became disyllabic on account of parasiting could be scanned as though they still possessed their monosyllabic forms, while later poets were less aware of this possibility. As the selection below indicates, verses requiring nonparasited forms for scansion can be found throughout *Beowulf*:

> Đǣr wæs hæleþa hleahtor (611a)
> wundor scēawian (840b)
> umborwesendum ǣr (1187a)
> ātertānum fāh (1459b)
> wundorsmiþa geweorc (1681a)
> lāc ond luftācen (1863a)
> þā mec sinca baldor (2428b)
> Frōfor eft gelamp (2941b)
> wundurscēawian (3032b)
> beadurōfes bēcn (3160a)

The occurrence of nonparasiting throughout *Beowulf* militates against the possibility that the poem is an amalgamation of discrete works composed at different times. The routine preservation of this archaic feature also raises doubts about the theory of scribal recomposition. If scribes during the ninth or tenth centuries had systematically recomposed the poem with the parasited forms common in contemporary poetry in mind, verses requiring nonparasiting for scansion could have been recomposed in ways that would obliterate this feature. For example, the order of the nouns in *wundor scēawian* (840b, 3032b) could have been reversed into *scēawian wundor, an acceptable type A verse, with the epenthetic vowel of *wundor* forming the second drop. Yet the transmitted text reads *wundor scēawian*, a verse that is unmetrical unless *wundor* is scanned as its earlier monosyllabic form (*wundr), thereby generating a type D verse.[4] Nonparasiting thus provides another firm indication that *Beowulf* is a unified, archaic composition.

---

[4]   The reason why scansion demands nonparasiting in *wundor scēawian*, but not in *scēawian wundor, is that the metrical behavior of *scēawian* varies based on its position in the verse, in accordance with

§170. Kaluza's law, the most significant metrical criterion for the absolute dating of *Beowulf* (see §§5–6, Chap. 1 above), provides arguably the
most compelling indication that the poem is the unified work of one archaic
poet. *Beowulf* is unique in the corpus of Old English poetry in its systematic
application or suspension of resolution under secondary stress on the basis
of etymological length distinctions that became phonologically indistinct
in Mercia before 725 (*HOEM*:§§170–183). The only adequate explanation
for this impressive regularity is that it was phonologically conditioned: the
Beowulf poet composed while the pertinent oppositions were still audible
in the language he spoke (*HOEM*:§§406–421; Neidorf and Pascual 2014).
The hypothesis of phonological conditioning collaterally explains why
other Old English poets, including relatively early ones, show little or no
awareness of the distinctions of etymological length known to the *Beowulf*
poet. For poets composing after such distinctions had collapsed, consistent
adherence to Kaluza's law became a linguistic impossibility. *Exodus* is the
only poem to approach *Beowulf* in its incidence of verses with resolution of
historically short desinences under secondary stress, though it contains one
notable exception, *gylpplegan gāres* (240a), where the consonantal desinence
of *-plegan* must be resolved (*HOEM*:§176; Fulk 2007b:320–322). *Beowulf*
evinces no such exceptions in verses of this sort, which distinguish the poem
by displaying knowledge of the etymological resolvability of fifteen different
desinences.[5] The fact that verses adhering to Kaluza's law appear throughout
Beowulf, as the selection below makes clear, is therefore of considerable
importance in the present context:

> lēof lēodcyning (54a)
> nȳdwracu nīþgrim (193a)
> frēowine folca (430a, 2357a, 2429a)
> gilpcwide Gēates (640a)
> morðorbealo māga (1079a, 2742a)
> lāðbite līces (1122a)
> frome fyrdhwate (1641a, 2476a)

Fulk's law (also known as the Rule of the Coda). If *scēawian* were in the onset of the verse, *-ian* would
occupy a single metrical position, but the same sequence occupies two positions when *scēawian* is
placed in the coda, necessitating the metrical suppression of the epenthetic vowel of *wundor*. On
Fulk's law, see *HOEM*:§§221–245 and Pascual 2013–2014:58.

[5]   *Beowulf* is most distinct from the rest of the corpus in its restriction of resolution under secondary
stress to endings that were historically short; other poems share its tendency to suspend resolution
for historically long desinences, but no poem exhibits a comparable incidence of verses like *frēowine
folca*. Pertinent statistics, accompanied by an incisive analysis, are presented in Fulk 2007b:317–324.

wīs wordcwida (1845a)
gearo gyrnwræce (2118a)
wīcstede weligne (2607a)
wyrm wōhbogen (2827a)
mōdceare mǣndon (3149a)

The regular and extensive adherence to Kaluza's law maintained throughout
Beowulf, and *Beowulf* alone, speaks in favor of the poem's unity and casts
the gravest doubt upon competing hypotheses. Obviously, we should not
expect to find a subtle linguistic regularity of this sort if *Beowulf* consisted of
several discrete works or if scribes thoroughly recomposed the poem during
its transmission. Kaluza's law furnishes especially telling evidence against
theories of scribal recomposition, since it is implausible that consistent
observation of the law would be maintained if scribes had read formulaically,
and spontaneously substituted words of their own conception for words of
authorial origin. Lexical substitutions could easily convert any verse that
adhered to Kaluza's law into a verse that violated it. For example, if *-wine*
in *frēowine folca* were replaced with *-cyning*, resolution of an etymologically
long desinence would be required to render the verse metrically viable.
Conversely, if *-cyning* in *lēof lēodcyning* were replaced with *-wine*, resolution
would need to be suspended by an etymologically short desinence for the
verse to contain four metrical positions. The ease with which exceptions to
Kaluza's law could have been generated renders the paucity of exceptions
one of the clearest signs that *Beowulf* retains the structural characteristics it
possessed when it was first committed to parchment.

§171. A crucial difference between the implications of contraction and
parasiting, on the one hand, and Kaluza's law, on the other hand, is worth
expounding upon. Since verses requiring noncontraction and nonparasiting
are well attested in other archaic poems, such as *Genesis A*, *Exodus*, and
Daniel, the presence of these metrical archaisms throughout *Beowulf* could
be accommodated to a disunity hypothesis, if one were to argue that all of
the discrete works comprising *Beowulf* were relatively early compositions.
The same cannot be said for the poem's adherence to Kaluza's law, which
distinguishes it even from *Genesis A*, the most conservative poem apart from
Beowulf with respect to metrical archaisms.[6] The exceptionally low incidence
of verses adhering to Kaluza's law in *Genesis A* appears to reflect a pattern
of avoidance induced by the poet's uncertainty about phonological opposi-

---

[6]   On the dating of *Genesis A* and its variety of archaic features, see Doane 2013:37–41;
HOEM:§§376–377; Cronan 2004; Neidorf 2013–2014.

tions that had recently collapsed (*HOEM*:§179). Because no other poem exhibits a knowledge of etymological length distinctions comparable to what is found in *Beowulf*, it is doubtful that *Beowulf* could consist of three or more separate poems. *Beowulf* is unique in its consistent correlation of resolution with etymology, maintained in subtle ways from the beginning to the end of the poem. In *nȳdwracu nīþgrim* (193a), the poet knows that the feminine ō-stem nominative singular is resolvable, whereas in *gearo gyrnwræce* (2118a), roughly two thousand lines later, the poet knows that the feminine ō-stem genitive singular is unresolvable. Knowledge of length distinctions in the prehistoric declension of the *i*-stem noun *cwide* is evinced first in *gilpcwide Gēates* (640a) and again twelve hundred lines later in differing metrical circumstances in *wīs wordcwida* (1845a). To all appearances, *Beowulf* seems to reflect one poet's coherent understanding of the phonology of his language and the ability of linguistic material to fill metrical positions.

§172. Another linguistic regularity in *Beowulf* that we should not expect to find if the poem had undergone extensive scribal recomposition is its pervasive use of unsyncopated verb endings (*-est*, *-eð*, *-ed*), a feature characteristic of Anglian compositions.[7] Unsyncopated forms occur throughout the transmitted text, and metrical considerations confirm that such forms are structurally required. Verses such as *sūþan scīneð* (606b), *gegān þenceð* (1535b), and *þæt þe gār nymeð* (1846b) would be rendered unmetrical if the syncopated verb forms characteristic of southern compositions (*scīnð*, *þyncð*, *nymð*) were substituted in place of the authorial forms. The consistent structural necessity of disyllabic forms from *beholen weorðeð* (414b) to *wīde weorðeð* (2913a) suggests that *Beowulf* reflects one Anglian poet's understanding of verb morphology and its relationship to metrical composition. Because the extant Old English poems of southern origin exhibit syncopated verb forms (*HOEM*:§§326–334)—for example *and þē sylfum dēmst* (87a) in *Judgement Day II*, where syncopation is metrically confirmed—it is improbable that late southern scribes should have substantially recomposed *Beowulf* without introducing this feature into the text. Remarkably, the only syncopated verb form transmitted in *Beowulf* is *cwið*, which appears in *þonne cwið æt bēore* (2041a) and *ond þæt word ācwyð* (2046b). *Beowulf* shares this ostensible peculiarity with the Vespasian Psalter, the purest representative of the Mercian dialect, where unsyncopated forms are the norm, with the sole exception of *cweðan* (*HOEM*:§353.12; *KB:Lang*. §25.1). The fact that syncopation in

---

[7]   Sievers's arguments (1884:273; 1885:464–475) for regarding this feature as an indicator of a poem's dialect of composition were validated in *HOEM*:§§318–375.

Beowulf is limited to a single verb known to have undergone syncopation in Mercian is a strong indication that *Beowulf* is one archaic Mercian poem transmitted with minimal scribal interference.

§173. The regularities discussed above suggest that scribes refrained from tampering with stressed lexemes, but there are also some telling signs in *Beowulf* that the scribes responsible for its transmission even refrained from introducing minor morphological changes into the text. *Beowulf* is unique in the corpus of Old English in its standard use of the archaic syntactic construction wherein a weak adjective modifies a noun without a determiner (i.e., a demonstrative or a possessive) preceding it.[8] The construction can be found throughout the poem, in verses such as *āngan dohtor* (375a, 2997b), *miclan dōmes* (978b), *bēahsele beorhta* (1177a), *Wīsa fengel* (1400b), *gamela Scylding* (1792a, 2105b), *herenīð hearda* (2474a), and *lǽnan līfes* (2845a). While the prevalence of this construction in any given work is a probable indicator of the work's antiquity, scholars have long recognized that its incidence cannot be used to establish a relative chronology, since this feature was particularly vulnerable to scribal alteration. The construction could often be obliterated without generating metrical defects: a scribe wishing to substitute the strong adjective form, for example, could alter *miclan dōmes* to *micles dōmes* without affecting the metrical structure of the verse. Studies of scribal variants in prose texts from Ashley C. Amos (1980:171–196) and Dorothy M. Horgan (1980) have, in fact, demonstrated that scribes occasionally tampered with relevant constructions in the texts they transmitted. The fact that the archaic use of the weak adjective was so vulnerable to scribal alteration makes its routine preservation in *Beowulf* all the more remarkable. The pervasive use of the weak adjective without a determiner in *Beowulf* suggests that its text might have enjoyed an exceptionally fortunate transmission, in which it never reached the hands of a scribe who would force its syntax to conform to later prose usage.

§174. The faithful adherence of *Beowulf* to Kuhn's law of sentence particles (*Satzpartikelgesetz*) provides another indication that the scribes who transmitted *Beowulf* could not have taken extensive liberties with its text.[9]

---

[8] The vast literature on this subject, originating with Lichtenheld (1873), is reviewed in Amos 1980:110–124. Amos doubts the chronological significance of this criterion, though she concedes that "*Beowulf* stands apart from the rest of Old English poetry and prose by its fairly standard use of the weak adjective without the definite article" (1980:124). The chronological significance of this feature has recently been reaffirmed in Fulk 2014:27–28 and Yoon 2014.

[9] The vast body of scholarship on the metrico-syntactic laws propounded in Kuhn (1933) is surveyed in Momma 1997. For a persuasive defense of the reality of Kuhn's law of sentence particles, see Donoghue 1997.

This law governs the metrical behavior of particles (i.e., words of variable stress, such as pronouns or finite verbs) by assigning ictus to them whenever they are displaced from the first drop of the verse clause. In its observance of this metrico-syntactic rule, *Beowulf* is, as Kuhn (1933) noted, the most conservative poem in any West Germanic language. Exceptions are exceedingly rare in *Beowulf*,[10] yet we should expect to find the text riddled with exceptions if scribes had substantially recomposed one-fifth of it, as Liuzza maintained. The ease with which exceptions could have been generated becomes apparent upon consideration of virtually any passage selected at random:

> Ne wæs þæt wyrd þā gen
> þæt hē mā mōste   manna cynnes
> ðicgean ofer þā niht.

> (734b–736a)

> That was no longer to be the case, that he would be able to feed on more of the human race beyond that night.

If a scribe had chosen to rearrange the order of the text in his exemplar, unmetrical verses and violations of Kuhn's law would have resulted. For example, if *wæs* were moved out of the first drop of the clause and placed after *gen*, it would receive ictus and thereby generate an unmetrical verse. Conversely, if a scribe moved *gen* into the drop by placing it before *þæt*, it would no longer be assigned ictus and the resulting verse would possess fewer than four metrical positions. The paucity of exceptions to Kuhn's law suggests that the scribes even restrained themselves from interpolating many function words of the semantically inconsequential sort into the text. Suppose that a scribe without an understanding of noncontraction sought to improve *on flett gæð* (2034b) by recomposing it as **on flett hē gæð*. The resulting verse would resemble an acceptable type B verse, but Kuhn's law would require ictus to be assigned to the interpolated *hē*, since it is displaced from the first drop of the clause. Opportunities to introduce violations of Kuhn's law abound, yet it is plain that the scribes refrained from taking them.

§175. Several syntactic regularities in *Beowulf* elevate the probability that it is a unified composition transmitted with limited scribal intervention. Because these regularities pertain to the poem's particular use of the

---

[10] On these exceptions, see Orton 1999. Many perceived exceptions to Kuhn's law actually demonstrate conformity to a complementary regularity, Pascual's law, which governs the metrical behavior of finite verbs (Pascual 2015).

conjunctions *siþþan* and *þā*, two proclitics prone to scribal alteration, they constitute further support for the notion that even minor features of the poem were preserved during its transmission. The most salient insight to emerge from Janet Bately's (1985) thorough study of the use of *siþþan* in the corpus of Old English poetry is that one particular construction is characteristic of *Beowulf*. With the exception of a passage in *The Dream of the Rood* (lines 48–49), the postponed use of *siþþan* to reveal a cause after its effect has been described is unique to *Beowulf*. A representative deployment of this *siþþan* construction occurs in the following passage:

> Denum eallum wæs,
> winum Scyldinga,   weorce on mōde
> tō geþolianne,   ðegne monegum,
> oncȳð eorla gehwǣm,   syðþan Æscheres
> on þām holmclife   hafelan mētton.

> 1417b–1421

> For all the Danes, friends of the Scyldings, it was painful to endure in their hearts, for many a thane, a distress to each of the men, when on the water-cliff they encountered Æschere's head.

Comparable passages exhibiting this suspenseful use of *siþþan* can be found throughout the poem (for example, lines 721–722, 1279–1282, 1588–1590, 2941b–2945). A similar tendency to invert temporal expectations is evident in the poem's *þā* ... *þā* constructions. Tom Shippey observed that in these constructions, the *Beowulf* poet consistently places the subordinate clause after the main clause, thereby reversing the expected order (i.e., 'when A did B, then A did C'), which is characteristic of prose texts and later poems like *The Battle of Maldon* (1993:177). Subtle syntactic regularities of this sort are best regarded as the linguistic consequences of the considered artistry of a single poet.

§176. *Beowulf* is also distinguished from the rest of the poetic corpus by its use of subordinating *þā* to mean "now that," a feature shared only with *Genesis A*. R. D. Fulk first observed this regularity and explained it as a linguistic archaism indicating that "subordinating *þā* had not yet developed a causal meaning separate from the temporal for the poet of either *Genesis A* or *Beowulf*" (2007c:625). The following passage provides a representative clause in which *þā* must be translated as "now that":

> þær him Hygd gebēad   hord ond rīce,
> bēagas ond bregostōl,   bearne ne truwode

þæt hē wið ælfylcum   ēþelstōlas
healdan cūðe,   ðā wæs Hygelāc dēad

2369–2372

there Hygd offered him treasury and rule, rings and throne; she did not
have confidence in her child that he would know how to hold his native
seats against foreigners, now that Hygelac was dead.

Because the regular use of *þā* in this manner is restricted to *Beowulf* and
Genesis A, the two poems with the highest incidence of metrical and lexical
archaisms, this semantic regularity should probably be construed as a sign of
chronological anteriority rather than of poetic idiosyncrasy. Nevertheless, the
presence of this regularity throughout *Beowulf* and the collateral absence of
uses of causal *þā* in which its temporal sense is dispensable (Fulk 2007c:627)
offer firm support for the unity of *Beowulf*. If *Beowulf* were three or more
discrete poems, we should not expect all of them to contain this syntactic
archaism. Similarly, it is doubtful that scribes could have substantially recomposed *Beowulf* without disturbing a subtle regularity involving precisely the
sort of function word that scribes felt licensed to alter or interpolate.

§177. Particularly compelling evidence for the scribal preservation of
minor features of the *Beowulf* poet's work is furnished in John D. Sundquist's
(2002) meticulous study of relative clause variation in *Beowulf*. Comparing
Beowulf with *Andreas*, *Maldon*, and the works of Cynewulf, Sundquist
analyzed the distribution of relative clauses introduced by the particle *þe*,
relative clauses introduced by a form of *sē*, and compound relative constructions with a combination of *sē* and *þe*. In this analysis, *Beowulf* was shown
to differ from the other works in several important respects, pertaining both
to the incidence of the relative clause types and the proximity of each clause
type to its antecedent. The most distinguishing feature of *Beowulf* is its
higher incidence of compound relative clauses introduced by both *sē* and *þe*,
which the poet tended to deploy with a distant antecedent. The construction
is exemplified twice in the passage cited below, first with *sē ðe* and again with
þone þe:

Swā mæg unfǣge   ēaðe gedīgan
wēan ond wræcsīð,   sē ðe waldendes
hyldo gehealdeþ.   Hordweard sōhte
georne æfter grunde,   wolde guman findan,
þone þe him on sweofote   sāre getēode

2291–2295

So a man if undoomed can readily survive distress and miserable plight who enjoys the ruler's favor. The hoard's keeper went looking intently over the ground, wanted to find the human who had caused it offense in its sleep.

The other poems contrast with *Beowulf* in exhibiting fewer of these constructions and a stronger preference for clauses with *þe* alone, which tend to be introduced in connection with an adjacent antecedent. Strong support for the unity of *Beowulf* therefore resides in the fact that the incidence of compound relative clauses with *sē* and *þe* remains stable throughout the poem: if *Beowulf* is divided into segments corresponding to the textual divisions maintained by Schücking and his followers, each segment can be seen to contain roughly the same proportion of these clauses (Sundquist 2002:264). Because this regularity involves the kind of linguistic variation of which speakers tend to be unconscious, it defies probability to regard its presence as anything other than a firm indication that *Beowulf* is the work of one poet, which was not substantially recomposed during its transmission.

§178. With respect to certain linguistic features, the unity of *Beowulf* is suggested not by the detection of singular qualities, but by the absence of signs of disunity. Daniel Donoghue's (1991) study of auxiliary verb usage in *Beowulf* found that no section of the poem differed consistently enough from any other section to justify credence in the hypothesis of composite authorship. Similarly, Klaus R. Grinda's (1984) survey of metrical and stylistic criteria pertaining to A3 verses, E verses, verbal stress, and alliterative line-linking turned up no firm evidence for the disunity of *Beowulf*. Divided into units corresponding to the hero's monster fights, the three sections of *Beowulf* often rank near to one another when the statistics from the poem are tabulated alongside those from the other long Old English poems (Grinda 1984:319–322). Thomas A. Bredehoft's (2014) catalogue of metrical and stylistic innovations also furnishes indirect evidence for the unity of *Beowulf*. Every poem known or conjectured to have been composed after 950 exhibits one or more salient innovations—for example verse rhyme, alliteration of *s* with *sc*, unclustered hypermetric lines, etc.—yet *Beowulf* exhibits no genuine examples of any of these features. If *Beowulf* represents an amalgamation of early and late poems, or an ancient poem that was thoroughly recomposed by eleventh-century scribes, it is remarkable that none of these innovations were introduced into its text. The absence of features that characterize late poems indicates that the entirety of *Beowulf* originated before such innovations entered into the poetic tradition.

§179. Lexical considerations provide a variety of decisive reasons to regard *Beowulf* as a unified composition. Words adduced in studies of the poem's antiquity constitute particularly strong evidence for its unity. An archaic lexical stratum consisting of words that appear to have become obsolete before the composition of ninth-century poetry and prose is preserved in *Beowulf*, *Genesis A*, *Exodus*, *Daniel*, *Maxims I*, and *Widsið* (Neidorf 2013–2014). The words that are attested only in one or more of these archaic works are not confined to one portion of *Beowulf*, but are distributed rather evenly throughout it. The point can be illustrated with *missere* 'half-year', whose restriction to *Beowulf*, *Genesis A*, and *Exodus* is a probable consequence of its early obsolescence (Cronan 2004:40; Neidorf 2013–2014:16–18). *Missere* can be found in the beginning, middle, and end of *Beowulf*, at 153b, 1498b, 1769b, and 2620b. A comparable distribution emerges for *fengel* 'ruler', a word whose restriction to *Beowulf* is also best explained as a result of obsolescence (Neidorf 2013–2014:30–31). *Fengel* is attested in both the Danish (1400b, 1475a) and the Geatish (2156a, 2345b) portions of the poem. Obviously, the presence of a simplex unique to *Beowulf* in passages separated by roughly one thousand lines supports the hypothesis that the same poet composed the entire work. Other words identified as probable archaisms occur throughout the poem: *gombe* 'tribute', appears in the beginning of the work (11a), *þengel* 'prince' falls in the middle (1507a), and *gædeling* 'kinsman, companion' is found towards its end (2617a, 2949b).[11]

§180. Semantic archaisms distributed throughout *Beowulf* lend further support to the notion that a single author's linguistic tendencies pervade the entire poem. *Beowulf* is distinct from much of the corpus of extant Old English literature in its preservation of earlier or etymological meanings of various words. In many cases, it is plain that the *Beowulf* poet composed before the development of theological overtones in homiletic discourse induced these words to lose their etymological meanings. The most salient semantic archaisms, noted by Fred C. Robinson, are *synn*, *fyren*, and *bealu*, which are used throughout *Beowulf* to denote "violence" or "hostility" rather than "sin" or "evil"; the words lack the theological connotations they possess in most other texts (1985:55–57). Dennis Cronan identified a similar pattern in the poem's preservation of the pre-Christian valences of *gylp*, *wlenco*, and *lofgeorn*: elsewhere, these are condemnatory terms for sinful behavior, but in *Beowulf* they possess positive connotations and refer to laudable

---

[11] For the rationale behind regarding these words as lexical archaisms see Cronan 2004:29, 40–41 and Neidorf 2013–2014:14, 16–18, 31–32.

aspects of heroic life (2003:400–401). To these words can be added *hrēow*, which, as Tom Shippey pointed out, consistently denotes "sorrow" rather than "penance," the meaning it came to possess in theological contexts (1993:173–175). Rafael J. Pascual (2014) likewise observed that *scucca* and *þyrs* are not yet terms for spiritual demons or devils, but must instead refer to the material monsters of Germanic folklore. The presence of these related semantic archaisms throughout *Beowulf* indicates that the entire work was composed prior to a variety of semantic shifts resulting from the institutional development of a Christian vernacular discourse.[12]

§181. Other linguistic regularities in *Beowulf* await identification in future studies, but the features enumerated above are sufficient to demonstrate that the poem is a unified composition. The entirety of *Beowulf* is both internally consistent and distinct from other works in its meter, syntax, phonology, morphology, lexicon, and semantics. Hypotheses of composite authorship or scribal recomposition appear improbable in the light of these regularities, which we should not expect to find if *Beowulf* contained substantial contributions from more than one author. The notion that *Beowulf* cannot be dated, or must be regarded as a late composition, because it might contain chronologically disparate strata—an argument most recently propounded by Audrey L. Meaney (2003:65–73)—appears especially untenable upon recognition of the fact that features indicative of archaic composition are distributed evenly throughout the poem. Close attention to the language of *Beowulf* leaves little room for doubt that the entire poem is the work of one archaic poet. Linguistic regularities indicate that the scribes responsible for the transmission of *Beowulf* did not substantially recompose the work they copied. The evidence suggests, contrary to recent theoretical scholarship, that scribes painstakingly preserved the poem's structural features, making no attempt to update or recontextualize the text beyond the modernization and Saxonization of its orthography. It is therefore more reasonable to regard *Beowulf* as a unified archaic poem than as anything else.

3. Methodological Considerations

§182. Direct examination of the linguistic evidence is the most reliable method for determining the relative probability of competing hypotheses

---

[12] Scott Gwara (2012) has identified another semantic archaism in *Beowulf*: the poem's consistent use of *giedd* in its etymological sense as a term for prophetic speech.

concerning the unity of *Beowulf*. When undertaken, such an examination effectively settles the question by identifying regularities whose presence cannot be adequately explained under hypotheses of composite authorship or scribal recomposition. Settling the question on an empirical basis will fail to persuade some observers, however, if various methodological barriers to credence in the hypothesis of unified archaic composition are not alleviated. The present section thus aims to address several methodological issues relevant to research on the transmission and unity of *Beowulf*. Its argumentation distinguishes sound methodological practices from unsound ones, in order to illustrate why the unitary hypothesis demands credence from reasonable observers. The issues raised here are, of course, also distinctly relevant to the textual study of Old English poems other than *Beowulf*. There is nothing less at stake here than the contemporary understanding of Anglo-Saxon literary and cultural history in general, constructed as it is upon a matrix of assumptions about the dating and transmission of poetic works. If obscurantist argumentation persuades scholars to withhold credence from the conclusions of philological scholarship, research will be vitiated and the advancement of knowledge will be impeded.

§183. The evidential basis for Liuzza's argument that scribes recomposed more than one-fifth of *Beowulf* in the course of its transmission is worth examining. Significantly, his argument is not premised upon the detection of linguistic or narrative inconsistencies in *Beowulf*; no internal evidence for such massive scribal intervention is offered. If *Beowulf* exhibits no compelling signs of disunity, why would it be rational to believe that scribes thoroughly recomposed it? Liuzza maintained this belief by interpreting the variant readings in parallel texts of Old English poems as evidence for routine intervention, with scribes purportedly producing substantial variants in approximately one-fifth (21.6%) of the verses they transmitted (1995:293). This statistic, which obscures the fact that the vast majority of these variants are metrically and semantically inconsequential, was shown to be erroneous when it was subjected to critical scrutiny (Fulk 2003:16–22). The analysis of textual variation conducted in the preceding chapter of this book identified additional reasons why Liuzza's basic interpretation of the evidence is untenable. The notion that variant readings in poems like *Daniel* and *Azarias* or *Soul and Body I* and *II* reflect the regular practice of Anglo-Saxon scribes can no longer be assumed, since it has been shown that variants in these texts stem from nonscribal sources, such as codicological damage and poetic revisers (§§142–144). Outside of these exceptional texts, variants tend to be irrelevant or detectable, involving the protraction of drops or the accidental replacement of authorial lexemes with inauthentic words of similar appearance (§§145–151).

§184. Closer examination of the corpus of parallel texts does not inspire confidence in the notion that there was an "Old English scribal tradition" (Liuzza 1995:291) wherein scribes introduced variants into the texts they transmitted with equal regularity. If one were to regard the variants in *Daniel* and *Azarias* as evidence for scribal practice, it should be obvious that these variants are of an entirely different character from those discernible in the parallel texts of *Solomon and Saturn I*. Similarly, the collection of minor variants in *Solomon and Saturn I* distinguishes its transmission from that of *The Gloria I*, whose parallel texts are nearly identical. The corpus of parallel texts therefore indicates that it would be a grave error to begin one's study of any given Old English poem with the a priori assumption that scribes substantially recomposed it during its transmission. The extant texts of *The Battle of Brunanburh*, for example, exhibit no amount of textual divergence comparable to what is found in *Soul and Body* or *Daniel* and *Azarias*. The assumption that variants in *Soul and Body* reveal the character and extent of undetectable variation in *Beowulf* and other works preserved in unique manuscript copies is plainly mistaken, since it is evident that many parallel texts do not exhibit comparable forms of variation.[13] Credence in Liuzza's argument thus requires one to overlook the findings of O'Donnell's (1996) comprehensive study of the variant readings in parallel texts. In particular, it requires one to ignore O'Donnell's conclusion that "the scribes did not take any specifically 'poetic' approach to the constituent verse" and that extensive variation in poetic texts was not an inevitable development during their transmission (1996:431).

---

[13] These considerations incidentally expose some errors of reasoning in the work of Moffat (1992), who argued on the basis of variants in *Soul and Body* that we should assume every extant poem to have received similar treatment at the hands of scribes. Moffat's conclusion, anticipating the argument of Liuzza, is summarized in the following remark: "What I am suggesting here is the possibility, indeed, the likelihood, that the Old English poetical manuscripts, because of the complex nature of scribal performance, are textured or layered in a way that demands an adjustment in the way we treat them. They should not be looked at, at least initially, as 'coherent' texts, that is, the unified product of a single mind.... Rather, the possibility must be faced that they are composite products of two, or very likely more, minds which were not necessarily working towards the same end" (1992:826). It should be noted that Moffat's understanding of scribal behavior differs considerably from that of O'Brien O'Keeffe and others, in that he regards the scribal contribution as generally detrimental, but he nevertheless believes it to be spontaneous and undetectable, because he attributes all of the variants in the parallel texts of *Soul and Body* to scribes. It appears altogether doubtful that the lexical variants in the Vercelli Book, which form the basis of Moffat's argument, should originate with a scribe rather than with the poet who revised and augmented an earlier *Soul and Body* poem.

§185. Erroneous beliefs about scribal behavior and textual transmission appear to stem in large part from the desire to undermine the conclusions of philological scholarship pertaining to the absolute and relative chronology of Old English poetry. Liuzza's argument for the scribal recomposition of *Beowulf* was given impetus not by the detection of linguistic inconsistencies, but by his conviction that scribal intervention should have obliterated the linguistic features that could enable scholars to determine its date of composition. The mere possibility of scribal recomposition, in his view, casts doubt upon "any argument which supposes that the linguistic and metrical details of a poem remained substantially unaltered during the course of its transmission" (1995:294). Liuzza thus aimed to deprive linguistic and metrical regularities in *Beowulf* of chronological significance by arguing that we should not expect to find such regularities in the text, even though we do actually find them. Methodologically unsound reasoning is apparent in this train of thought, as Fulk observed:

> This is illogical: when regularities occur in the data, the rational response is not 'These regularities are invalid because they ought not to occur'—that is properly absurd—but 'What is the most plausible explanation for these regularities?' The claim that scribal change should render it impossible to detect significant metrical differences among poems lacks both sense and relevance if regular differences do occur. And they do: this point is apparently not in dispute, as it is conceded by Liuzza.
>
> 2003:22

Reasoning similar to Liuzza's is evident in the work of Amos (1980:167–170), when she maintains that the uncertainties of scribal transmission undercut the validity of various dating criteria. Her objection has little relevance to the dating of a work such as *Beowulf*, which exhibits an array of linguistic archaisms, since it is plain that such features have not been obliterated during its transmission. Scribal recomposition could lead scholars to mistake an archaic poem for a late poem, but it could never cause a late poem to be mistaken for an archaic one (*HOEM*:§33). That is to say, scribes might well obliterate a work's adherence to Kaluza's law or diminish its regular use of the weak adjective without a determiner, but they surely could not introduce such features into a text that originally did not possess them. Because the archaic qualities of *Beowulf* were evidently preserved during its transmission, the possibility that scribes might have eliminated linguistic archaisms poses no grave danger to our estimation of the poem's date of composition. Indeed, it is possible that scribes removed archaic features from *Beowulf* that would require us to date it even earlier, but it would make little sense to invest credence in such a possibility without compelling reasons to do so.

§186. There is a noticeable chasm between beliefs about the possible extent of scribal intervention and the evidence for scribal behavior, in the form of erasures and corrections, in the extant manuscript of *Beowulf*. To be sure, the extant manuscript sheds light on the methods and concerns of only the two final scribes, but if these scribes did not substantially recompose the text, that is sufficient to invalidate the assertion that the composition of *Beowulf* was effectively contemporary with the production of its extant manuscript. Kiernan's arguments to this effect have been refuted at length (§137), but Liuzza articulated a similar claim when he contended that routine scribal recomposition was so thorough that "the only meaningful date for the 'effective composition' of *Beowulf* is that of the manuscript" (1995:294–295). If the scribes of Cotton Vitellius A.xv substantially recomposed one-fifth of *Beowulf* while copying it, it is remarkable that their creative interventions left no paleographical traces. Erasures and alterations are discernible throughout the extant manuscript, yet these uniformly function to correct mechanical errors or regularize spellings.[14] Nowhere in the manuscript is there evidence that the scribes rejected words of authorial origin and replaced them with graphically dissimilar words of their own. For example, we never find *dryhten* erased and replaced with *cyning*, nor do we find *guma* erased and replaced with *rinc*, or anything like that. Representative of both scribes' tendencies, rather, are the alterations of *sæde* to *sægde* (90b), *wlocn* to *wlonc* (331b), *ængum* to *ænigum* (793b), *findaan* to *findan* (1378b), *fāc* to *fāh* (2217a), *bil* to *bill* (2777b), and *þīo* to *þīow* (2961a). These alterations indicate that our scribes felt licensed to alter only the orthographical form, not the lexical identity, of antecedent readings. Scribal intervention appears to have been limited to the modernization and Saxonization of earlier spellings.

§187. The textual corruptions discussed throughout the preceding chapters of this book corroborate the constrained interpretation of scribal behavior suggested by the trivial character of the manuscript's erasures and alterations. Most of the corrupt readings in the transmitted text of *Beowulf* exhibit considerable graphemic overlap with the authorial readings that must have preceded them. This is evident, for example, in the corruptions of *wærc* into *weorc* (§60), *feðer* into *fæder* (§65), *hæle* into *helle* (§78), *eafoð* into *earfoð* (§77), *nefne* into *næfre* (§61), *dēoð* into *þēod* (§54), *læn* into *lēan*

---

[14] The scribal self-alterations, enumerated in Orchard 2003–2004:68–75, are discussed in depth elsewhere in the present book: see §§22, 44, 56, 66, 102, 110, 112–116. For illustrations of this phenomenon see figures 1–5 (chap. 2), 7 (chap. 3).

(§50), *Ēomēr* into *geōmor* (§91), *Ūnferð* into *Hūnferð* (§92), *Hrēðrīc* into *hrēðrinc* (§94), *Scilfingas* into *scildingas* (§101), and *Ēotum* into *eotenum* (§§103–104). The consistent presence of graphemic overlap in these cases makes it clear that the text's corruptions cannot be regarded as evidence for the view that scribes spontaneously altered antecedent readings in order to participate in literary creation. The close resemblance between corrupt readings and authorial readings indicates that errors were introduced into the text in the course of a mechanical effort to transmit the poem accurately and preserve its structural characteristics. Historical processes of linguistic and cultural change made it difficult for the scribes to modernize and Saxonize the text's orthography without misconstruing the lexical identity of antecedent readings and accidentally generating corruptions. Errors in the extant manuscript of *Beowulf* thus reflect the difficulties experienced by scribes transmitting a work composed long before they were born. Such errors are not signs of creative intervention.

§188. The notion that the scribal contribution to the transmission of *Beowulf* could be both massive and undetectable is rendered doubtful by the one instance in the extant manuscript where a word arising directly from the mind of one of the final scribes can be identified. The interpolation appears in the transmitted version of the following passage:

>   Meoduscencum hwearf
> geond þæt [heal]reced   Hæreðes dohtor,
> lufode ðā lēode   līðwæge bær
> hæleðum tō handa.

>   1980b–1983a

> Hæreth's daughter wound her way through the house with mead-vessels,
> treated the people kindly, brought drinking cups to the heroes' hands.

The scribe initially transmitted verse 1981a as *geond þæt reced*, a sequence deficient in both meter and alliteration. In response either to his perception of the verse's formal defects or his recognition that the exemplar was damaged, the scribe inserted the word *sīde* 'broad' in superscript between *þæt* and *reced* (figure 8). Julius Zupitza observed: "*sīde* added over the line in the same hand I think, but with another ink; a stop shows where it is to be inserted" (1959:91). The resulting verse, *geond þæt sīde reced*, makes adequate sense, but it remains transparently defective, since it fails to alliterate with the off-verse, *Hæreðes dohtor*. The scribe evidently could not think of a word capable of repairing both the metrical and alliterative defects, such as *heal-*, which editors routinely supply after deleting *sīde* from the text. The ineptitude of the scribe's effort to repair the verse casts the gravest doubt upon the idea that this scribe could have freely recomposed the poet's work without introducing obvious defects into the text. Whenever the scribes altered the substance of the antecedent text—whether out of confusion, whim, or an earnest desire to repair lacunae—traces of their intervention are evident in the aberrations that result. It should be plain by now that substantial and undetectable scribal recomposition cannot be assumed with regard to *Beowulf*. The hypothesis of unity demands credence, and its overwhelming credibility has important methodological consequences for the practice of textual criticism and for our understanding of the poem's relationship to its manuscript context.

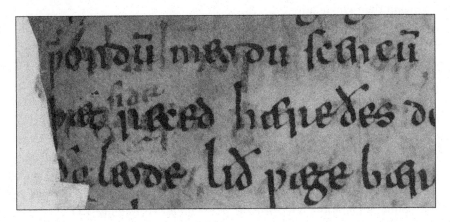

Figure 8. Scribal interpolation of *sīde* before *reced*, line 1981a (fol. 176v).

4. Textual Criticism

§189. The critical effort to detect scribal errors and restore authorial readings in the text of *Beowulf* would be severely undermined if scribes substantially recomposed the poem they copied. Textual criticism depends first upon the identification of spurious readings that constitute aberrations from the poem's norms, and then upon our ability to determine the antecedent reading that can remove such aberrations from the text (§§15–21). If *Beowulf* were a heterogeneous accretion, this enterprise could hardly be undertaken, since the poem would then have few features that characterize the entirety of its text. Yet it has been demonstrated above that numerous linguistic regularities pervade *Beowulf* and distinguish it from other extant poems. This demonstration corroborates the lexemic theory of scribal behavior and validates the hypothesis that *Beowulf* is a single archaic composition transmitted with minimal interference. Credence in the lexemic theory and the unity of *Beowulf* strengthens conviction, in turn, in the editorial effort to identify corruptions and recover genuine readings. The scribes responsible for the poem's transmission evidently strove to preserve its structural characteristics, while limiting their intervention to the orthographical form of each word they transmitted. *Beowulf* thus remains a more or less integral whole, with an array of individual words accidentally corrupted as the scribes modified their spellings. Because *Beowulf* retained its integrity, the corruptions that entered its text generate aberrations that facilitate their detection and demand their emendation.

§190. Recognition of authorial regularities preserved in *Beowulf* enables the textual critic to affirm with confidence that certain readings in the transmitted text could not reflect the compositional practices of the poet. For example, the poet's strict fidelity to the rules governing the construction of expanded type D* verses renders it improbable that the few defective D* verses in the transmitted text are genuine.[15] The improbability of their authenticity is elevated by the invariable presence of an obvious impetus for corruption in each defective verse (*KB:T.C.* §§30–31). Because expanded D* verses contain five metrical positions (typically SxSsx), classical poets restricted them to the on-verse and signaled this metrical license by means of double alliteration. The *Beowulf* poet composed roughly 150 D* verses adhering to these rules (Bliss 1967:123), distributed throughout his work, such as *mǣre mearcstapa* (103a), *sīde sǣnassas* (223a), *eorlum ealuscerwen* (769a), *scēotend Scyldinga* (1154a), *drēfan dēop wæter* (1904a), *helpan hildfruman* (2649a), and *sōhte searonīðas* (3067a). In light of this regularity, there can be little doubt that the verse transmitted as *ymbesittendra* (2734a) is not genuine, since it lacks double alliteration. Obviously, a scribe replaced *ymb-* with *ymbe-*, whose additional syllable created a fifth metrical position, thereby corrupting the authorial *ymbsittendra*, a standard type D verse that does not require double alliteration. Likewise, because the transmitted *wīca nēosian* (1125b) scans as a D* verse with single alliteration in the off-verse, it is clear that *nēosian* is a scribal substitute for *nēosan*, and that the genuine verse is *wīca nēosan*, a standard type A verse transmitted elsewhere in the manuscript (125b). Every defective D* verse in the extant manuscript can be

---

[15] For the essential scholarship on D* verses see §51, n. 8 above.

explained as a consequence of the lexemic approach to transmission. *Bēow Scyldinga* (53b) was corrupted into the dubious D* verse *Bēowulf Scyldinga* because a scribe presumed the name of the Danish progenitor to be an erroneous form of the name of the Geatish protagonist. *Ofost wīsode* (1663b) became the implausible D* verse *oftost wīsode* through the corruption of the authorial lexeme into a genuine word of similar appearance. The rules governing the construction of D* verses assist the effort to detect and emend corruptions in several other cases.[16]

§191. Deviations from the authorial norm in the transmitted text of *Beowulf* consistently result from minor changes made to individual words. The corruptions discussed throughout this book have demonstrated that the scribes responsible for the transmission of *Beowulf*, like many other Anglo-Saxon scribes, concentrated entirely on the orthographic form of the present lexeme while copying. Reading isolated words rather than continuous texts, these scribes paid little attention to the sense or meter of what they copied. Their job was to modernize and Saxonize the orthography of the text, not to discern its formal qualities or interpret its deeper meaning. The validation of the lexemic theory, effected through its ability to explain a wide array of phenomena in the Old English poetic manuscripts, disposes of several arguments frequently marshaled when scholars call for the retention of suspected corruptions. Perhaps the most common assumption rendered untenable by the lexemic theory is that a reading's authenticity is ensured by the fact that it survived the scrutiny of the scribes. It has been periodically maintained since the work of Johannes Hoops (1932a:9) that metrically defective verses should not be emended because the scribes must have judged them formally acceptable according to their own standards.[17] Lines lacking alliteration have been defended on the same grounds. Wilhelm G. Busse, for example, contended that such lines "were evidently acceptable as such for the scribe and, it may be supposed, for a contemporary audience as well" (1981:202). Studying the transmission of *Beowulf* undermines the credibility of such reasoning by revealing the labors of scribes who focused exclusively on the acceptability of the text's orthography, not its metrics or alliteration.

---

[16] For other corruptions that generate spurious D* verses, see §§45, 51, 81, 86. Additional discussion of the corruptions mentioned in the paragraph above can be found in §§68, 81–82, 89–90.

[17] This argument is widespread in conservative textual criticism: Kiernan, for example, defends the authenticity of several corruptions by asserting that the scribes would not have transmitted spurious readings that disturb the formal regularities of the work (1981:186–188). Such a defense necessarily shares Hoops's assumption that the scribes pondered questions of meter and alliteration while performing their mechanical task. See also Niles 1994 and Taylor and Davis 1982.

The many corruptions that result in transparent nonsense render it doubtful in the extreme that these scribes experienced the poem they transcribed as a coherent work with formal properties, rather than as a series of discrete lexemes. The fact that the 150 scribal self-corrections discernible in the manuscript are concerned entirely with matters of spelling is an unambiguous declaration of the occupational interests of these scribes.

§192. The validation of the lexemic theory requires the reformation of text-critical discourse in another crucial respect: arguments for the emendation or retention of suspected corruptions can no longer derive much support from considerations of the apparent accuracy or conscientiousness of an individual scribe. Scholars have recently sought to elevate the authority of the Old English poetic manuscripts by regarding erasures and corrections in them as evidence for the meticulousness of the copyists who produced them (see, for example, Muir 2005). Kiernan doubted that the transmitted text of *Beowulf* could exhibit much corruption, since the scribes' sporadic modification of their work purportedly indicated that "the *Beowulf* MS was subjected to intelligent scrutiny" (1981:191). Yet it is now clear that the scribal concentration on orthographic form did not safeguard the text from corruption: this practice merely ensured that most of the transmitted corruptions happen to possess the form of genuine lexemes. The diligence of the scribe does not guarantee the authenticity of the text. The scribe who corrupted *Bēow* into *Bēowulf* was probably a conscientious scribe alert to the errors committed by antecedent copyists, but his personal qualities cannot be imagined to increase the probability that the poet composed a verse like *Bēowulf Scyldinga*. Judgments as to whether a scribe was "good" or "bad" are not necessarily relevant to questions of textual criticism: *Wīca nēosian* is a corrupt verse, but the scribe who transmitted it can be considered a competent scribe. His job was to regularize spellings in the text, so he frequently altered *nēosan* to *nēosian* without regard for the metrical defects generated thereby. The scribe is competent, but the text is implausible. The two considerations have little to do with each other.

§193. The common understanding of the notion of scribal error must therefore be reconsidered in the light of the lexemic theory and the transmission of *Beowulf*. The introduction of error into the transmitted text is often regarded as a random and unpredictable phenomenon related to human frailty. Many critics appear to believe that erroneous forms are committed to parchment only when fatigue or carelessness induces the otherwise reliable scribe to stray. This belief is expressed whenever a scholar defends two identical corruptions on the grounds that a scribe is unlikely to have committed the same error twice. Such arguments are common in *Beowulf* textual criticism, where they have been deployed in defense of such implausibilities as *Bēowulf Scyldinga* and the presence of giants in the Finnsburh episode.[18] It should be clear by now that the serial alteration of *Bēow* to *Bēowulf* or *Ēotum* to *eotenum* is not a random development, but is rather a principled consequence of the lexemic approach to transmission. When the scribes processed discrete lexemes in their exemplar, conscious deliberation informed their decisions about how to modernize, Saxonize, or correct forms that were perceived to be nonstandard or erroneous. It is therefore no surprise that such deliberation should have resulted in the transmission of the same corruption multiple times. Many corruptions occur in more than one place in the transmitted text: *wrætte* was twice corrupted into *wræce* (§18), *eafoð* was twice corrupted into *earfoð* (§77), *ondslyht* and *ondlēan* were twice corrupted into *hondslyht* and *hondlēan* (§80), *wærc* was corrupted three times into *weorc* (§60), and *Ūnferð* was corrupted four times in *Hūnferð* (§92). The scribal substitution of *nēosian* for *nēosan* engendered three corrupt verses (§68), while the scribal inflection of uninflected infinitives spoiled the meter on five occasions (§45). Analogical restoration of syncopated vowels (e.g., the alteration of *secga ǣngum* to *secga ǣnigum*) produced no fewer than eight unmetrical verses (§66). Corruptions are not random, but they remain corruptions, insofar as that term denotes forms or verses that cannot plausibly reflect the compositional practices of the *Beowulf* poet.

§194. Because scribal alterations no longer appear to be the arbitrary expressions of the subjectivity of individual scribes, the implications of the lexemic theory extend to the textual criticism of the rest of the Old English poetic corpus as well. The presence of identical corruptions in multiple manuscripts—the examples are manifold[19]—indicates that the scribes who produced these codices were trained professionals with similar aims. They were engaged in a collective enterprise of modernizing and Saxonizing the orthography of a corpus of predominantly Anglian poetic texts, many of which had been composed one to three centuries earlier. Consequently, corruptions in these texts often stem from the methodical deliberation of

---

[18]   See for example Earl 1994:22–25; Kaske 1967:287; Tupper 1910:170; and Vickrey 2009:34.

[19]   For example, corruptions resulting from the substitution of LWS *gehwǣre* (for *gehwǣm*) and the scribal inflection of uninflected infinitives are found in the *Beowulf* manuscript and the other poetic codices; see §47. The corruption of *wærc* into *weorc* is found in the transmitted text of several works beside *Beowulf*; see Fulk 2004. The substitution of LWS *dydon* for *dēdon* generates corrupt verses in multiple poetic texts; see Sievers 1885:498; *HOEM*:§355.4. Other errors in the poetic codices similar to those found in the *Beowulf* manuscript are discussed in §§154–157 above.

scribes and cannot be defended on the grounds that accidents should not happen twice. To return to the faulty rhymes in the text of Cynewulf's *Elene* transmitted in the Vercelli Book (§§130–131), defenses of their authenticity have been erected upon the claim that scribes are unlikely to have introduced the same corruption multiple times (Rogers 1971; Stanley 1993). Pointing to defective rhymes that result from the substitution of southern forms in *Christ II* (from the Exeter Book) and *Judith* (from the *Beowulf* manuscript), Patrick W. Conner argued for the authorial creation of these faulty rhymes by reasoning: "I do not think it very probable that the three scribes in question would have all changed Anglian forms in the same way" (1996:33). The improbabilities generated by such reasoning are considerable: if one were to credit Conner's argument, one would have to believe that numerous poets coincidentally composed unmetrical verses only when they contained *gehwǣre*, *dydon*, or inflected infinitives. The appearance in multiple poetic manuscripts of unmetrical verses resulting from precisely these forms indicates that scribal alterations reflect the imperatives of an institutional program, not an individual's subjectivity. It is therefore entirely to be expected that three or more discrete scribes would have obliterated Anglian rhymes through the substitution of southern forms. We are dealing here with an impersonal phenomenon.

5. Manuscript Context

§195. The unity of *Beowulf* and the lexemic approach to its transmission have important implications for our understanding of the poem's manuscript context and its place in literary history. Because *Beowulf* essentially remains the unified work of an archaic Mercian poet, it is methodologically suspect to interpret the poem in the eleventh century merely because its extant manuscript copy happened to be produced at that time. Linguistic regularities in *Beowulf* and paleographical evidence in the manuscript align to confirm that the scribes who produced the extant manuscript did not substantially recompose the poem. *Beowulf* was not adapted or recontextualized for its eleventh-century audience. To the contrary, *Beowulf* was transmitted with minimal interference, with the result that it still retains the structural characteristics it possessed when it was first committed to parchment in Mercia around the year 700. Consequently, the date of the *Beowulf* manuscript is no more relevant to the interpretation of the poem than the dates of Carolingian or Renaissance manuscripts are to the interpretation of the classical works they preserve. Little would be gained, and much would be lost, if scholars insisted on interpreting Catullus's poetry in the fourteenth-century context of its earliest extant manuscripts rather than in the late Roman Republic context of its composition. By the same token, interpretations of *Beowulf* should be situated in an early Mercian context if they are to be persuasive and historically plausible.

§196. Recently, scholars have come to believe that the tenth- and eleventh-century dates of the extant poetic manuscripts provide a secure basis for situating interpretations of Old English poetry "in the late Anglo-Saxon period, the period in which we know the poems to have been read" (Magennis 1996:5). An assumption essential to the validity of this practice is that the corpus of Old English poetry was linguistically and culturally transparent to the readers of its late southern manuscripts. The present study has demonstrated, however, that linguistic and cultural changes rendered a substantial portion of *Beowulf* unintelligible to the scribes who transmitted it. Corruptions of archaisms, Anglianisms, and proper names pervade the transmitted text of the poem, which often exhibits manifest nonsense as a result. If scholars feel impelled to reconstruct the reading experience of eleventh-century Anglo-Saxons who held the *Beowulf* manuscript, the difficulties that engendered these corruptions should form the central focus of their reconstruction. To read an edited text of *Beowulf*, which contains roughly three hundred emendations, in an eleventh-century context is to engage in a practice that is firmly ahistorical, since it is certain that late audiences did not have access to that cleanly legible text. An interpretation of *Beowulf* reliant upon a nuanced understanding of its language and a deep grasp of its constituent heroic-legendary traditions is an interpretation belonging to the period of its composition, not the period of its reception. Such an interpretation appears to have become a historical impossibility by the eleventh century.

§197. To be sure, there is much to be learned from paying close attention to the extant poetic manuscripts and the unedited texts they transmit. The present study has demonstrated that the *Beowulf* manuscript is a valuable source of information for the history of the English language and the changing nature of Anglo-Saxon culture. The corruptions that pervade the manuscript offer fascinating insights into the difficulties that late Anglo-Saxons experienced while wrestling with the text of a poem composed more than two centuries before they were born. Confronting this text without the wealth of scholarly resources available to a modern editor, the scribes often had little choice but to alter unfamiliar names and lexemes into common words of similar appearance in their desperate effort to produce a legible text. Because the corruptions in the manuscript relate so frequently to processes of linguistic and cultural change, they cannot be disregarded as the random by-products of scribal carelessness. The *Beowulf* manuscript tells us much more about the impersonal and inexorable movements of history than it does about the relative merits of its final scribes. The corruptions bear eloquent witness to the manifold changes that took place in England during the three centuries separating the period of the poem's composition from the period of its extant manuscript.

Appendix

J. R. R. TOLKIEN'S *BEOWULF* TEXTUAL CRITICISM

Two major events in *Beowulf* textual scholarship took place in the decade prior to this book's publication. The first of these events was the publication in 2008 of the fourth edition of Klaeber's *Beowulf*, edited by Robert D. Fulk, Robert E. Bjork, and John D. Niles. This edition immediately and deservedly became the scholarly standard, and its invaluable contribution to textual scholarship is signaled by the numerous references to *KB* that pervade the present book.[1] Virtually every textual problem is addressed there, and readers are provided with balanced assessments of the relative merits of competing solutions. On many textual difficulties, the book provides a definitive account of the reasons why emendation is either necessary or superfluous, with the result that a reference to *KB* often directs the reader to a summation of the entire scholarly tradition. The comprehensiveness of the fourth edition represents the successful continuation of the editorial and pedagogical aims of Frederick Klaeber (1863–1954), whose earlier editions of the poem digested a century of philological scholarship and transmitted the fruits of what had been a largely German tradition to generations of Anglophone scholars.[2] For newcomers to *Beowulf* textual scholarship, the fourth edition of Klaeber's *Beowulf* performs the indispensable service of rendering accessible both the earlier philological tradition and every significant advance of the past century. The value of this service may increase in the coming years, on account of the other major recent event, which is likely to cause more than a few individuals to develop a newfound interest in *Beowulf* textual scholarship.

[1] For an appreciative assessment of Klaeber's *Beowulf* from its first edition to its fourth edition, see Shippey 2009.

[2] Klaeber's editorial perspective and pedagogical concerns are assessed in Fulk 2007f.

J. R. R. Tolkien's *Beowulf: A Translation and Commentary*, edited from his unpublished papers by his son Christopher, appeared in the middle of 2014 and came to my attention only after a complete draft of the present book had been composed. Because the views of the most celebrated Anglo-Saxonist and fantasy author of the twentieth century will possess special interest for many readers, I decided not to incorporate Tolkien's conclusions piecemeal into my book, but instead to compose this appendix, which summarizes his general views on the transmission of *Beowulf* and assesses his positions on various textual issues relevant to my arguments. In Old English studies, Tolkien's best-known work is his 1936 lecture to the British Academy, "*Beowulf*: The Monsters and the Critics," a work of literary criticism that has exerted unparalleled influence on the interpretation of the poem. Yet Tolkien identified himself principally as a philologist, not a literary critic, so an estimation of his prowess in textual criticism may help to balance contemporary understanding of the character of his medieval scholarship.[3] Such estimation is only now possible, on account of the publication of the lectures on *Beowulf* that Tolkien delivered during his tenure as Rawlinson and Bosworth Professor of Anglo-Saxon at Oxford University (1925–1945). Christopher's decision to print these lectures as the commentary accompanying his father's translation was sound, since they are as much concerned with textual criticism as they are with literary interpretation.[4] Beyond the insights they afford into Tolkien's medieval scholarship, the lectures also contain many astute observations and intriguing suggestions worth assimilating into mainstream textual scholarship on *Beowulf*.

Tolkien's general understanding of the transmission of *Beowulf* accords remarkably well with conclusions reached in recent philological research, which are supported and extended in the present book. Though he nowhere presents the evidence behind this conclusion—it fell upon subsequent generations of scholars to assemble and analyze the full range of evidence—Tolkien has no doubt that *Beowulf* is a Mercian poem that was composed and committed to parchment in the first half of the eighth century. Toward

---

[3] Because his lecture inspired much scholarship that might be characterized as formalist, some scholars have mistakenly regarded Tolkien as a practitioner of "New Criticism"; for correctives, see Drout 2011 and Branchaw 2014.

[4] Christopher Tolkien notes in his preface: "He did indeed explicitly intend that the series of lectures on *Beowulf* which I have used in this book should be a 'textual commentary', closely concerned with verbal detail.... [T]he lectures in question were addressed to an audience of students whose work on Old English was in part based on the demanding language of *Beowulf*, and his purpose was to elucidate and illuminate, often in precise detail, that part of the original text that was prescribed for study" (2014:viii–ix).

the beginning of the commentary, the *Beowulf* poet is described as "a man of the West Marches" (2014:150) and the extensive duration of the work's transmission is laid out in unambiguous terms: "Our manuscript is c. 1000, something like 250 years after the poem was made" (2014:146).[5] As will be seen below, much of Tolkien's textual criticism rests upon the argument that linguistic and cultural changes that took place during the three centuries of the poem's transmission resulted in the trivialization of obsolete words and the obliteration of long-forgotten proper names. By consistently relating textual problems to diachronic change, Tolkien went considerably further than many of his contemporaries in anticipating the conclusions of this book and seeing the larger picture that emerges when many similar corruptions are studied alongside one another. Although a handful of Tolkien's arguments can no longer be credited, the problems surrounding a few particulars should not substantially detract from our appreciation of the accuracy of his views in general.

The notion that corruptions result from scribal unfamiliarity with legendary material known to the poet and his original audience is articulated several times in Tolkien's commentary. Discussing the corruption of *Bēow* (18a, 53b) into *Bēowulf*, Tolkien suggests that during the lifetime of the two scribes, "knowledge of the legendary and old dynastic matter had grown dim" (2014:146). The point is reiterated in a later discussion, where Tolkien writes: "By the time our late copy of *Beowulf* was made, the ancient traditions were already becoming dim, and since they were obscure to copyists, references to them were liable to corruption" (2014:237–238). On the question of Beow's presence in the poem, Tolkien takes the position adopted in the present book (§§89–90). He regards the alignment of metrical and genealogical evidence in support of Beow as confirmation that the alteration of this name into Beowulf stems not from the mind of the poet, but from "two scribes both extremely ignorant of and careless with proper names" (2014:148). Tolkien supplements these considerations with perceptive literary-critical remarks on the obtrusive character of this alteration and the consequent improbability that the *Beowulf* poet genuinely renamed the son of Scyld Scefing.[6] In its thoroughness and soundness, Tolkien's assess-

---

[5]   Such views are consonant with those expressed in the British Academy lecture: "I accept without argument throughout the attribution of *Beowulf* to the 'age of Bede'—one of the firmer conclusions of a department of research most clearly serviceable to criticism: inquiry into the probable date of the effective composition of the poem as we have it" (1936:262).

[6]   Tolkien observes that the replacement of *Bēow* with *Bēowulf* "is certainly an *alteration*—yet a purposeless one, and therefore unlikely to be one made by the poet, an artist, a man very sensitive to

ment of the Beow controversy resembles his treatment of the Jutes versus giants question in the lectures edited by A. J. Bliss and published in 1982 under the title of *Finn and Hengest*. There, an array of philological considerations led Tolkien to the firm conclusion that scribes corrupted *Ēotum* 'Jutes' into *eotenum* 'giants', on account of their unfamiliarity with "the name of the Jutes," which "only occurs occasionally in the poem, and in obscure and allusive contexts, and was doubtless in the tenth century no longer generally known" (Tolkien 2006:63).[7]

On most of the corruptions of proper names, Tolkien held positions comparable to those maintained in the present book,[8] but there are some differences worth identifying. In one case, Tolkien's commentary called my attention to an inaccurately transmitted proper name that could reasonably be added to those surveyed in chapter 3. I had not considered the variation in the spellings of the name of Heorogar significant enough to merit inclusion, but Tolkien's observations persuade me to modify my initial view. He points out that the spellings *Heorogār* (61) and *Hiorogār* (2158) represent the successful transmission of the name of Hroðgar's elder brother, whereas the spelling *Heregār* (467b) represents a form that is best regarded as a corruption. A trenchant rationale for this position is then provided:

> Variation in the form of personal names, even well-known ones, by which the first element preserves the alliteration but is changed into some other more or less similar element, is frequent. It is nonetheless a form of error, of scribal origin: the actual names of individuals no doubt had one correct form only, for formal use. Confusion of *heoro-* and *here-* was specially easy, since they looked much alike, while both belonged to a similar sphere of meaning.
>
> 2014:247

In sum, the trivialization of *heoro* 'sword' to *here* 'army' in the transmitted form *Heregār* is an error that was probably facilitated by unfamiliarity with the name and the legendary figure who bore it. The line of reasoning informing Tolkien's argument could also be applied to the variation in the

---

repetitions and significant correspondences. Yet no one has ever been able to show that this correspondence is anything but a nuisance and a distraction. Beowulf of the Geats has no lineal connexion at all with Beowulf of the Scyldings, and never alludes to him, as he surely would when he came marching into Heorot; or else Hrothgar would, when Beowulf the Geat's lineage is under discussion" (2014:147).

[7]   This interpretation accords with the views adopted in the present book (§§103–105), which are presented at greater length in Neidorf 2015a.

[8]   This is made especially clear in Tolkien 2006:62–63.

spellings of Weohstan's name. Most of the time, the name is successfully transmitted as *Wēohstān* or *Wīhstān* (2613b, 2862b, 3076b, etc.), but in one instance it appears as *Wēoxstānes* (2602b). The rarity of the latter spelling raises the possibility that it is not a mere orthographic variant, but is rather the consequence of the trivialization of *wēoh* 'pagan shrine' to the preterite form of *weaxan* 'to grow'—a corruption perhaps facilitated by a scribe's interpretation of *Wēohstanes* as a sequence of discrete lexemes rather than the fixed name of a legendary hero.

Arguments concerning scribal unfamiliarity with the poem's proper names figure into several of Tolkien's more questionable proposals. The alteration of *hild* to *hilde* in the unmetrical verse *hilde onsǣge* (2076b) is said to have been motivated by a scribe's refusal to construe *Hondsciō* as a proper name: "The scribe probably (as some editors since) could not believe in a man named Handshoe = Glove, and so took the line to mean 'a glove ... fell with war (hostile intent) [*hilde*] upon the doomed man'" (2014:343). The suggestion is plausible, though the level of engagement with the text it implies slightly exceeds what is normal for our scribes. Tolkien also detects a corrupt proper name in the manuscript reading *hæ num* (1983a), which was originally *hæðnum* before a scribe erased the *ð*. He contends that misconstruction of the dative plural form of the *Hæðnas* ethnonym (Old Icelandic *Heiðnir*) as its homograph *hæðnum* 'heathens' prompted a scribe to erase the *ð* in recognition of the improbability that the poet would refer to the Geats as heathens. An argument then follows linking the *Hæðnas* to Queen Hygd, which endeavors to account for the unexpected statement that she delivers mead *Hæðnum tō handa* 'into the hands of the *Hæðnas*' (2014:318–320). Nevertheless, a sudden reference to Hygd's otherwise unnamed people remains doubtful, and Tolkien's explanation for the erasure of *ð* seems to attribute too much critical awareness to the scribe. The solution accepted in the fourth edition of Klaeber's *Beowulf*—that authorial *hæleðum* 'heroes' was trivialized into *hæðnum* 'heathens'—appears far more credible to me (cf. §78). How to explain the erasure of *ð* and the unintelligible reading (*hæ num*) that results? Probably the scribe caught his error, began the process of correcting it to *hæleðum*, and simply forgot to finish the job, leaving a sequence of letters that meant nothing.[9]

The aberrant manuscript reading *Gēatena* (443b), explained here as a corruption of *Gēata* perhaps influenced by *Ēotena* (§102), led Tolkien down

---

[9] This would not be the only case in the manuscript where the process of scribal self-correction was left incomplete; for a comparable instance, see Robinson 1996:54–57.

a path of error that resulted in several implausible claims. He maintained that *Gēatena* represents a corruption of *Gotena*, the genitive plural of *Gotan* 'Goths', and that the poet was here conflating the Goths and the Geats in the belief that they were originally the same ethnic group (2014:237–240). In support of this conflation hypothesis, Tolkien argues that the poem contains two compounds where *hrēð-* should be construed as a shortened form of the *Hrēðgotan* ethnonym (cf. *Widsið* 57b). The structure of the lines containing these supposed *hrēð-* compounds, however, cannot accommodate the word divisions credited by Tolkien. The lines are correctly edited in *KB* as follows:

> mægenhrēð manna.   Nā þū mīnne þearft (445)
> sigehrēð secgum,   swā þīn sefa hwette. (490)

According to Tolkien, the words comprising the on-verses in these two lines should be divided into *mægen Hrēðmanna* and *sige Hrēðsecgum*. What renders this proposal untenable is the regularity known as Krackow's law (1903), which holds that the first element of a genuine compound must participate in the alliterative scheme of the line in which it appears. The fact that neither line exhibits *h*-alliteration is a clear sign of the spuriousness of *Hrēðmanna* and *Hrēðsecgum*.[10] The elimination of these two ethnonyms undermines, in turn, the basis for Tolkien's strained interpretation of the textual history of *Gēatena*.

When his attention turned to textual problems involving ordinary language, Tolkien's imagination was more constrained. In this realm, a number of suggestions are offered that are both intriguing and plausible, while simultaneously relevant to the arguments of the present book, insofar as they corroborate the lexemic theory of scribal behavior or the claim that language change resulted in frequent corruption. A particularly interesting case, considering the emphasis placed on monsters in Tolkien's British Academy lecture, emerges during his consideration of the following passage, which Beowulf speaks when introducing himself to Hroðgar:

> selfe ofersāwon,   ðā ic of searwum cwōm,
> fāh from fēondum,   þǣr ic fīfe geband,
> ȳðde eotena cyn   ond on ȳðum slōg
> niceras nihtes,   nearoþearfe drēah
>
> 419–422

---

[10] It should be noted that Tolkien has not been alone in crediting the improbable verse *mægen Hrēðmanna*; this is in fact the reading of verse 445a printed in Dobbie 1953.

they themselves had seen when I emerged from ambushes stained with the
blood of enemies, where I tied up five, laid waste a family of ogres, and on
the waves killed sea-serpents by night, endured dire straits

Tolkien contends that *fīfe* 'five' represents a scribal error for neuter plural *fīfel*
'monsters'. This emendation was first proposed in Grein (1857), but it has
never been widely accepted. Tolkien offers some persuasive reasons to credit
the authenticity of *fīfel*, however. That a scribe should trivialize *fīfel* into
the numeral it resembles is not surprising, since "this word was practically
forgotten, and is only preserved [outside of *Beowulf*] in one of the fragments
of the Old English poem *Waldere*" (2014:231). Tolkien then observes that
within *Beowulf*, the word occurs in the phrase *fīfelcynnes eard* (104b) 'the
troll-kind's home', which refers to the habitat of Grendel (an *eoten*) and
thereby "shows connexion of *fīfel* with *eoten*" (2014:231). The apposition
of *fīfel geband* with *ȳðe eotena cyn* makes good sense, since *fīfel* "seems to
have represented the *eoten*-kind in their huge, clumsy, lumpish and stupid
side: so Old Norse *fīfl*, 'clown, boor, fool'" (2014:231). It could be added
that the presence of the numeral in 420b appears rather out of place there,
and that the emendation would seem to improve the passage considerably.
The scribal trivialization of the unfamiliar *fīfel* into the quotidian *fīfe* appears
rather probable in the light of Tolkien's arguments.

An original and rather ingenious emendation is proposed in Tolkien's
commentary on the following passage, which has long attracted the attention
of textual critics, and is edited in *KB* as follows:

> eoforlīc scionon
> ofer hlēorber[g]an   gehroden golde,
> fāh ond fȳrheard;   ferhwearde hēold
> gūþmōd grīmmon.
>
> 303b–306a

boar-images gleamed, covered with gold, over cheek-guards, patterned and
fire-hardened; the warlike, helmeted man accorded them safe conduct.

Interpretation of the transmitted passage involves several difficulties, the
most salient of which is the manuscript's *gūþmōd grummon*. The problems
of sense and grammar emanating from this reading lead most editors to
emend it, and the solution adopted in *KB* is perhaps the most economical
available: they emend the meaningless *grummon* to a compound *grīm-mon*
'helmeted man', thereby removing the apparently plural verb and providing
a singular subject for *hēold*. Tolkien, on the other hand, argues that *grummon*

represents a corruption of *grīma* 'mask'. This word makes admirable sense here, since it continues the poet's focus on the decorated helmet.[11] Scribal unfamiliarity with *grīma* is not improbable, and further difficulties with the passage may be indicated by "the retention of a number of 'dialectal', i.e. not West Saxon forms, which would probably have been altered if the scribe felt more confidence: *scionon, beran* for *bergan* (W.S. *beorgan*); *ferh* for *feorh*" (2014:202). Tolkien interprets the scribe's reluctance to modernize and Saxonize the text's spellings as an indication that "the passage puzzled the scribe, either because it was already corrupted or in places hard to read, or because he could not make much sense out of it, or for both reasons combined" (2014:202). Such an interpretation is plausible, and the conception of scribal behavior it assumes accords rather well with the arguments for lexemic transmission put forward in the present book.

One emendation that originated with Tolkien and is propounded in his commentary had actually been known for some time, since it was bruited in a textual note from Bruce Mitchell (1989:315), who duly attributed the idea to his teacher at Oxford. This emendation is designed to remove an awkward feature from the following passage:

> Foran æghwylc wæs,
> steda nægla gehwylc,   stȳle gelīcost,
> hæþenes handsporu   hilderinces,
> egl' unhēoru.

984b–987a

> At the end of each was, all the places of the nails, very like steel, the horrible, disagreeable hand-vestiges of the heathen combatant.

The combination of *æghwylc* and *gehwylc* has raised doubts among textual critics on account of the suspicious proximity of the two pronouns, which uncharacteristically take the same referent. Some editors remedy the problem by deleting *gehwylc* (e.g. Thorpe 1855), though this leaves the unmetrical sequence *steda nægla*, which must then be altered in some way in order for it to possess four metrical positions. Tolkien disposes of the problem much more economically: he contends that *æghwylc* is a corruption of *æghwǣr* 'at

---

[11] The editors of *KB* remark that *gūþmōd* "would not ... very convincingly describe the helmet" (*KB*:136). To this objection, Tolkien preemptively responded: "It is true that *gūþmōd grīma* 'the war-spirited mask' would appear to require transfer of an epithet proper to a warrior to his armour. This is not a grave difficulty: arms can be described as *fūs* or *fūslīc*, that is 'eager to advance, eager for battle'. But the *grīma* or mask probably more or less represented a *face*, human or animal, and *gūþmōd* was the expression of this face" (2014:203–204).

all places', conditioned by the scribe's anticipation of *gehwylc* (2014:298–301). This solution is considerably superior to its alternatives, and it has already been accepted in the editions of Jack (1995) and Mitchell and Robinson (1998). The editors of *KB* understandably refrain from emending the passage, on the grounds that the transmitted text is not "indisputably defective" (*KB*:175), but it must be said that Tolkien's emendation improves the sense of the passage, while also being paleographically plausible. The corruption of an authorial reading (*ǣghwǣr*) into a genuine word that is visually similar (*ǣghwylc*) is entirely to be expected from our scribes.

Another transmitted reading that has long attracted attention from textual critics is *hādor*, an adjective construed as a noun, "brightness," in the sentence: *siððan ǣfenlēoht under heofenes hādor beholen weorþeð* 'after the evening light becomes hidden under the brightness of heaven" (413b–415). Editors have been divided in their treatment of *hādor*, with some retaining the transmitted form and others emending it to *haðor* 'confinement' (*KB*:141). Tolkien favored emendation to *haðor* on semantic grounds, arguing that "it seems nonsense to say that the evening-light is hidden *under* the brightness of the sky" (2014:225). He also noted the exceptional rarity of this poetic word, which renders its trivialization all the more likely (2014:225). Subsequent metrical research has vindicated the position Tolkien adopted. The disyllabic anacrusis in *under heofenes hādor* was shown by Bliss (1967:§§46–47) to generate a pattern that the *Beowulf* poet strictly avoided. Fulk (2005:146), meanwhile, has demonstrated that this metrical problem cannot be alleviated by scanning *hādor* as a nonparasited monosyllable, since the word appears to have been etymologically disyllabic. Meter thus requires emendation to *haðor*, the corruption of which might reflect scribal unfamiliarity with poetic diction or the interchangeable use of *d* and *ð* to represent the dental fricative at an earlier stage of the poem's textual history.[12] In either case, the instance lends incremental support to this book's contention that many transmitted corruptions result from linguistic and cultural changes that took place in the centuries between the period of the poem's composition and the period of its extant manuscript.

On the whole, Tolkien's commentary is a welcome contribution to *Beowulf* textual criticism, with many valuable observations grounded in a sound understanding of the poem's transmission. To be sure, the commentary contains some implausibilities, perhaps the most salient of which is the claim that Hroðgar's homily (lines 1700–1784) underwent revision and expansion

---

[12]   On confusions of *d* and *ð* in the *Beowulf* manuscript and their chronological significance, see §54.

at the hand of Cynewulf.[13] Beyond its inherent improbability, linguistic considerations falsify the claim decisively, since the passage contains many metrical archaisms that are both characteristic of *Beowulf* and rare in the corpus of Cynewulf's poetry.[14] It should be noted, however, that Tolkien regarded the purported intervention of Cynewulf as an unrepresentative incident in the textual history of a poem that otherwise preserved its structural characteristics during the course of its transmission. Dissenting from generations of scholars who adhered to the *Liedertheorie* and deemed *Beowulf* a heterogeneous accretion, Tolkien was an early and vocal proponent of the view that the poem essentially remains the unified work of one archaic poet. He influentially articulated this position in his British Academy lecture, and it finds eloquent expression in his commentary as well:

> *Beowulf* is a work, as we have it, of a single hand and mind—comparable to a play (say *King Lear*) by Shakespeare: thus it may have varied sources; minor discrepancies due to imperfections in the handling and blending of these; and may have suffered some "corruption" (e.g. occasional deliberate tinkering or editing, and many minor casual errors) in the course of tradition between author and our copy. But it makes a unified artistic impression: the impress of a single imagination, and the ring of a single poetic style. The minor "discrepancies" detract little from this, as a rule (2014:170).

Tolkien's British Academy lecture gave rise to numerous literary-critical arguments for the compositional unity of *Beowulf*, the most prominent being those propounded in the monographs of Bonjour (1950) and Brodeur (1959). Such arguments deprived the *Liedertheorie* of currency and exerted considerable influence in subsequent decades, yet the rise of dubious

---

[13]   After deeming Hroðgar's homily "too long," "not throughout suitable," and similar in content to a passage from *Christ II*, Tolkien argues "that Cynewulf's own hand has retouched the king's address: has in fact turned it from a *giedd* into a genuine homily" (2014:311). His commentary also elaborates the view propounded in his British Academy lecture (1936:287–289) that lines 175–188 are a scribal interpolation, on the grounds that their theological perspective is discordant with the rest of the poem (2014:169–181). Tolkien's claim has found some adherents (Whitelock 1951:78; Hill 1994:68–71), but the passage has been convincingly reconciled with the rest of the poem by Wentersdorf (1981) and Russom (2010).

[14]   Particularly strong counterevidence materializes in the occurrence of three verses that adhere to Kaluza's law by restricting resolution to etymologically short desinences: *lēodbealo longsum* (1722a), *ecghete eoweð* (1738a), and *mōdceare micle* (1778a). There are also two verses that exhibit nonparasiting: *wōm wundorbebodum* (1747a) and *symbelwynne drēoh* (1782b). The presence in 1769b of the lexical archaism *missere*—a word whose attestation is restricted to *Beowulf*, *Exodus*, and *Genesis A* (see Cronan 2004:40)—also tells against Cynewulfian composition. On the chronological significance of Kaluza's law and nonparasiting, see §§4–6 and 169–711.

theories of scribal behavior have made it fashionable once again to regard *Beowulf* as a heterogeneous work. *The Transmission of Beowulf* has aimed to restore credence in the compositional unity of *Beowulf* by providing the first comprehensive defense of this position on linguistic and textual grounds. In doing so, it vindicates an entire tradition of *Beowulf* research galvanized by Tolkien, whose views had a stronger philological basis than perhaps even he realized.

GLOSSARY OF TERMS

Alliterative Rule of Precedence: The first lift of the line must participate in its alliterative scheme. The word occupying this lift must receive prosodic stress greater than or equal to that of the word occupying the second lift. Thus, a finite verb (a particle) cannot take precedence over a noun or an adjective (a stress-word); and when a verse contains two words that receive equivalent degrees of prosodic stress, the first of these two words must alliterate.

Anacrusis: Extrametrical syllables permitted under strict conditions to appear before the first lift in verses of types A and D.

Anglian: An umbrella term for the dialects spoken in the midland and northern regions of England, which exhibit salient differences in phonology, morphology, and lexicon from the dialects spoken in the southern regions.

Emendation: An editorial intervention, involving the alteration of at least one letter, that restores sense, meter, and/or alliteration to the work when its transmitted text appears to be defective on account of scribal error.

Four-Position Principle: The standard verse in classical Old English poetry consists of precisely four metrical positions. The position is realized as a stressed syllable, a resolved sequence of a stressed short syllable and its unstressed successor, or a variable sequence of unstressed syllables. Licensed exceptions to the four-position principle are limited to verses of type A3 and D*.

Fulk's Law: The metrical behavior of trisyllabic noncompounds with short medial syllables (for example *scēawian*) depends upon their position in the verse. When placed in the onset, such words fill two metrical positions, but when placed in the coda, they fill three metrical positions. Also known as the Rule of the Coda.

Ictus: The metrical prominence a syllable must possess in order to make position and preserve the structure of the verse. Metrical ictus often, but not always, correlates with prosodic stress, the acoustic emphasis a syllable receives in ordinary linguistic usage.

Kaluza's Law: The application of resolution to an open syllable under secondary stress depends upon the etymological length of the following syllable. Resolution takes effect if the desinence was short in Proto-Germanic or shortened in prehistoric Old English, but it is suspended if the desinence was historically trimoraic or consonantal.

Krackow's Law: The first element of a genuine compound word must participate in the alliterative scheme of the line in which it appears.

Kuhn's Law of Sentence Particles: Ictus is assigned to particles (words of intermediate prosodic stress, such as finite verbs) whenever they are displaced from the first drop of the verse clause. Thus, a particle may be nonictic if it appears either before the first lift of the clause or (if the first lift begins the clause) between the first and second lifts.

Late West Saxon: A southern English dialect in use during the tenth and eleventh centuries, which provided the linguistic norms for the literary language employed in the majority of the surviving texts of Old English works.

Lexemic Theory of Scribal Behavior: The scribes responsible for the transmission of Old English poetry concentrated on individual lexemes while copying in order to modernize and Saxonize their orthography. Considerations of sense and meter were subordinated, when not ignored entirely, to the imperative to regularize orthography.

Non-Structural Features: Aspects of the text of *Beowulf*, such as spelling and word division, that scribes could alter during its transmission without disturbing the sense, meter, or alliteration of the poem. Many of these features must originate with scribes rather than with the poet; this is particularly clear with regard to the fitt divisions in the extant manuscript (see Fulk 2006).

Pascual's Law: The metrical behavior of a finite verb at the head of the off-verse depends upon its ability to participate in the alliterative scheme of the line. A finite verb that would normally form a drop must instead form a lift if it alliterates. By identifying the conditions under which finite verbs form drops or lifts in the off-verse, this law accounts for many perceived exceptions to Kuhn's Law of Sentence Particles.

Resolution: When metrical stress is assigned to a syllable that is both light and open, its unstressed successor is absorbed into a single metrical position.

Saxonization: The systematic conversion of Anglian (or Kentish) forms into their southern equivalents during the textual transmission of works originally composed in non-West Saxon dialects.

Text: One particular concrete manifestation of a work, which may differ from the work as it was first recorded by possessing textual corruptions. The nonstructural features of the text (for example spelling, punctuation, capitalization, and word division) have no essential connection to the work, since they may originate not with its author but with scribes or amanuenses.

Terasawa's Law: Old English poets avoid the use of compounds in which an unstressed syllable at the end of the first constituent precedes a resolvable sequence at the beginning of the second constituent. This law accounts for the ostensibly random variation in the form of the first constituent in compounds such as *hildfruma* or *hildlata* versus *hildebord* or *hildemæcg*.

Trivialization: The unconscious or deliberate replacement of an unfamiliar reading with a more familiar one. This term may also refer to textual alterations that simplify a work's syntax or remove poetic features that distinguish its language from colloquial speech.

BIBLIOGRAPHY

Abels, R. 2009. "What Has Weland to Do with Christ? The Franks Casket and the Acculturation of Christianity in Early Anglo-Saxon England." *Speculum* 84: 549–581.

Amos, A. C. 1980. *Linguistic Means of Determining the Dates of Old English Literary Texts*. Cambridge, MA: Medieval Academy of America.

———. 1982. "An Eleventh-Century *Beowulf*?" *Review* (Charlottesville, VA) 4: 333–345.

Andrew, S. O. 1948. *Postscript on Beowulf*. Cambridge: Cambridge University Press.

Anlezark, D. 2006. *Water and Fire: The Myth of the Flood in Anglo-Saxon England*. Manchester: Manchester University Press.

———, ed. 2009. *The Old English Dialogues of Solomon and Saturn*. Woodbridge: D. S. Brewer.

Aurner, N. S. 1921. "Hengest: A Study in Early English Hero Legend." *University of Iowa Humanistic Studies* 2: 1–76.

Bammesberger, A. 1996. "The Emendation of *Beowulf* l. 586." *Neuphilologische Mitteilungen* 97: 379–382.

Baker, P. S. 1984. "A Little-Known Variant Text of the Old English Metrical Psalms." *Speculum* 59: 263–281.

Bately, J. 1985. "Linguistic Evidence as a Guide to the Authorship of Old English Verse: A Reappraisal, with Special Reference to *Beowulf*." In *Learning and Literature in Anglo-Saxon England: Studies Presented to Peter Clemoes on the Occasion of His Sixty-Fifth Birthday*, edited by M. Lapidge and H. Gneuss, 409–431. Cambridge: Cambridge University Press.

Biddle, M., and B. Kjølbye-Biddle. 1985. "The Repton Stone." *Anglo-Saxon England* 14: 233–292.

Bjork, R. E., ed. 1996. *Cynewulf: Basic Readings*. New York: Garland.

————, ed. and trans. 2013. *The Old English Poems of Cynewulf*. Cambridge, MA: Harvard University Press.

Bjork, R. E., and J. D. Niles, eds. 1997. *A Beowulf Handbook*. Lincoln: University of Nebraska Press.

Bjork, R. E., and A. Obermeier. 1997. "Date, Provenance, Author, Audiences." In Bjork and Niles 1997, 13–34.

Björkman, E. 1918. "Bēow, Bēaw und Bēowulf." *English Studies* 52: 145–193.

Bliss, A. J. 1967. *The Metre of Beowulf*. Rev. ed. Oxford: Blackwell.

Bonjour, A. 1950. *The Digressions in Beowulf*. Oxford: Blackwell.

Branchaw, S. 2014. "Contextualizing the Writings of J. R. R. Tolkien on Literary Criticism." *Journal of Tolkien Research* 1: 1–36.

Bredehoft, T. A. 2014. "The Date of Composition of *Beowulf* and the Evidence of Metrical Evolution." In Neidorf 2014a, 97–111.

Brodeur, A. G. 1953. "The Structure and Unity of *Beowulf*." *PMLA* 68: 1183–1195.

————. 1959. *The Art of Beowulf*. Berkeley: University of California Press.

————. 1970. "*Beowulf*: One Poem or Three?" In *Medieval Literature and Folklore Studies: Essays in Honor of Francis Lee Utley*, edited by J. Mandel and B. A. Rosenberg, 3–26. New Brunswick, NJ: Rutgers University Press.

Brunner, K. 1965. *Altenglische Grammatik: Nach der angelsächsischen Grammatik von Eduard Sievers*. Tübingen: M. Niemeyer.

Bullough, D. A. 1993. "What has Ingeld to do with Lindisfarne?" *Anglo Saxon England* 22: 93–125.

Busse, W. G. 1981. "Assumptions in the Establishment of Old English Poetic Texts: P. J. Lucas's Edition of *Exodus*." *Arbeiten aus Anglistik und Amerikanistik* 6: 197–219.

Cable, T. 1974. *The Meter and Melody of Beowulf*. Urbana: University of Illinois Press.

Calder, D. G. 1979. "The Study of Style in Old English Poetry: A Historical Introduction." In *Old English Poetry: Essays on Style*, edited by D. G. Calder, 1–65. Berkeley: University of California Press.

Campbell, A., ed. 1938. *The Battle of Brunanburh*. London: W. Heinemann.

————. 1959. *Old English Grammar*. Oxford: Clarendon Press.

————. 1962. "The Old English Epic Style." In *English and Medieval Studies Presented to J. R. R. Tolkien on the Occasion of his Seventieth Birthday*, edited by N. Davis and C. L. Wrenn, 13–26. London: Allen & Unwin.

Campbell, J. J. 1951. "The Dialect Vocabulary of the Old English Bede." *Journal of English and Germanic Philology* 50: 349–71.

Carr, C. T. 1939. *Nominal Compounds in Germanic*. London: H. Milford.

Chadwick, H. M. 1912. *The Heroic Age*. Cambridge: Cambridge University Press.

Chambers, R. W. 1959. *Beowulf: An Introduction to the Study of the Poem with a Discussion of the Stories of Offa and Finn*. 3rd ed., with a supplement from C. L. Wrenn. Cambridge: Cambridge University Press.

Child, C. G. 1906. "*Beowulf*, 30, 53, 132, 2957." *Modern Language Notes* 21: 198–200.

Clark, G. 2009. "The Date of *Beowulf* and the Arundel Psalter Gloss." *Modern Philology* 106: 677–685.

———. 2014. "Scandals in Toronto: Kaluza's Law and Transliteration Errors." In Neidorf 2014a, 219–234.

Clarke, M. G. 1911. *Sidelights on Teutonic History during the Migration Period, being Studies from Beowulf and other Old English Poems*. Cambridge: Cambridge University Press.

Clemoes, P. 1995. *Interactions of Thought and Language in Old English Poetry*. Cambridge: Cambridge University Press.

Colgrave, B., ed. 1956. *Felix's Life of St. Guthlac*. Cambridge: Cambridge University Press.

Conner, P. W. 1996. "On Dating Cynewulf." In Bjork 1996, 23–55.

Craigie, W. A. 1923. "Interpolations and Omissions in Anglo-Saxon Poetic Texts." *Philologica* 2: 5–19.

Cronan, D. 2003. "Poetic Meanings in the Old English Poetic Vocabulary." *English Studies* 84: 397–425.

———. 2004. "Poetic Words, Conservatism, and the Dating of Old English Poetry." *Anglo-Saxon England* 33: 23–50.

———. 2014. "*Beowulf* and the Containment of Scyld in the West Saxon Royal Genealogy." In Neidorf 2014a, 112–137.

Doane, A. N. 1994. "The Ethnography of Scribal Writing and Anglo-Saxon Poetry: Scribe as Performer." *Oral Tradition* 9: 420–439.

———, ed. 2013. *Genesis A: A New Edition, Revised*. Tempe: ACMRS.

Dobbie, E. V. K. 1937. *The Manuscripts of Cædmon's Hymn and Bede's Death Song*. New York: Columbia University Press.

———, ed. 1953. *Beowulf and Judith*. New York: Columbia University Press.

Donoghue, D. 1987. *Style in Old English Poetry: The Test of the Auxiliary*. New Haven: Yale University Press.

———. 1991. "On the Non-Integrity of Beowulf." *SELIM* 1: 29–44.

———. 1997. "Language Matters." In *Reading Old English Texts*, edited by K. O'Brien O'Keeffe, 59–78. Cambridge: Cambridge University Press.

Drout, M. D. C. 2011. "'*Beowulf*: The Monsters and The Critics' Seventy-Five Years Later." *Mythlore* 30: 5–22.

Dümmler, E., ed. 1895. *Epistolae Karolini Aevi II*. Monumenta Germaniae Historica, Epistolae 4. Berlin: Weidmann.

Dumville, D. N. 1976. "The Anglian Collection of Royal Genealogies and Regnal Lists." *Anglo-Saxon England* 5: 23–50.

———. 1988. "Beowulf Come Lately: Some Notes on the Paleography of the Nowell Codex." *Archiv für das Studium der neueren Sprachen und Literaturen* 225: 49–63.

———. 1998. "The *Beowulf* Manuscript and How Not to Date It." *Medieval English Student's Newsletter* 39: 21–27.

Dumville, D., and S. Keynes, eds. 1983–. *The Anglo-Saxon Chronicle: A Collaborative Edition*. Cambridge: D. S. Brewer.

Earl, J. W. 1994. *Thinking About Beowulf*. Stanford: Stanford University Press.

Ellis Davidson, H. R. 1958. "Weland the Smith." *Folklore* 69: 145-159.

Evans, S. S. 1997. *The Heroic Poetry of Dark-Age Britain: An Introduction to its Dating, Composition, and Use as a Historical Source*. Lanham: University Press of America.

Flasdieck, H. M. 1950. "OE *Nefne*: A Revaluation." *Anglia* 69: 135–171.

Frank, R. 1991. "Germanic Legend in Old English Literature." In *The Cambridge Companion to Old English Literature,* edited by M. Godden and M. Lapidge, 88–106. Cambridge: Cambridge University Press.

———. 2007. "A Scandal in Toronto: *The Dating of Beowulf* a Quarter-Century On." *Speculum* 82: 843–864.

Fulk, R. D. 1982. "Review Article: Dating *Beowulf* to the Viking Age." *Philological Quarterly* 61: 341–359.

———. 1987. "Unferth and His Name." *Modern Philology* 85.2: 113–127.

———. 1989. "An Eddic Analogue to the Scyld Scefing Story." *Review of English Studies* 40: 313–322.

———. 1992. *A History of Old English Meter*. Philadelphia: University of Pennsylvania Press.

———. 1995. "Kuryłowicz on Resolution in Old English." In *Kuryłowicz Memorial Volume*, vol. 1, edited by W. Smoczyński, 491–497. Cracow: Universitas.

———. 1996a. "Cynewulf: Canon, Dialect, and Date." In Bjork 1996, 3–21.

———. 1996b. "Inductive Methods in the Textual Criticism of Old English Verse." *Medievalia et Humanistica* 23: 1–24.

———. 1997. "Textual Criticism." In Bjork and Niles 1997, 35–53.

———. 2003. "On Argumentation in Old English Philology, with Particular Reference to the Editing and Dating of *Beowulf.*" *Anglo-Saxon England* 32: 1–26.

———. 2004. "Old English *weorc*: Where Does It Hurt? South of the Thames." *ANQ* 17: 6–12.

———. 2005a. "Some Contested Readings in the *Beowulf* Manuscript." *Review of English Studies* 56: 192–223.

———. 2005b. "Some Lexical Problems in the Interpretation and Textual Criticism of *Beowulf* (Verses 414a, 845b, 986a, 1320a, 1375a)." *Studia Neophilologica* 77: 145–155.

———. 2006. "The Origin of the Numbered Sections in Beowulf and in Other Old English Poems." *Anglo-Saxon England* 35: 91–109.

———. 2007a. "Archaisms and Neologisms in the Language of *Beowulf.*" In *Studies in the History of the English Language III: Managing Chaos; Strategies for Identifying Change in English*, edited by C. M. Cain and G. Russom, 267–287. Berlin: Mouton de Gruyter.

———. 2007b. "Old English Meter and Oral Tradition: Three Issues Bearing on Poetic Chronology." *Journal of English and Germanic Philology* 106: 304–324.

———. 2007c. "Old English *þa* 'now that' and the Integrity of *Beowulf.*" *English Studies* 88: 623–631.

———. 2007d. "Some Emendations and Non-Emendations in 'Beowulf' (Verses 600a,976a, 1585b, 1663b, 1740a, 2525b, 2771a, and 3060a)." *Studies in Philology* 104: 159–174.

———. 2007e. "The Etymology and Significance of Beowulf's Name." *Anglo-Saxon* 1: 109–136.

———. 2007f. "The Textual Criticism of Frederick Klaeber's *Beowulf.*" In *Constructing Nations, Reconstructing Myths: Essays in Honour of T. A. Shippey*, edited by A. Wawn, with G. Johnson and J. Walter, 131–153. Turnhout: Brepols.

———, ed. and trans. 2010a. *The Beowulf Manuscript: Complete Texts, and the Fight at Finnsburg.* Cambridge, MA: Harvard University Press.

———. 2010b. "The Roles of Phonology and Analogy in Old English High Vowel Deletion." *Transactions of the Philological Society* 108: 126–144.

———. 2014. "*Beowulf* and Language History." In Neidorf 2014a, 19–36.

Fulk, R. D., R. E. Bjork, and J. D. Niles, eds. 2008. *Klaeber's Beowulf: Fourth Edition.* Toronto: University of Toronto Press.

Gerritsen, J. 1989a. "Emending *Beowulf* 2253—Some Matters of Principle, with a Supplement on 389–90, 1372, & 240." *Neophilologus* 73: 448–452.

———. 1989b. "Have with You to Lexington! The *Beowulf* Manuscript and *Beowulf.*" In *In Other Words: Transcultural Studies in Philology, Translation and Lexicography Presented to Hans Heinrich Meier*, edited by J. Lachlan Mackenzie and R. Todd, 15–34. Dordrecht: Foris.

———. 1998. "*Beowulf* Revisited." *English Studies* 79: 82–86.

Girvan, R. 1935. *Beowulf and the Seventh Century: Language and Content.* London: Methuen.

Godden, M., and S. Irvine, eds. 2009. *The Old English Boethius: An Edition of the Old English Versions of Boethius's De Consolatione Philosophiae with a Chapter on the Metres by M. Griffith and Contributions by R. Jayatilaka.* 2 vols. Oxford: Oxford University Press.

Gradon, P. O. E., ed. 1958. *Cynewulf's Elene.* New York: Appleton-Century-Crofts.

Grein, C. W. M., ed. 1857. *Bibliothek der angelsächsischen Poesie.* Vol. 1. Göttingen: Wigand.

Grinda, K. 1984. "Pigeonholing Old English Poetry: Some Criteria of Metrical Style." *Anglia* 102: 305–322.

Grundtvig, N. F. S., ed. 1820. *Bjowulfs Drape: Et Gothisk Helte-Digt fra forrige Aar-Tusinde, af Angel-Saxisk paa Danske Riim.* Copenhagen: A. Seidelin.

Gwara, S. 2012. Paradigmatic Wisdom and the Native Genre *giedd* in Old English. *Studi Medievali* 53: 783–852.

Harris, J. 2014. "A Note on the Other Heorot." In Neidorf 2014a, 178–190.

Hartman, M. E. 2007. "Stressed and Spaced Out: Manuscript Evidence for Beowulfian Prosody." *Anglo-Saxon* 1: 201–220.

Hill, T. D. 1994. "The Christian Language and Theme of *Beowulf.*" In *Companion to Old English Poetry*, edited by R. H. Bremmer, Jr. and H. Aertsen, 63–77. Amsterdam: VU University Press.

Hirsch, E. D., Jr. 1967. *Validity in Interpretation.* New Haven: Yale University Press.

Hogg, R. M. 1992. *A Grammar of Old English.* Vol.1, *Phonology.* Oxford: Blackwell.

Hogg, R. M., and R. D. Fulk. 2011. *A Grammar of Old English.* Vol.2, *Morphology.* Oxford: Wiley-Blackwell.

Hoops, J. 1932a. *Beowulfstudien.* Heidelberg: C. Winter.

————. 1932b. *Kommentar zum Beowulf.* Heidelberg: C. Winter.

Horgan, D. M. 1980. "The Lexical and Syntactic Variants shared by Two of the Later Manuscripts of King Alfred's Translation of Gregory's *Cura Pastoralis.*" *Anglo-Saxon England* 9: 213–221.

Housman, A. E., ed. 1926. *M. Annaei Lucani Belli Civilis Libri Decem.* Oxford: B. Blackwell.

————. 1961. "The Application of Thought to Textual Criticism." In *Selected Prose,* edited by J. Carter, 131–150. Cambridge: Cambridge University Press.

Hutcheson, B. R. 1995. *Old English Poetic Metre.* Cambridge: D. S. Brewer.

Jack, G., ed. 1995. *Beowulf: A Student Edition.* Rev. reprint. Oxford: Clarendon Press.

Jordan, R. 1906. *Eigentümlichkeiten des anglischen Wortschatzes: Eine wortgeographische Untersuchung mit etymologischen Anmerkungen.* Heidelberg: C. Winter.

Kaluza, M. 1896. "Zur Betonungs- und Verslehre des Altenglischen." In *Festschrift zum siebzigsten Geburtstage Oskar Schade,* 101–134. Königsberg: Hartungsche verlagsdruckerei.

————. 1909. *Englische Metrik in historischer Entwicklung dargestellt.* Berlin: E. Felber.

Kaske, R. E. 1967. "The *Eotenas* in *Beowulf.*" In *Old English Poetry: Fifteen Essays,* edited by R. P. Creed, 285–310. Providence: Brown University Press.

Kelly, B. 1982. "The Formative Stages of *Beowulf* Textual Scholarship: Part I." *Anglo-Saxon England* 11: 247–274.

————. 1983. "The Formative Stages of *Beowulf* Textual Scholarship: Part II." *Anglo-Saxon England* 12: 239–275.

Kemble, J. M., ed. 1835. *The Anglo-Saxon Poems of Beowulf, the Scop or Gleeman's Tale, and the Fight at Finnesburg.* 2nd ed. London: Pickering.

Ker, N. R. 1957. *Catalogue of Manuscripts Containing Anglo-Saxon.* Oxford: Clarendon Press.

Keynes, J. M. 1921. *A Treatise on Probability.* London: Macmillan.

Kiernan, K. S. 1995. "The Legacy of Wiglaf: Saving a Wounded *Beowulf.*" In *Beowulf: Basic Readings,* edited by P. S. Baker, 195–218. New York: Garland Library.

————. 1996. *Beowulf and the Beowulf Manuscript.* Reprint ed. with supplements, Ann Arbor: Michigan University Press. First published 1981, New Brunswick: Rutgers University Press.

Kitson, P. R. 1997. "When Did Middle English Begin? Later Than You Think." In *Studies in Middle English Linguistics*, edited by J. Fisiak, 221–269. Berlin: Mouton de Gruyter.

Klein, S. S. 2006. *Ruling Women: Queenship and Gender in Anglo-Saxon Literature*. Notre Dame: University of Notre Dame Press.

Kluge, F. 1922. *Nominale Stammbildungslehre der altgermanischen Dialekte*. 3rd ed. Halle: M. Niemeyer.

Kock, E. A. 1922. "Interpretations and Emendations of Early English Texts, IX." *Anglia* 46: 63–96.

Krackow, O. 1903. *Die Nominalkomposita als Kunstmittel im altenglischen Epos*. Weimar: Druck von R. Wagner Sohn.

Krapp, G. P., and E. V. K. Dobbie, eds. 1931–1953. *The Anglo-Saxon Poetic Records*. 6 vols. New York: Columbia University Press.

Kuhn, H. 1933. "Zur Wortstellung und -betonung im Altgermanischen." *Beiträge zur Geschichte der deutschen Sprache und Literatur* 57: 1–101.

Kuryłowicz, J. 1949. "Latin and Germanic Metre." *English and Germanic Studies* 2: 34–38.

Lapidge, M. 1982. "*Beowulf*, Aldhelm, the *Liber Monstrorum*, and Wessex." *Studi Medievali* 23: 151–192.

———. 1993. "The Edition, Emendation, and Reconstruction of Anglo-Saxon Texts." In *The Politics of Editing Medieval Texts*, edited by R. Frank, 131–157. New York: AMS Press.

———. 1994. "On the Emendation of Old English Texts." In *The Editing of Old English*, edited by D. G. Scragg and P. E. Szarmach, 53–67. Cambridge: D. S. Brewer.

———. 2000. "The Archetype of *Beowulf*." *Anglo-Saxon England* 29: 5–41.

———. 2003. "Textual Criticism and the Literature of Anglo-Saxon England." In Scragg 2003, 107–136.

———. 2006. "An Aspect of Old English Poetic Diction: The Postpositioning of Prepositions." In Walmsley 2006, 153–180.

Lehmann, W. P. 1969. "On Posited Omissions in the *Beowulf*." In *Studies in Language, Literature, and Culture of the Middle Ages and Later*, edited by E. B. Atwood and A. A. Hill, 220–229. Austin: University of Texas.

Leneghan, F. 2005. "Making Sense of Ker's Dates: The Origins of *Beowulf* and the Paleographers." *Proceedings of the Manchester Centre for Anglo-Saxon Studies Postgraduate Conference* 1: 2–13.

Lichtenheld, A. 1873. "Das schwache Adjektiv im Altenglischen." *Zeitschrift für deutsches Altertum und deutsche Literatur* 16: 325–393.

Liuzza, R. M. 1995. "On the Dating of *Beowulf.*" In *Beowulf: Basic Readings*, edited by P. S. Baker, 281–302. New York: Garland.

Lucas, P. J. 1990. "The Place of *Judith* in the *Beowulf*-Manuscript." *Review of English Studies* 41: 463–478.

———, ed. 1994. *Exodus.* Rev. ed. Exeter: University of Exeter Press.

Magennis, H. 1996. *Images of Community in Old English Poetry.* Cambridge: Cambridge University Press.

Magoun, F. P., Jr. 1958. "*Béowulf A*: A Folk-Variant." *Arv: Journal of Scandinavian Folklore* 14: 95–101.

———. 1963. "*Béowulf B*: A Folk-Poem on Beowulf's Death." In *Early English and Norse Studies Presented to Hugh Smith in Honour of his Sixtieth Birthday*, edited by A. Brown and P. Foote, 127–140. London: Methuen.

Malone, K. 1929. "The Daughter of Healfdene." In *Studies in English Philology: A Miscellany in Honor of Frederick Klaeber*, edited by K. Malone and M. B. Ruud, 135–158. Minneapolis: University of Minnesota Press.

———. 1930. "When Did Middle English Begin?" In *Curme Volume of Linguistic Studies*, edited by J. T. Hatfield, W. Leopold, and A. J. Friedrich Zieglschmid, 110–117. Baltimore: Waverly Press.

———. 1939. "Notes on *Beowulf* IX–XI." *Anglia* 63: 103–112.

———. 1940. "Ecgtheow." *Modern Language Quarterly* 1: 37–44.

———. 1951. "A Note on *Beowulf* 2466." *Journal of English and Germanic Philology* 50: 19–21.

———, ed. 1963. *The Nowell Codex: British Museum Cotton Vitellius A.XV, Second MS.* Copenhagen: Rosenkilde & Bagger.

Meaney, A. L. 2003. "Scyld Scefing and the Dating of *Beowulf* Again—Again." In Scragg 2003, 23–73.

Mellinkoff, R. 1980. "Cain's Monstrous Progeny in *Beowulf*, Part II: Post-Diluvian Survival." *Anglo-Saxon England* 9: 183–197.

Menner, R. J. 1952. "The Date and Dialect of *Genesis A* 852–2936." *Anglia* 70: 285–294.

Mitchell, B. 1985. *Old English Syntax.* 2 vols. Oxford: Clarendon Press.

———. 1989. "*Beowulf*: Six Notes, Mostly Syntactical." *Leeds Studies in English* 20: 311–318.

Mitchell, B., and F. C. Robinson, eds. 1998. *Beowulf: An Edition with Relevant Shorter Texts.* Oxford: Blackwell.

Moffat, D., ed. 1990. *The Old English Soul and Body.* Wolfeboro: D. S. Brewer.

———. 1992. "Anglo-Saxon Scribes and Old English Verse." *Speculum* 67: 805–827.

Momma, H. 1997. *The Composition of Old English Poetry*. Cambridge: Cambridge University Press.

Muir, B. J. 2006. "Issues for Editors of Anglo-Saxon Poetry in Manuscript Form." In Walmsley 2006, 181–202.

Müllenhoff, K. 1869. "Die innere Geschichte des Beowulfs." *Zeitschrift für deutsches Altertum* 14: 193–244.

Napier, A. S. 1901. "The Franks Casket." In *An English Miscellany: Presented to Dr. Furnivall in Honour of his Seventy-Fifth Birthday*, edited by W. P. Ker, A. S. Napier, and W. W. Skeat, 362–381. Oxford: Clarendon Press.

Neidorf, L. 2013a. "Beowulf before *Beowulf*: Anglo-Saxon Anthroponymy and Heroic Legend." *Review of English Studies* 64: 553–573.

———. 2013b. "Scribal Errors of Proper Names in the *Beowulf* Manuscript." *Anglo-Saxon England* 42: 249–269.

———. 2013c. "The Dating of *Widsið* and the Study of Germanic Antiquity." *Neophilologus* 97: 165–183.

———. 2013–2014. "Lexical Evidence for the Relative Chronology of Old English Poetry." *SELIM* 20: 7–48.

———, ed. 2014a. *The Dating of Beowulf: A Reassessment*. Cambridge: D. S. Brewer.

———. 2014b. "Germanic Legend, Scribal Errors, and Cultural Change." In Neidorf 2014a, 37–57.

———. 2014c. "Introduction." In Neidorf 2014a, 1–18.

———. 2015a. "Cain, Cam, Jutes, Giants, and the Textual Criticism of *Beowulf*." *Studies in Philology* 112: 599–632.

———. 2015b. "On the Epistemology of Old English Scholarship." *Neophilologus* 99: 631–646.

———. 2016a. "Metrical Criteria for the Emendation of Old English Poetic Texts." In Neidorf, Pascual, and Shippey 2016, 52–68.

———. 2016b. "The Pejoration of *Gædeling*: From Old Germanic Consanguinity to Middle English Vulgarity." *Modern Philology* 113: 441-59.

———. Forthcoming. "The Composite Authorship of *The Dream of the Rood*." To appear in *Anglo-Saxon England* 45.

Neidorf, L., and R. J. Pascual. 2014. "The Language of *Beowulf* and the Conditioning of Kaluza's Law." *Neophilologus* 98: 657–673.

Neidorf, L., R. J. Pascual, and T. Shippey, eds. 2016. *Old English Philology: Studies in Honour of R. D. Fulk*. Cambridge: D. S. Brewer.

Newton, S. 1993. *The Origins of Beowulf and the Pre-Viking Kingdom of East Anglia*. Cambridge: D. S. Brewer.

Niles, J. D. 1994. "Editing *Beowulf*: What Can Study of the Ballads Tell Us?" *Oral Tradition* 9: 440–467.

O'Brien O'Keeffe, K. 1990. *Visible Song: Transitional Literacy in Old English Verse*. Cambridge: Cambridge University Press.

O'Donnell, D. P. 1996. *Manuscript Variation in Multiple-Recension Old English Poetic Texts: The Technical Problem and Poetical Art*. PhD diss., Yale University.

———. 2005. *Cædmon's Hymn: A Multi-Media Study, Edition, and Archive*. Cambridge: D. S. Brewer.

Oliver, L. 2002. *The Beginnings of English Law*. Toronto: University of Toronto Press.

Orchard, A. 2003a. *A Critical Companion to Beowulf*. Cambridge: D. S. Brewer.

———. 2003b. *Pride and Prodigies: Studies in the Monsters of the Beowulf Manuscript*. 2nd ed. Toronto: University of Toronto Press.

———. 2003–2004. "Reading *Beowulf* Now and Then." *SELIM* 12: 49–81.

Orrick, A. H. 1956. "*Reðes ond Hattres, Beowulf* 2523." *Modern Language Notes* 71: 551–556.

Orton, P. R. 1979. "Disunity in the Vercelli Book *Soul and Body*." *Neophilologus* 63: 450–460.

———. 1999. "Anglo-Saxon Attitudes to Kuhn's Laws." *Review of English Studies* 50: 287–303.

———. 2000. *The Transmission of Old English Poetry*. Turnhout: Brepols.

Osborn, M. 1978. "The Great Feud: Scriptural History and Strife in *Beowulf*." *PMLA* 93: 973–981.

Palmer, R. B. 1976. "In His End is His Beginning: *Beowulf* 2177–2199 and the Question of Unity." *Annuale Medievale* 17: 5–21.

Pascual, R. J. 2013–2014. "Three-Position Verses and the Metrical Practice of the *Beowulf* Poet." *SELIM* 20: 49–79.

———. 2014. "Material Monsters and Semantic Shifts." In Neidorf 2014a, 202–218.

———. 2015. "On a Crux in *Beowulf*: The Alliteration of Finite Verbs and the Scribal Understanding of Metre." *Studia Neophilologica* 87: 171–185.

———. 2016. "Sievers, Bliss, Fulk, and Old English Metrical Theory." In Neidorf, Pascual, and Shippey 2016, 17–33.

Pasternack, C. B. 1995. *The Textuality of Old English Poetry*. Cambridge: Cambridge University Press.

Patterson, L. 1987. *Negotiating the Past: The Historical Understanding of Medieval Literature*. Madison: University of Wisconsin Press.

Pope, J. C. 1957. "The Emendation 'Orethes ond Attres,' *Beowulf* 2523." *Modern Language Notes* 72: 321–328.

———. 1966. *The Rhythm of Beowulf: An Interpretation of the Normal and Hypermetric Verse-Forms in Old English Poetry.* Rev. ed. New Haven: Yale University Press.

———. 1988. "The Irregular Anacrusis in *Beowulf* 9 and 402: Two Hitherto Untried Remedies, with Help from Cynewulf." *Speculum* 63: 104–113.

Popper, K. 1985. *Popper Selections.* Edited by D. Miller. Princeton: Princeton University Press.

Pulsiano, P. 1985. "*Cames cynne*: Confusion or Craft?" *Proceedings of the PMR Conference* 7: 33–38.

Remley, P. G. 2002. "*Daniel*, the *Three Youths* Fragment, and the Transmission of Old English Verse." *Anglo-Saxon England* 31: 81–140.

Rieger, M. 1871. "Zum *Beowulf.*" *Zeitschrift für deutsche Philologie* 3: 381–416.

Robinson, F. C. 1985. *Beowulf and the Appositive Style.* Knoxville: University of Tennessee Press.

———. 1996. "*Beowulf* in the Twentieth Century." *Proceedings of the British Academy* 94: 45–62.

Rogers, H. L. 1971. "Rhymes in the Epilogue to *Elene*: A Reconsideration." *Leeds Studies in English* 5: 47–52.

Russom, G. 1987. *Old English Meter and Linguistic Theory.* Cambridge: Cambridge University Press.

———. 2002. "Dating Criteria for Old English Poems." In *Studies in the History of the English Language: A Millennial Perspective*, edited by D. Minkova and R. Stockwell, 245–266. Berlin: Mouton de Gruyter.

———. 2010. "Historicity and Anachronism in *Beowulf.*" In *Epic and History*, edited by D. Konstan and K. A. Raaflaub, 243–261. Malden: Wiley-Blackwell.

Schönfeld, M. 1911. *Wörterbuch der altgermanischen Personen- und Völkernamen.* Heidelberg: Carl Winters Universitätsbuchhandlung.

Schücking, L. L. 1905. *Beowulfs Rückkehr: Eine kritische Studie.* Halle: M. Niemeyer.

Scragg, D. G., ed. 2003. *Textual and Material Culture in Anglo-Saxon England: Thomas Northcote Toller and the Toller Memorial Lectures.* Cambridge: D. S. Brewer.

Sebo, E. 2011. "Beowulf Hondbana: The Literary Context for Emending Line 1520b." *Neophilologus* 95: 639–648.

Seiler, A. 2008. "The Scripting of Old English: An Analysis of Anglo-Saxon Spellings for *w* and *þ*." *Sprachwissenschaft* 33: 139–172.

Shaw, P. A. 2013. "Adapting the Roman Alphabet for Writing Old English: Evidence from Coin Epigraphy and Single-Sheet Charters." *Early Medieval Europe* 21: 115–139.

Shippey, T. A. 1993. "Old English Poetry: The Prospects for Literary History." In *Proceedings of the Second International Conference of SELIM (Spanish Society for English Medieval Language and Literature)*, edited by A. León Sendra, 164–179. Córdoba: SELIM.

———. 1997. "Structure and Unity." In Bjork and Niles 1997, 149–174.

———. 2005. "The Merov(ich)ingian Again: *damnatio memoriae* and the *usus scholarum*." In *Latin Learning and English Lore: Studies in Anglo-Saxon Literature for Michael Lapidge*, 2 vols, edited by K. O'Brien O'Keeffe and A. Orchard, 1:389–406. Toronto: University of Toronto Press.

———. 2007. "Afterword." In *Beowulf and Lejre*, edited by J. D. Niles, 469–480. Tempe: ACMRS.

———. 2009. Review Article, "Klaeber's *Beowulf* Eighty Years On: A Triumph for a Triumvirate." *Journal of English and Germanic Philology* 108: 360–376.

———. 2014. "Names in *Beowulf* and Anglo-Saxon England." In Neidorf 2014a, 58–78.

Sievers, E. 1884. "Miscellen zur angelsächsischen Grammatik." *Beiträge zur Geschichte der deutschen Sprache und Literatur* 9: 197–300.

———. 1885. "Zur Rhythmik des germanischen Alliterationsverses." *Beiträge zur Geschichte der deutschen Sprache und Literatur* 10: 209–314, 451–545.

———. 1893. *Altgermanische Metrik*. Halle: M. Niemeyer.

Sisam, K. 1953a. "Anglo-Saxon Royal Genealogies." *Proceedings of the British Academy* 39: 287–348.

———. 1953b. *Studies in the History of Old English Literature*. Oxford: Clarendon Press.

———. 1965. *The Structure of Beowulf*. Oxford: Clarendon Press.

Stanley, E. G. 1981. "The Date of *Beowulf*: Some Doubts and No Conclusions." In *The Dating of Beowulf*, edited by C. Chase, 197–211. Toronto: University of Toronto Press.

———. 1984. "Unideal Principles of Editing Old English Verse." *Proceedings of the British Academy* 70: 231–273.

———. 1993. Review of Fulk 1992. *Æstel* 1: 175–182.

———. 2002. "Paleographical and Textual Deep Waters: <a> for <u> and <u> for <a>, <d> for <ð> and <ð> for <d> in Old English." *ANQ: American Notes and Queries* 15: 64–72.

Stevick, R. D. 1959. "Emendation of Old English Poetic Texts: *Beowulf* 2523." *Modern Language Quarterly* 20: 39–43.

——. 1968. *Suprasegmentals, Meter, and the Manuscript of Beowulf*. The Hague: Mouton.

——, ed. 1975. *Beowulf: An Edition with Manuscript Spacing Notation and Graphotactic Analyses*. New York: Garland.

Ström, H. 1939. *Old English Personal Names in Bede's History: An Etymological-Phonological Investigation*. Lund: C. W. K. Gleerup.

Sundquist, J. D. 2002. "Relative Clause Variation and the Unity of Beowulf." *Journal of Germanic Linguistics* 14: 243–269.

Suzuki, S. 1996. *The Metrical Organization of Beowulf: Prototype and Isomorphism*. Berlin: Mouton de Gruyter.

Swanton, M., ed. 1987. *The Dream of the Rood*. Rev. ed. Exeter: University of Exeter.

——, ed. 2010. *The Lives of Two Offas: Vitae Offarum duorum*. Crediton: Medieval Press.

Sweet, H. 1978. *A Second Anglo-Saxon Reader: Archaic and Dialectal*. 2nd ed., revised by T. F. Hoad. Oxford: Clarendon Press.

Taylor, P. B., and R. E. Davis. 1982. "Some Alliterative Misfits in the *Beowulf* MS." *Neophilologus* 66: 614–621.

ten Brink, B. 1888. *Beowulf: Untersuchungen*. Strassburg: K. J. Trübner.

Terasawa, J. 1994. *Nominal Compounds in Old English: A Metrical Approach*. Copenhagen: Rosenkilde & Bagger.

——. 2011. *Old English Meter: An Introduction*. Toronto: University of Toronto Press.

Thorpe, B., ed. 1855. *The Anglo-Saxon Poems of Beowulf, the Scop or Gleeman's Tale, and the Fight at Finnesburg*. London: Reeves & Turner.

Tolkien, J. R. R. 1936. "*Beowulf*: The Monsters and the Critics." *Proceedings of the British Academy* 22: 245–295.

——. 1950. "Prefatory Remarks on Prose Translation of *Beowulf*." In *Beowulf and the Finnesburg Fragment: A Translation into Modern English Prose*, translated by J. R. Clark Hall and revised by C. L. Wrenn, ix–xliii. London: G. Allen & Unwin.

——. 2006. *Finn and Hengest: The Fragment and the Episode*. Edited by A. J. Bliss. London: Harper Collins. First published 1982, London: G. Allen & Unwin.

——. 2014. *Beowulf: A Translation and Commentary, together with Sellic Spell*. Edited by C. Tolkien. Boston: Houghton Mifflin Harcourt.

Townend, M. 2002. *Language and History in Viking Age England: Linguistic Relations between Speakers of Old English and Old Norse*. Turnhout: Brepols.

Tristram, H. L. C., ed. 1985. *Sex Aetates Mundi: Die Weltzeitalter bei den Angelsachsen und den Iren*. Heidelberg: C. Winter.

Tupper, F., Jr. 1910. "Textual Criticism as a Pseudo-Science." *PMLA* 25: 164–181.

Vickrey, J. F. 2009. *Beowulf and the Illusion of History*. Bethlehem, PA: Lehigh University Press.

Vinaver, E. 1939. "Principles of Textual Emendation." In *Studies in French Language and Medieval Literature, Presented to Professor Mildred K. Pope, by Pupils, Colleagues, and Friends*, edited by C. E. Pickford, 351–369. Manchester: Manchester University Press.

Walmsley, J., ed. 2006. *Inside Old English: Essays in Honour of Bruce Mitchell*. Oxford: Blackwell.

Wentersdorf, K. 1981. "*Beowulf*: The Paganism of Hrothgar's Danes." *Studies in Philology* 78: 91–119.

Westphalen, T. 1967. *Beowulf 3150–55: Textkritik und Editionsgeschichte*. Munich: Wilhelm Fink Verlag.

Weyhe, H. 1905. "Beiträge zur westgermanischen Grammatik." *Beiträge zur Geschichte der deutschen Sprache und Literatur* 30: 55–141.

———. 1906. "Beiträge zur westgermanischen Grammatik." *Beiträge zur Geschichte der deutschen Sprache und Literatur* 31: 43–90.

Whitelock, D. 1951. *The Audience of Beowulf*. Oxford: Clarendon Press.

Willis, J. 1972. *Latin Textual Criticism*. Urbana: University of Illinois Press.

Wilson, R. M. 1952. *The Lost Literature of Medieval England*. London: Methuen & Co.

Wormald, C. P. 2006. "*Beowulf*: The Redating Reassessed." In *The Times of Bede: Studies in Early English Christian Society and its Historian*, edited by S. Baxter, 71–81, 98–105. Malden: Blackwell.

Wrenn, C. L. 1943. "The Value of Spelling as Evidence." *Transactions of the Philological Society* 42: 14–39.

Yoon, H. C. 2014. "Weak Adjectives and Definiteness in Old English." *Studies in Modern Grammar* 80: 69–95.

Zupitza, J. 1959. *Beowulf: Reproduced in Facsimile from the Unique Manuscript, British Museum MS. Cotton Vitellius A.XV*. 2nd ed., with an introductory note by N. Davis. London: Oxford University Press.

INDEX OF VERSES

INDEX OF SUBJECTS

MYTH AND POETICS
A SERIES EDITED BY
GREGORY NAGY

CPSIA information can be obtained
at www.ICGtesting.com
Printed in the USA
BVOW03*0310170417
480715BV00002B/3/P